APPROACHING PSYCHOANALYSIS

David L. Smith

APPROACHING PSYCHOANALYSIS

AN INTRODUCTORY COURSE

David Livingstone Smith

KARNAC

LONDON   NEW YORK

First published 1999 by
H. Karnac (Books) Ltd.
6 Pembroke Buildings
London NW10 6RE

Reprinted 2005

British Library Cataloguing in Publication Data
A C.I.P. for this book is available from the British Library

ISBN: 1 85575 157 7

Edited, designed, and produced by Communication Crafts

www.karnacbooks.com

To my parents, David and Rose

ACKNOWLEDGEMENTS

I would like to thank Brett Kahr for implanting the idea for this book in my head and periodically watering it with encouragement, as well as reading the manuscript 20,000 feet above the Atlantic Ocean.

At many times during the course of writing my computer became clinically insane, and were it not for the expert assistance of Benjamin Smith this would have driven me to desperation.

Sasha Smith deserves thanks for her word-processing skills and cheerful presence.

Thanks to Adolf Grünbaum and to Robert Langs for reading sections of the manuscript and providing helpful comments.

Thanks to Regent's College for teaching me more about human nature than I could possibly have acquired from the psychoanalytic literature.

Thanks to Camila Batmanghelidjh for providing a way out.

Thanks to Cesare Sacerdoti of Karnac Books, who was endlessly patient as my bizarre trajectory through personal and professional crisis delayed the completion of the manuscript. I hope that the final product has proved worth the wait.

Thanks to Mariam Scudamore, for her support and encouragement.

Thanks to my psychoanalytic students, who have, over the years, forced me to learn my subject in order better to teach it. You are more present in this book than you may realize.

Thanks to Harry Schlepperman, a goldmine of information on the history of psychoanalysis.

Finally, very special thanks to Subrena Smith for much more than I could ever put into words.

CONTENTS

ix

Introduction

Words of hypocrisy include saying such things as "such-and-
such a person is good or bad, to be followed or to be
shunned", when such words really mean "I like him or dislike
him, I want to believe in him or disbelieve him".

Kasab of Mazar

Psychoanalysis has been around for more than a century and
has proliferated widely. I wrote this book to provide an
introduction to what I consider to be the main currents in
psychoanalytic thought.

I have taught introductory and advanced courses on various
aspects of psychoanalysis for nearly two decades. During this time,
I have been struck by the lack of an accessible, non-doctrinaire,
critical textbook that covers an appropriate range of contributions.
One day a friend and colleague said, "Why don't you write one
yourself?" And so I have.

1

How to use this book

You will not know all about psychoanalysis simply by reading this book. If you are new to the subject, this book will provide you with a compass to help you navigate through the strange seas of psychoanalysis. One of the problems facing beginners is that psychoanalytic books are written in one of the many obscure dialects of *psychoanalese*. Mastering the language is half the problem. I hope that the present work will carry you some distance towards that end.

Although psychoanalytic thinking is quite diverse, its history follows a certain Hegelian logic. Unsolved problems, contradictions, and unacknowledged clinical or theoretical issues have given rise to new psychoanalytic "schools". It is easier to comprehend and appreciate, say, Melanie Klein's work if one has a grasp of just why it is that she said what she did when she did. I have therefore tried to capture the dialectic of the development of psychoanalysis.

Although I have emphasized how this book may be used as a guide for the uninitiated, it will also repay the attention of more seasoned psychoanalytic aficionados. Very few practitioners possess a sound, reasonably well-rounded psychoanalytic education. The present text can be used to fill in some of the gaps. The book also contains new material that has not been published elsewhere.

What is included

I have devoted the first half of the book to a discussion of Freud's work. Given the scope and complexity of Freud's contributions, I have had to leave quite a bit out of these chapters. However, as many later writers take him as a point of departure for their own innovations, I return to Freud from time to time during the second section of the book, elaborating points that could not be included within the first eight chapters.

I have had to make a selection of authors to cover in the second half of the book. Of the very numerous contributors to psychoanalytic thought, I have selected a cast of seven stars.

Wilhelm Reich is significant primarily as the originator of the first systematic approach to psychoanalytic practice. Reich created the first clinical seminar ('supervision group") at the Vienna Psycho-Analytic Institute. It was at this seminar that he hammered out his method of "character analysis", which extended the insights of Freud's new ego psychology into the domain of psychoanalytic treatment. Reich's work has had a profound and often unacknowledged influence on a number of later psychoanalytic writers.

While Reich was developing his method of character analysis in Vienna, Melanie Klein was establishing herself in England as the originator and leader of a new psychoanalytic movement. Born in Vienna, Klein emigrated to England on the invitation of Freud's British bulldog Ernest Jones. Klein pioneered the psychoanalytic treatment of young children and later on extended these ideas in her work with adults. She is widely acknowledged as a psychoanalytic titan, and her approach has been a dominant influence on British and Latin American psychoanalysis.

Just as the Kleinian movement was gathering momentum, National Socialism was flexing its muscles. Shortly after the *Anschluss* of Austria, the Freud family arrived as refugees in London. Melanie Klein had been locked in bitter rivalry with Sigmund's daughter Anna for a number of years, and their arrival fed the flames of conflict between the Kleinians and those who retained allegiance to a more Freudian vision. A third group of British analysts refused to line up behind either of the warring women and became known as the "Independent" Group. By far the most prominent of these was D. W. Winnicott, a paediatrician–psychoanalyst. Winnicott was one of the first major psychoanalytic figures who did not come from a marginalized ethnic group. With his roots lodged deeply in the security of the British, Methodist middle class, his work on infantile development and therapeutic technique infused psychoanalysis with a new sensibility.

The North American Freudians found the British analytic idiom deeply uncongenial. There were, however, some members of the North American psychoanalytic community who were enthusiastic about integrating British concepts with mainstream American ego psychology. Chief amongst these was Otto Kernberg, who came to specialize in the "borderline personality organization". The second major intellectual influence on Kernberg was the work of Margaret Mahler, the Hungarian psychoanalyst-pae-diatrician who worked out an elaborate, observationally based model of child development. Kernberg married the theories of Klein, Hartmann, Mahler, and others to beget a systematic approach to treatment of borderline conditions. Chapter eleven presents contributions by Mahler and Kernberg.

An idea must wait for its time in order to flourish. During the early years of psychoanalysis, emphasis was given to sexuality and the unconscious. One of the earliest members of Freud's circle, Paul Federn, was primarily interested in variations in what he (and Freud) called "I-feeling". Concern with the experiential aspects of human existence was carried forward by the humanistic psychotherapists. This movement, which included psychoanalytic apostates like Fritz Perls and Eric Bern, as well as the home-grown American psychologist Carl Rogers, achieved an efflorescence during the 1960s. It was at this moment that the Viennese-born Heinz Kohut, past president of the Chicago Psychoanalytic Association, launched his dissident approach. Kohut's "psychoanalytic Self Psychology", the subject of chapter twelve, grew out of the inability of mainstream ego psychology to deal with primitive but non-psychotic personality disorders. Unlike Kerberg, who was faced with a similar dilemma, Kohut revived the old Federnian emphasis on conscious experience.

From Freud onwards, psychoanalysts have unashamedly called their discipline a "science". But is it a science? Many philosophers have called this into question. Chapter thirteen explores the work of Adolf Grünbaum. Grünbaum, a philosopher of science, entered the debate on the scientificity of psychoanalysis because of his opposition to the views of Karl Popper, another philosopher who had offered trenchant criticisms of Freudian thinking. Although refuting Popper's own position, Grünbaum's work has confronted the psychoanalytic world with a mighty challenge to its intellectual credentials.

Finally, we come to the work of Robert Langs, which is the subject of chapter fourteen. Langs trained as a classical Freudian psychoanalyst before developing his own radical and unsettling theory that patients unconsciously monitor their analysts' every move and produce incisive encoded commentaries identifying the real implications of the analyst's conduct.

As well as its seven stars, my story of psychoanalysis involves a supporting cast who enter, leave, and sometimes re-enter the narrative as it unfolds across time. These include the creative but undisciplined Sándor Ferenczi, Freud's "grand vizier" who mentored Klein and Mahler and anticipated aspects of the work of Winnicott and Langs; August Aichhorn, Margaret Mahler's analyst-lover who worked with the young criminals on the streets of Vienna; Helene Deutsch, the imperious director of the Vienna training institute who pronounced Mahler psychotic; Edith Jacobson, the communist who refused to break her oath of confidentiality when the Gestapo wanted information about one of her patients and who was imprisoned for her principles. There are yet others who play bit parts (although their contribution to psychoanalysis was sometimes immense): Ernest Jones, Karl Abraham, Otto Fenichel, Joan Riviere, and many others.

What has been left out

Psychoanalysis has been around a long time, and there is a lot of it. As an author, I was confronted with the need to make choices. What I chose to cover was a function of (a) the role each author has played in the development of psychoanalysis, (b) competition for space, and (c) my personal estimation of the value of each author's work.

I have had to leave out a lot of Freud. Freud's massive, brilliant contribution cannot possibly be captured in a few chapters of an introductory text. I have therefore chosen to concentrate on the fundamentals. I have also entirely excluded Freud's huge contribution to aesthetics, literary criticism, historiography, sociology, and anthropology.

There are many authors who I think have made important contributions to psychoanalytic thought whom I have left out or relegated to minor roles. These include Ferenczi, Hartmann, Mahler, Bowlby, Fairbairn, Michael Balint, and Anna Freud. There are other writers whom I esteem but have not mentioned because their work is not yet widely recognized within the psychoanalytic community. Chief amongst these are the evolutionary psychoanalysts, who combine psychoanalysis with contemporary Darwinian thinking.

Perhaps the most glaring omission is the lack of any discussion of Jacques Lacan. This renegade French psychoanalyst spawned a movement that has had a continually accelerating impact on clinical and theoretical psychoanalysis, as well as on the use of psychoanalysis in the humanities. The Lacanian approach is perhaps the most widely practised form of psychoanalysis in the world.

Some of my prejudices

Given the epigraph to this Introduction, I think that it is only fair that I place some of my prejudices on the table.

I have emphasized the wide proliferation of the Lacanian approach. Why have I excluded it from this book then? I have excluded it because I do not understand it. I have so little sympathy with the approach that I cannot even criticize it properly. The Lacanian approach is a different kind of animal, and the interested natural historian of psychoanalysis will have to look elsewhere for information about it.

With regard to Klein, whom I *have* included, I have very strong reservations about her work. However, I do think that she was a woman with very powerful and important intuitions, which she was unable properly to articulate. In spite of my antipathy, I have tried very hard to be fair in my presentation of her ideas.

I am very strongly prejudiced in favour of Sigmund Freud. Although I believe that Freud is often mistaken, his mistakes are *profound*. My enthusiasm for Freud will doubtless be apparent in the chapters devoted to him.

Finally, I must make it clear that I am an advocate of Langs's communicative approach to psychoanalysis having pioneered its development in Britain, and I am therefore in danger of being insufficiently critical of his work in spite of my sincere efforts to be objective and even-handed.

It is my sincere hope that readers will not automatically take on board my own evaluations of the psychoanalytical theories described in this book, but will use the book as a stimulus to independent investigation and critical thought.

PART ONE

THE WORK OF SIGMUND FREUD

CHAPTER ONE

Mind and nature:
the context of Freud's work

You call something a "mystery" when you will not see it.

Musa Farawani

Sigmund Freud was born Sigismund Schlomo (Solomon) Freud in the Moravian (Czech) village of Freiberg in 1856. The son of a Jewish wool-merchant from the northern province of Galicia, Freud was only one generation away from the mediaeval culture of traditional, rural Jewry. In 1859, the Freud family moved to Leipzig in search of employment and then wandered on to Vienna, where they settled in the Leopoldstadt district, living in slum conditions until they were able to improve their circumstances. There has been considerable dispute about the reasons for this move from Freiberg. Perhaps the most colourful theory is that it was connected with a counterfeiting ring of which the Freuds may have been a part (Gedo, 1986).

Vienna was one of the two capitals (the other being Budapest) of the magnificent, sprawling Austro-Hungarian Empire. During the latter half of the nineteenth century, the population of Vienna swelled with immigrants from the more far-flung provinces and many of them, like the Freuds, were Jews in search of opportunity. The liberal policies of the Emperor Franz Josef encouraged the assimilation of Jews into the mainstream of European cultural life. Vienna was perhaps the pinnacle of European cultural achievement and innovation in both the arts and the sciences. Those Jews seeking integration into this world therefore moved from a deeply traditional culture to the cutting edge of modernity. Freud was, as it were, midway between the *shtetl* and high European culture.

After graduating from secondary school, Freud entered the University of Vienna and eventually settled on the study of biology (although he read widely and took classes with luminaries such as the physicist Josef Stefan and the philosopher Franz Brentano). Freud's interests led him to specialize in neuroscience, a field that—as I shall describe—was the centre of intense disputes that had important implications for the most fundamental ways that we conceive of ourselves as human beings. Freud carried out research in Ernst Brücke's prestigious if primitive Physiological Institute, where he befriended or was befriended by Josef Breuer, a well-established physician. In his youth, Breuer had studied under Ewald Hering, who is best known for his work on the physiological mechanisms underpinning colour vision, and the research jointly undertaken by Hering and Breuer led to the discovery of the role of the vagus nerve in the self-regulating mechanism of breathing (the eponymous Hering–Breuer reflex). Hering was also the author of a celebrated lecture on unconscious mental activity (Butler, 1880); Freud later described this lecture as a "masterpiece" (Levine, 1926).

Breuer had also done important work on the function of the semicircular canal of the ear. He became Freud's friend, mentor, and financial sponsor. It was also Breuer who introduced Freud to the practice of psychotherapy.

During his time at the Physiological Institute, Brücke advised Freud that there were poor financial prospects facing him as a researcher, and he advised him to obtain a medical qualification. Freud accordingly extended his education and, on 5 September 1885, obtained his medical qualification. Freud opened his private practice on Easter Sunday, 1886. This characteristic swipe at the Roman Catholic majority in Vienna displays an important feature of Freud's personality: his desire to combat the hypocrisies of Christian culture, a motive that certainly had a decisive impact on his future work.

Freud came to establish himself as an expert in cerebral hemiplegias (paralyses) in children. He also became deeply involved in the new field of aphasiology—the study of speech disorders caused by damage to the brain. Freud's third major interest during the early period of his career was the disorder then known as *hysteria*. In 1885, Freud obtained a small grant enabling him to travel to Paris to study with Jean Martin Charcot, a world authority on neurology who had developed a special interest in hypnosis and hysteria. Freud's earliest contributions to psychology and psychotherapy centred on his investigations of hysteria.

Psychology, neuroscience, and psychiatry

Freud's work can only be properly understood and appreciated in the context of its rightful place in the history of ideas. Freud was a member of an international intellectual community that included psychologists, neuroscientists, psychiatrists, and philosophers. Although each of these groups was concerned with the study of the mind, each approached it from its own particular vantage point.

Psychologists wanted to understand the nature of normal mental processes. Psychology had become a scientific discipline in its own right largely through the efforts of Wilhelm Wundt, who attempted to harness the methods of experimental science to discipline the process of introspection. In his laboratory in Leipzig, Wundt and his colleagues exposed trained subjects to controlled stimuli, measured reaction-times, and solicited first-person reports. Inspired by the successes of the physicists, the new scientific psychologists hoped to identify the fundamental constituents of the psyche, the atoms of mental life. Within a few years, psychological laboratories began to spring up elsewhere in Europe and North America.

Neuroscientists studied the relationship between the mind and the brain. Neuroscience emerged during the first half of the nineteenth century. Nineteenth-century neuroscientists were confined to study damaged brains: in the absence of modern imaging techniques, it was not possible to study intact living brains. However, if a patient was found who had suffered brain damage, it was possible to determine which if any mental functions were disturbed by this damage. The neuroscientists gathered numerous cases of "trauma" suffered by living brain tissue, and they used these to try to determine the role of brain structures in normal mental life.

Psychiatrists situated themselves within the tradition of clinical medicine: they were concerned with understanding the nature of mental aberrations. Scientific psychiatry was born in the middle of the nineteenth century with the work of Wilhelm Griesinger. Griesinger's slogan "Mind diseases are brain diseases" illustrated the impact of neuroscience on the new psychiatry.

Nineteenth-century philosophy defined the basic assumptions and world-view in which the psychologists, neuroscientists, and psychiatrists worked. The conceptual horizons of the sciences of mind were fixed by one immensely significant tradition in the history of philosophy: the dualistic legacy of the seventeenth-century polymath René Descartes.

Descartes held that mind and body were made from two distinct "substances". He believed that the body is made out of physical substance and exists in space, whereas the mind is made of immaterial substance and exists only in time. In contrast to the spiritual nature of mind, the body is nothing but a complicated machine. Over the next few centuries, other philosophers proposed novel forms of dualism. In one form or another, dualism remained the prevailing view of the relationship between mind and brain until the twentieth century.

In addition to his work on the relationship between mind and body, Descartes had a theory about the relationship of the mind with itself. He believed that our minds are transparent to themselves: that is, we automatically and incorrigibly know whatever is going on in our minds. In other words, Descartes held that all mental states are *conscious* and that consciousness is an intrinsic characteristic of anything mental. If all mental states are conscious, then introspection is the only sensible method for psychological research.

During the nineteenth century, dualism became more and more difficult to entertain seriously. Nineteenth-century developments in the fields of evolutionary biology, physics, and neuroscience sharply contradicted the older dualistic theories. These developments had a momentous effect on our relationship to ourselves. The new knowledge challenged extremely ancient and deeply rooted beliefs about the human soul.

The unconscious before Freud

The other aspect of the Cartesian package—the view that all mental phenomena are conscious—was also being challenged by new work in the sciences. Hypnosis, psychiatry, and neuroscience conspired to demonstrate the existence of *unconscious* mental processes: mental states existing outside of awareness. Researchers struggled to make these observations square with the received view that all mental states are conscious.

Some writers claimed that consciousness can be *split*. A portion of one's consciousness is split off or dissociated from one's main consciousness. According to this view, apparently unconscious mental processes are actually manifestations of split-off portions of consciousness itself.

Another alternative was to claim that so-called unconscious mental states are really nothing more than neurophysiological states. They are not *mental* at all. They are merely capable of *giving rise* to mental states. According to this view, when we forget something, it is not simply inaccessible: it literally *disappears* as an idea. Each time that we remember it, the underlying neurophysiological state simply generates it anew.

Hysteria

Freud's earliest psychological work, which was done in collaboration with Josef Breuer, concerned the causes, dynamics, and treatment of hysteria. It is therefore important to describe something of the context in which Breuer and Freud advanced their ideas.

"Hysteria" was a term used for a rather heterogeneous group of illnesses. Sufferers from hysteria might experience epileptiform fits, mysterious pains, paralyses and other motor disabilities, and sensory distortions such as hallucinations or fall victim to states of dissociation. What defined all of these symptomatic pictures as "hysterical" was the absence of any anatomical or physiological explanation for them.

The concept of hysteria had been around for a very long time. The earliest reference to it is found in the writings of the ancient Egyptians, who believed hysteria to be an exclusively feminine disorder and attributed it to the dislocation of the womb, which was imagined as wreaking havoc as it slithered its way around the inside of a woman's body. The Egyptian theory of the dynamics of hysteria was taken up by the Greeks. In fact, it was Hippocrates who first used the term "hysteria" (from the Greek for womb, *hystera*).

During the Middle Ages, Saint Augustine proclaimed that the disease was caused by witchcraft. As being a victim of the super-natural disease denoted the heretic, the patients so diagnosed came into the hands of the Inquisition. They were questioned un-der torture for having exposed themselves to the allure of the devil or witchcraft and were punished for it—often by death (Veith, 1977).

During the Renaissance, the German physician Paracelsus re-jected mediaeval superstition in favour of the ancient uterine theory of hysteria. During the seventeenth century, post-mortem examinations of hysterical women demonstrated that hysteria was not accompanied by pathological changes to the womb. Charles Le Pois and Thomas Sydenham rejected the traditional womb theory. It was Sydenham who first described hysteria as a *psychological* disorder and, in rejecting the womb theory, could assert that males could also suffer from it. Sydenham recommended a *physical* treat-ment regime of soothing medication, iron supplements, blood-let-ting, and vigorous exercise. By 1845, Ernst von Feuchtersleben, a Viennese psychiatrist, was recommending psychotherapy (includ-ing the analysis of the patient's dreams) as the treatment of choice.

This progressive trend was obstructed by Wilhelm Griesinger and his followers, whose descriptions of the "hysterical personality" seethed with contempt. Griesinger initiated a revival of the medieval attitude of *moral disapproval*, this time clothed in scientific rather than theological garb.

One of the voices opposing this chorus of disapproval was that of Jean-Martin Charcot. The son of a carriage builder, Charcot studied medicine and, after making a number of brilliant contributions to neurology, was given the chair of pathological anatomy at the University of Paris and was soon appointed to the chair of diseases of the nervous system. His medical reputation was equalled only by that of Louis Pasteur.

Charcot believed that hysteria was a constitutionally rooted neurological disorder which disposes certain individuals to respond hysterically to traumatic events and that the process of suggestion played a role in the generation of hysterical symptoms. He attempted to show this by demonstrating that hysterical individuals can be hypnotically induced to simulate neurotic symptoms and that these could also be *removed* by means of hypnosis.

Charcot's approach to hypnotism brought him into conflict with a group known as the "Nancy School", which was lead by Ambroise Liébeault, a rural physician, and Professor Hyppolyte Bernheim, of the University of Nancy. Charcot had claimed that susceptibility to hypnotic suggestion was *physiologically* determined, and rooted in a hysterical disposition. Liébeault and Bernheim asserted that hypnosis was a wholly *psychological* process and that susceptibility to it was not indicative of a pathological disposition. Bernheim accordingly claimed that hysteria was not an illness. It was, he believed, only an exaggeration of a natural tendency shared by all human beings confronted with emotional trauma. The dispute between the Charcotians and the Nancy School became rather acrimonious and was carried out both in the scholarly journals and in national newspapers such as *Le Temps*.

Perhaps the most important contributor to the literature on hysteria immediately after Charcot was Pierre Janet. Janet had been Charcot's student at the Salpêtrière. He emphasized the psychological character of hysterical afflictions and emphasized the role of "subconscious" ideas in hysteria. Janet believed that hysteria could be provoked by physical illness or by emotional shock, although he emphasized the former.

Therapy

The forms of psychotherapy current in the nineteenth century included psychosocial interventions such as suggestion (Bernheim), environmental management (Charcot), and forms of psychological analysis (Feuchtersleben).

The use of medication was an age-old approach to hysteria and was declining in popularity by the late nineteenth century. Doctors administered drugs that often complicated the original hysteria with a physician-induced addiction (Decker, 1991).

One of the most popular treatment modalities for hysteria was the Weir Mitchell "rest cure". Silas Weir Mitchell [1829–1914] was an American neuroscientist and also the author of poetry and "pop" novels. In 1877, he published his first book on the treatment of hysteria: the bizarrely titled *Fat and Blood*. Mitchell believed that hysterical women tended to be thin and lacked blood. He therefore proposed that the physical health of the patient was to be built up by means of a period of enforced rest supplemented by massage and electrotherapy. Mitchell combined his rest cure with "moral therapy"—efforts to influence patients psychologically to abandon the hysterical lifestyle.

Electrotherapy was a highly regarded method for treating hysteria. Treatment could go on for anything from a few months to several years. Electricity was applied either locally or generally and provoked a number of unpleasant side-effects (Decker, 1991).

Hydrotherapy, a less "high-tech" approach, was also widely employed for the treatment of hysteria. The most common form of hydrotherapy involved a high-pressure jet of cold water being directed at the patient. Alternatively, patients were tightly wrapped in cold, wet sheets.

Nineteenth-century technologies for treating hysteria were primitive, sometimes brutal, and unrelated to any sophisticated psychological understanding of the hysterical process (for a detailed discussion of these and more bizarre treatments, see Altschuler, 1965). This situation was decisively altered by the ground-breaking work undertaken by Joseph Breuer and his young collaborator Sigmund Freud, and it is to this development that we will now turn.

CHAPTER TWO

Freud, Breuer, and hysteria:
the cathartic method

If you laid your finger on my shoulder, it would affect you like
fire running through your veins. The possession of the least
place on my body will give you sharper joy than the conquest
of an empire. Offer your lips! My kisses taste like fruit ready to
melt into your heart! Ah! how you'll lose yourself in my hair,
breathing the scent of my sweet-smelling breasts, marvelling
at my limbs, and scorched by the pupils of my eyes, between
my arms, in a whirlwind.

Gustave Flaubert, *The Temptation of Saint Anthony*

In July 1883, Vienna was in the grips of a heatwave. On 13 July,
the 27-year-old Sigmund Freud left the laboratory at the Physiological Institute and made his way to the home of Josef and
Matilda Breuer on the Brandtstätte. After arriving, Freud was invited to have a bath to wash off the sweat and grime of the day. He
and the Breuers dined together, and Sigmund and Josef sat up
talking far into the night. One of the matters on Breuer's mind was
his patient Bertha Pappenheim, whom he had ceased treating for
hysteria and had committed to a sanatorium the day before.

Later that month, Breuer invited Freud to accompany him on holiday to his summer home in Gmunden in the Austrian Alps. Once in Gmunden, Breuer found time to pour his heart out to Freud about his patient Bertha Pappenheim. Bertha had relapsed and was in intense physical and psychological pain. Breuer evidently described her condition as "quite unhinged" and expressed the wish that she would *die* so as to be released from her misery (Jones, 1953, p. 247).

In spite of this outcome, Freud pressed Breuer for the details of his treatment of Bertha. Bertha, who was presented as "Fräulein Anna O." in Breuer and Freud's *Studies on Hysteria* (Freud, 1895d), suffered from a variety of "hysterical" symptoms which began during the period when she was nursing her dying father. These included sensory disturbances, motor disturbances (including paralysis), multiple personality, and speech disturbances.

Bertha Pappenheim was, like many Jews of her generation, the offspring of an arranged marriage. She was born in 1859 into the wealthy household of Siegmund Pappenheim. Bertha's illness began in the spring of 1880 with facial spasms and the symptoms of neuralgia. In the summer of the same year, Siegmund Pappenheim fell ill with peripleuritis while the family were on holiday in the Salzkammergut. Bertha took on night-time nursing duties. Waiting for the arrival of a surgeon on the evening of 17 July, Bertha fell asleep, then woke in the middle of the night to tend to her father. Exhausted, she began to doze, with her right arm draped over the back of her chair, and she experienced a hallucination. A menacing black snake emerged from the wall and was moving towards her father. Terrified, she tried fend it off, but her right arm had gone to sleep. The fingers of her right hand were transformed into little snakes with death's heads. Bertha tried to pray but could remember only an English nursery rhyme (Freud, 1895d).

Breuer visited the 21-year-old Bertha every day. He observed a clinical picture of ever-increasing gravity involving fugue states, multiple personality, hallucinations, aphasia, and mutism. Noticing that she normally entered a dreamy state during the evening, which she called her "clouds", he found that encouraging Bertha to invent stories associated with words that she had uttered during her hallucinatory states earlier in the day would bring about a

measure of relief. According to Breuer, this unusual treatment regime caused all of Bertha's symptoms to vanish by 1 April 1881.

On 5 April, Siegmund Pappenheim died, and Bertha suffered a
serious relapse. She could no longer feed herself, lost the capacity
to understand her native tongue, and again experienced visual
disturbances.

Alarmed at the possibility of suicide, Breuer wanted Bertha to
be medically supervised during periods when he was to be absent.
He therefore removed her from home and had her lodged at a villa
near Inzerdorf, outside Vienna. Her symptoms improved until the
summer holiday interrupted visits from Breuer and the Pappenheim family. Breuer returned from his holiday to find her in a
wretched condition. He took Bertha to Vienna and managed to get
her to resume telling him stories, which now began increasingly to
focus on the content of her hallucinations and of recent events.
Breuer noticed during this week of intensive psychotherapy that
when his patient recounted incidents relating to the onset of one or
another of her symptoms, the symptom in question disappeared.
Breuer systematically attempted to trace each of Bertha's symptoms back to the point of its emergence, at first confining these
efforts to her evening periods of autohypnosis, but later supplementing these with morning sessions of hypnotic regression. On 7
June 1882, Bertha reproduced under hypnosis the original event
that marked the onset of her illness in the summer of 1880 (the
hallucination of the snakes, described above). According to
Breuer's published account (Freud, 1895d), this marked the conclusion of her treatment.

However, Breuer's original report on the treatment (Hirschmüller, 1978) shows that from spring of 1882 Bertha suffered from
an agonizing neuralgia and intense convulsions. She was treated
with morphine and choral and became severely addicted to these.
Bertha developed paranoid ideas. Breuer had her admitted to the
Bellvue sanatorium on 12 July 1882. A year later she was admitted
to the Inzerdorf sanatorium. It is little wonder that Breuer expressed to Freud the wish that Bertha might die so as to be
released from her misery. In short, "the impression he [Breuer]
gives in *Studies on Hysteria* that the patient was completely cured
does not square with the facts" (Hirschmüller, 1978, pp. 106–107).

Breuer had other reasons to be distressed at the fate of Bertha Pappenheim. It seems that his wife, Matilda, had become jealous of Breuer's relationship with Bertha and that the unilateral termination of the treatment owed something to this situation. There is some (shaky) evidence that Freud told his student and patron Marie Bonaparte that Matilde Breuer attempted suicide in response to her husband's involvement with his patient (Borch-Jacobsen, 1996). Breuer later described his treatment of Bertha as an "ordeal" which devastated his way of life (Hirschmüller, 1978, p. 130).

According to Freud (1925), Breuer abruptly terminated his treatment of Bertha because he realized that she was in love with him and wanted to bear him a child. Although it is impossible to corroborate Freud's claim, Hirschmüller asserts that "It seems . . . beyond dispute that there was a conflict between his personal and medical interest in the case and a certain fear of the consequences of such a deep relationship" (p. 130).

Freud believed that Breuer had been caught unawares by Bertha's "transference-love" (see chapter seven). As we shall see, it was only decades later that psychoanalysts began seriously to consider their *own* contributions to the analytic relationship. Indeed, if Freud's reconstruction is correct, we must wonder whether Breuer had in fact committed a sexual act with Bertha Pappenheim.

We know that Bertha was on Breuer's mind during July 1883— the month that she was admitted to the Inzerdorf sanatorium and the first anniversary of his termination of her treatment. When Breuer and Freud travelled together from Vienna to Gmunden during the final week of July, Breuer presented Freud with a book for him to read on the outward journey. The book made a very deep impression on Freud. It was Gustave Flaubert's *The Temptation of Saint Anthony* (1874).

Freud's collaboration with Breuer

Although Bertha's treatment was far from successful, the phenomena that Breuer observed were certainly suggestive. Freud mentioned Breuer's work briefly to Charcot, who seemed uninterested.

Upon his return from Paris, Freud opened his private practice and Breuer referred patients to him. Breuer, in the role of general practitioner, supervised the general health of these patients while Freud, the clinical neurologist, attended to their psychological symptoms.

Freud was unhappy with the conventional methods of treatment for neurotic disorders. He began using hypnotic suggestion in 1887 in order to *suggest symptoms away*. It was not until May 1889 that he began experimenting with the method of treatment that Breuer had developed with Bertha Pappenheim, an approach that Breuer and Freud christened the "cathartic method".

Between 1886 and 1892, Freud and Breuer worked together in the treatment of a number of cases. The two men also attempted to use their clinical observations in conjunction with then current neurophysiological ideas to develop a theory of hysteria. Their first joint publication was entitled "Preliminary communication" and was published in two parts in a scholarly journal in 1893 (Freud, 1895d).

In May 1895, Breuer and Freud published the ground-breaking *Studies on Hysteria* (Freud, 1895d). The *Studies* included Breuer's account of Bertha Pappenheim ("Anna O.") and five case studies by Freud, as well as a chapter on the aetiology and dynamics of hysteria written by Breuer and a chapter on psychotherapy by Freud. The earliest cases show Freud using Bernheim's method of suggestion for the treatment of hysteria, but by the time we reach the final case, that of "Elisabeth von R", Freud has developed a sophisticated method of analytical psychotherapy.

The Freud/Breuer theory rested on a principle first developed by the psychophysiologist Gustav Theodor Fechner. Fechner believed that the nervous system strives to maintain an optimal level of arousal, and that arousal in excess of this must be "discharged" so as to restore equilibrium. Fechner called this the "principle of stability". According to Freud and Breuer, hysteria is based on an obstruction of this fundamental process: states of emotional arousal cannot be discharged. Instead, the "strangulated affects" take the form of hysterical symptoms.

The next explanatory task confronting this theory is to give some account of why it is that some people appear to be unable to discharge their emotional energies. Freud held that discharge was rendered impossible by the fact that it would give rise to states of extreme emotional conflict. Emotion is blocked in order to prevent the experience of mental anguish. Freud argued that in cases of hysteria the emotions that have been suppressed would, if acknowledged, give rise to terrible feelings of shame and guilt.

It is not immediately clear how it is that one can suffer an emotional state while simultaneously keeping it out of awareness. In order to resolve this problem, Freud and Breuer drew on the French tradition of neuropathology, arguing that emotional conflict brings about a *splitting of consciousness*. The hysteric's consciousness becomes divided, and that portion of consciousness harbouring the "pathogenic idea"—the awareness of the suppressed emotional state—becomes dissociated from his or her "main" consciousness.

The task of the psychotherapist must be to reinstate the patient's capacity to express blocked pathogenic emotions. To reach this point, the patient must become aware of the suppressed emotional state. The psychotherapy of hysteria was conceived as a laborious process of determining just what it is that the patient is suppressing, convincing the patient that he or she is engaged in such a state of self-deception, and facilitating a full emotional "catharsis" of the suppressed mental state. Freud held that the experience of full emotional catharsis will invariably eliminate hysterical symptoms.

CHAPTER THREE

The very core of nature:
the beginnings of psychoanalysis

> All I was trying to do was explain defence, but just try to explain something from the very core of nature! I had to work my way through the problem of quality, sleep, memory—in short, all of psychology.
>
> Sigmund Freud

Freud's work with Breuer was not yet psychoanalysis. Although the technique of psychotherapy that Freud evolved during the 1890s was in many respects that of psychoanalysis, the theory that he used to explain his clinical observations was decidedly pre-psychoanalytic. In the present chapter, I discuss the beginnings of psychoanalytic technique in the free-association method and Freud's first distinctively psychoanalytic model of the architecture of the soul.

The evolution of psychoanalytic technique

Freud's movement away from hypnotic suggestion therapy seems to have begun in 1891 (Freud, 1891d). The situation was different when it came to the use of hypnotic *regression* with the aim of recovering suppressed memories, but here, too, there were disadvantages. Freud found that he could not create a state of hypnotic "somnambulism" in all of his patients. He needed some alternative method of making contact with their dissociated states, and it was desirable to find a way of doing this while the patient is in a waking state. Bernheim had once demonstrated to him that events experienced during hypnotic trance are only *apparently* forgotten, and that subjects can be induced to recall them by means of light pressure of a hand on the forehead combined with insistence that they *can* remember (Freud, 1895d).

Freud decided on the basis of this experiment that his patients *knew* of their dissociated pathogenic ideas. He needed only to give them the appropriate command. He would place his hand on the patient's forehead and say:

> You will think of it under the pressure of my hand. At the moment at which I relax my pressure you will see something in front of you or something will come into your head. Catch hold of it. It will be what we are looking for.—Well, what have you seen or what has occurred to you? [p. 110]

Freud seems to have initiated this "pressure method" during the treatment of Elisabeth von R in late 1892 (Macmillan, 1991), although he did not completely abandon the therapeutic use of hypnosis until early 1895. The transition to the pressure technique had important theoretical ramifications. He had previously believed that, as hysteria was caused by a splitting of consciousness, it was necessary to induce an altered state of consciousness in the patient in order to enter into the *condition seconde*. The success of the pressure technique therefore cast doubt on the dissociative theory of hysteria.

Freud's next step was the creation of the method of "free association", which he came to call the "fundamental rule of psychoanalysis". Freud's use of the free-association method was rooted in a long-standing philosophical belief in what he called "psychical determinism". The concept of psychical determinism was based on the philosophy of scientific naturalism: the view that the mind is a part of nature and that mental phenomena are not essentially different from any other natural events. One of the central doctrines of nineteenth-century scientific naturalism was the doctrine of "determinism": the view that all events are *caused* and that causal relations conform to the laws of nature. For Freud, as for other scientific psychologists, mental events are cemented to other events just as securely as physical events are. None of us stand outside the great causal web of nature. This principle had practical implications. If all mental states are causally related to other mental states—if no thought, memory, or emotion is random—it follows that any thought coming to mind, no matter how bizarre or trivial, must in some sense be *meaningful*. Freud also had some conception of the causal pathways through which psychical determinism was transmitted. In common with many of his colleagues he believed that the mind was *associatively* structured (Macmillan, 1991). According to this view, sequences of ideas are connected by associative links.

Freud developed the free-association method gradually between 1892 and 1896. This development was certainly influenced by experiences like the following, recorded in the case study of "Emmy von N" (Freud, 1895d).

> I took the opportunity of asking her ... why she had gastric pains and where they came from. ... Her answer, which she gave rather grudgingly, was that she did not know. I requested her to remember by tomorrow. She then said in a definitely grumbling tone that *I was not to keep on asking her where this and that came from, but to let her tell me what she had to say.* I fell in with this. [pp. 62–63, emphasis added]

The term "free association" is a rough translation of the German *freier Einfall. Freier*, of course, means "free". The translation of *Einfall* is more problematic. *Einfall* is a "falling into mind"—a thought suddenly coming into mind "out of the blue". The concept has a passive quality: one *finds* oneself with *Einfalle*. They are, as Freud sometimes put it, "involuntary ideas". Freud's "free association" is the attitude of allowing things to involuntarily come to mind. Referring to himself in the third person, Freud (1904a) describes the procedure as follows:

> Without exerting any other kind of influence, he [Freud] invites them to lie down in a comfortable attitude on a sofa, while he himself sits on a chair behind them outside their field of vision. He does not even ask them to close their eyes, and avoids touching them in any way, as well as any other procedure which might be reminiscent of hypnosis. . . . He asks the patient to "let himself go" in what he says, "as you would do in a conversation in which you were rambling on quite disconnectedly and at random". Before he asks them for a detailed account of their case history he insists that they must include in it whatever comes into their heads, even if they think it unimportant or irrelevant or nonsensical; he lays special stress on their not omitting any thought or idea from their story because to relate it would be embarrassing or distressing to them. In the course of collecting this material of otherwise neglected ideas, Freud made the observations which became the determining factor of his entire theory. [pp. 250–251)

Freud also sometimes described free association as *freie Assoziation*—which clearly translates as "free association". Freud could treat *Einfall* and *Assoziation* synonymously because of his commitment to the theory of psychical determinism. Freud did not believe that *Einfalle* just drop unbidden into the mind: in spite of appearances, these thoughts are in fact associations generated by other ideas that are *concealed from consciousness*. Although apparently freakish and random, they are in fact part of the causal/associative web constituting the structure of the mind. Thus:

> . . . when conscious purposive ideas are abandoned, concealed purposive ideas assume control of the current of ideas, and . . . superficial associations are only substitutes by displacement for suppressed deeper ones. [Freud, 1900a, p. 531]

Freud's use of hypnosis, and later his pressure technique, expressed a certain mistrust of nature. It implied that some special *effort* ("concentration") was required in order to induce the mind to yield up its secrets. In contrast to this, the method of free association was based on the principle of letting nature speak her mind.

An architecture of mind

Prior to the spring of 1895, Freud's view of the structure of the mind was a vague amalgam of the philosophical, neurophysiological, and psychiatric views current at the time. During the early 1890s, his rapidly expanding clinical experience as a psychotherapist did not always cohere with these views.

Following in the tradition of French neuropathology, Freud believed that hysteria was caused by a splitting of consciousness. In his therapy, he attempted to eliminate hysterical symptoms by eliminating their cause. He therefore attempted to unify the apparently dissociated consciousness of the hysteric. However, even when hysterical symptoms were removed, Freud's patients often *still* did not recognize the previously split-off pathogenic memories as their own. They were *accepted*, but not *remembered*. This observation raised very serious theoretical problems, for according to the Freud/Breuer theory this state of affairs should be impossible. The restoration of unity to a fractured consciousness should result in the patient immediately recognizing the previously dissociated memories as her own.

Confronted with these problems, Freud began in late March or early April 1895 to reassess his conception of the mind. This was slow going, and it was not until 20 October that he reported substantial progress (Freud, 1887–1904, p. 146). His thoughts were written down in a document that is now called the "Project for a Scientific Psychology" (1950a [1887-1902]). The fundamental ideas hammered out in the "Project" became the basis for much of Freud's future psychoanalytic theorizing.

Freud's "Project" achieved two important aims. First, it announced a philosophical revolution in Freud's thought. Freud explicitly rejected the dualistic views (described in chapter one) in favour of a *materialistic* solution to the mind–body problem. He described mental processes as identical to brain processes. Although this position is now a philosophical orthodoxy, in Freud's day it was quite a radical and unusual stance.

Freud's "Project" also rejected the thesis of mental transparency, no longer regarding the mind as invariably conscious of its own contents and operations. This in turn had implications for psychological research. Introspection could no longer be relied upon as an investigative procedure because introspection can only tell us about those aspects of mental life that happen to be conscious.

Having disposed of these Cartesian assumptions, Freud was free to develop a model of the mind which was not absolutely based upon consciousness. His model, greatly simplified, is as follows.

The mind/brain can be imagined as composed of three systems of neurones (nerve cells) which are represented by the Greek letters phi, psi, and omega. Any model of the mind needs to allow for the fact that we take in information from the external world. The "Phi System" consists of all the sensory channels that lead from the external world into the mind; it is, in contemporary jargon, an "input system". Once inside the mind, such information is analysed and laid down in memory; Freud's "Psi System" is just this— it is the sector of the brain that processes and stores information. The "Omega System" is the part of the brain that produces consciousness. Information passing from Phi to Omega results in a perception: the consciousness of something in the external world. Information passing from Psi to Omega makes us conscious of something in our mind: of our thoughts or memories. Omega (consciousness), is therefore the end-point of two streams of information (just as Omega is the final letter of the Greek alphabet), one coming from the mind and the other coming from the world. In contemporary parlance, it is an "output system".

There are two particularly striking features of this model. First, notice that thinking and consciousness are entirely separate. We only become conscious of our thinking when it enters the Omega System. Thinking is therefore in itself *unconscious*. It is also noteworthy that, in Freud's model, consciousness cannot *do* anything: it is only a site where information coming from the depths of the mind and the external world is displayed, rather like a computer monitor displays the output of the computer.

Freud laid down some principles in the "Project" describing how such information becomes conscious. He regarded perceptions—information from the external world—as immediately conscious. When we perceive something in the external world, "raw sensations" cross our consciousness before we can make any sense of what it is that we are perceiving. We do not have such unmediated access to our own thoughts. In order for a thought to become conscious, it must come into contact with something sensory. Freud believed that *language* provides this link between thinking and consciousness. Language is sensory: it is heard or seen (as in writing or sign language). It is also richly symbolic. For Freud, then, *for a thought to become conscious, it must be translated into language* (even if this only takes place in one's head). It follows from this that *a thought can be prevented from becoming conscious by disrupting or distorting the process of translation.* Freud called this "repression".

Freud was now in a position to replace the unwieldy split-consciousness theory of the *Studies on Hysteria* with a theory of repressed, unconscious mental states. It was not the case, he reasoned, that hysteria is underpinned by a splitting of consciousness. It was rather that certain trains of thought were *prevented* from becoming conscious. This new formulation went some distance towards resolving the clinical problems with which he had been grappling. Freud's patients did not remember having thought this or that, because these conflict-laden thoughts had been prevented from entering consciousness in the first instance. They had been *repressed* (see chapter five).

The concept of resistance

Freud believed that repressed ideas were actively excluded from consciousness because of their emotionally distressing character. Repression was therefore something more than a failure to accurately translate thought into language: it was a *motivated* failure. There was a force within the patient that actively prevented "traumatic" ideas—ideas that would generate particularly intense states of guilt or shame—from entering consciousness. Such ideas cannot be consciously articulated, because their relationship with language has been disrupted. During the process of psychotherapy, this opposing force or "counter-will" is expressed as an irrational opposition to the therapeutic procedure. Freud named this "resistance" [*Widerstand*].

Enter sexuality: the actual neuroses

Once Freud had established himself in private practice, it was not hysterics who made up most of his caseload. Freud was most often called upon to treat *neurasthenics* (Macmillan, 1991).

The concept of neurasthenia (literally, "weakness of the nerves") as a disease came from the work of van Deusen (1868–1869). It was George Beard (1869) who placed neurasthenia in the limelight. Beard described the symptoms of neurasthenia as a state of depletion involving loss of appetite, headaches, hypochondriasis, sexual dysfunctions, loss of energy, and so on. He believed that neurasthenia was caused by a loss of a hypothetical nerve-force. Beard's work stimulated a good deal of interest, and by the mid-1880s several hundred books had been written on the subject (Macmillan, 1991). Freud seems to have begun seriously studying neurasthenia around 1887. By late 1892, Freud had come to believe that neurasthenia was caused by certain forms of sexual activity: excessive masturbation and incomplete intercourse to prevent conception.

Freud reached the conclusion in 1892 or 1893 that Beard's neurasthenia actually covered two distinct disorders, and he distinguished neurasthenia from "anxiety neurosis". Anxiety neurosis, characterized by anxiety, depression, and hypersensitivity, was caused, Freud believed, by sexual abstinence. The symptoms of anxiety neurosis were "substitutes or surrogates for the physiological reactions that should have taken place during orgasm" (Macmillan, 1991, p. 137). Freud's hypothesis was a continuation of an ancient medical tradition. Mediaeval physicians believed that "seed" was ejaculated into the womb by both men and women during intercourse. Seed retained too long in the body was held to become "corrupt" and to cause various maladies. Whereas men were encouraged to discharge this seed into lovers, women were treated by midwives, who would evacuate the vagina with their fingers and with pessaries. By the sixteenth century, the possibility that women obtained sexual pleasure from these procedures became a matter of concern to the clergy (Schleiner, 1997).

Freud classified neurasthenia and anxiety neurosis as "actual neuroses" (from the German *actuelle*, meaning "contemporary").

Unlike the "psychoneuroses" (hysteria, obsessional neurosis, and phobia), the actual neuroses were not seen as amenable to psychotherapy. The treatment of choice was sexual counselling designed to enable the patient to abandon unhealthy sexual practices. It was Freud's work with the actual neuroses, in conjunction with the clinical experience of hysteria garnered during his period of collaboration with Breuer, that led him to the conjecture that the psychoneuroses might also have a specifically sexual basis. It is to the first form of this conjecture that we will now turn.

CHAPTER FOUR

Screens and seductions:
the rise and fall
of the seduction theory

> That building without a firm base: Do not build it high; Or, if
> you do—be afraid.
>
> Sa'adi of Shiraz

During the course of the late 1880s and the early 1890s,
Freud moved from the stance of the neurologist who
studies the effects of nervous disorders to that of the psychologist primarily interested in studying the *stories* that people
tell about themselves and others. Freud believed that it was only
by means of listening to patients' stories that it is possible to draw
valid conclusions about the hidden aspects of their souls, their
unconscious mental life.

The seduction theory

Freud's "seduction theory" was first publicly advanced in the
spring of 1896. Although it was privately retracted in September
1897, public retraction did not come until 1906, a full nine years

after the private retraction. Here is how Freud, writing nineteen years later, described the seduction theory and its retraction:

> The majority of my patients reproduced from their childhood scenes in which they were sexually seduced by some grown-up person. With female patients the part of the seducer was almost always assigned to their father. I believed these stories, and consequently supposed that I had discovered the roots of the subsequent neurosis. ... If the reader feels inclined to shake his head at my credulity, I cannot altogether blame him. [1914d, p. 34]

Why credulity? "I was", wrote Freud in 1933, "driven to recognize in the end that these reports were untrue" (1933a, p. 120). Unfortunately, as we shall see, Freud himself was a purveyor of misinformation about this period of his own work.

The "seduction theory" remains one of the most sensational of Freud's contributions, and a great deal of very misleading material continues to be written about it. This trend was accelerated, if not initiated, by Jeffrey Masson, whose best-selling *Assault on Truth* (1984) asserted that Freud had, in the early 1890s, been told by his patients that they had been sexually abused by their fathers. Masson claims that Freud at first bravely endorsed these anguished accusations but was later driven by his fear of social opprobrium to claim that the confessions of his patients were merely fantasies stemming from infantile sexual desire *for* their fathers. Apart from its negative evaluation of Freud's abandonment of the seduction theory, Masson's story is essentially the same as that later promulgated by Freud himself.

Freud announced the seduction hypothesis in three papers written and published in the spring of 1896: "Heredity and the Aetiology of the Neuroses" (1896a), "Further Remarks on the Neuro-Psychoses of Defence" (1896b) and "The Aetiology of Hysteria" (1896c). According to these papers, hysteria is *always* caused by the repressed memory of a childhood sexual experience. Freud specified that the experience must have occurred early in childhood and must have involved the stimulation of the child's genitals by another person.

The early sexual experience does not immediately produce hysterical symptoms. Instead, it undergoes a period of incubation.

The concept of the "incubation" of a neurosis had been invoked by Breuer in his case of "Anna O." and by Charcot before him. Unlike these authors, Freud provides a principled explanation of why incubation occurs. At first, the memory of the sexual event is of no great psychological consequence. Later, when the child reaches puberty and becomes sexually aware, the memory of the early sexual event is reinforced by a massive amount of energy and becomes powerfully reactivated. The hysteric now understands the memory differently. It has become an emotionally charged memory of a *taboo sexual act* and produces mental conflict. In order to reduce or eliminate the conflict, the memory is rendered unconscious (repressed). Although unconscious, it continues to exert its influence and finds disguised expression in the production of hysterical symptoms.

Freud calls the power of a memory to produce its effects at a later date *Nachträglichkeit*—usually translated as "deferred action". During the interval between the infantile "seduction" and puberty, the memory accrues *negative* value. It becomes much more *emotionally disturbing* and is eventually pushed out of awareness, finding disguised expression only in the form of neurotic symptoms. Freud also believed that the origins of other disorders, such as obsessional neurosis and paranoia, could be explained in terms of variations on the formula initially worked out for hysteria.

Cioffi (1974) appears to have been the first scholar to remark on the fact that, contrary to Freud's later accounts (1906a, 1914d, 1925d, 1933a), the hysterical patients whose experiences provided the evidential base for the seduction theory definitely did *not* routinely report experiences of seduction to Freud. How could they? Freud's theory required that the memory be *unconscious* in order to produce its pathological effects. One cannot report something that is unconscious! What was Freud's data base? He describes inducing experiences in his patients which he calls "reproductions". What did the "reproductions" involve? Schimek (1987) tells us that

> The patients produced the material in response to Freud's continuing pressure (verbal and physical), and his repeatedly asking "What did you see?" or "What occurred to you?" They seem to have produced visual scenes, often of hallucinatory intensity, accompanied with some display of affect, physical sensations, and motoric gestures. . . . The reproduction of the

seduction scenes may have often been a kind of minor hysteri-cal attack, with both verbal and non-verbal expression, in a somewhat altered state of consciousness (Freud mentioned the similarities between the pressure technique and hypnosis). Freud readily admits that the occurrence, if not the main con-tents, of these episodes was strongly influenced by his insistent suggestions and relentless pressure. [pp. 943–944]

Freud *believed* that the "reproductions" were portrayals of the original traumatic "scenes": his patients did not *tell* him that they had been sexually abused (Schimek, 1985). He *reconstructed* (or constructed) these *hypothetical* scenes "on the basis of his interpre-tation of a variety of more or less disguised and partial manifesta-tions and 'reproductions'" (p. 944).

Freud had to exert considerable pressure upon his patients—to use what he called "the strongest compulsion of the treatment"—in order to induce the reproductions. Freud admitted that his patients did not recall the reconstructed events and his conjectures seem never to have received corroboration, and he began to ques-tion the validity of the seduction theory in June or July 1897. By August, he was "tormented by grave doubts" (Freud, 1887–1904, p. 261). On 21 September 1897, he wrote to Fliess retracting the seduction theory.

Although Freud continued for several years to entertain the possibility that the theory was correct (Masson, 1984), this was the beginning of the end for the seduction theory.

Critics sometimes claim that in rejecting his seduction theory Freud denied the existence and importance of the sexual abuse of children. Freud never doubted the existence of the sexual abuse of children or the harmful effects of such experiences. In rejecting the seduction theory, he merely rejected his own unsupported dogma that the cause of hysteria is always an unconscious memory of sexual abuse.

Freud's self-analysis

Freud was a naturally introspective man, but this trait must be distinguished from the more formal process of self-analysis which he began to undertake in the mid-1890s. Freud had good reasons for embarking on his self-analysis, one of which was frankly therapeutic. Freud suffered from mild psychoneurotic symptoms such as anxiety and depression during the 1890s (Jones, 1953). These negative moods disappeared when he was abroad, giving way to a state of restlessness and elation. Freud also suffered from a travel phobia, suffering attacks of anxiety when embarking. The second reason was research. Although developed as a method of treatment, psychoanalysis was a research instrument for investigating unconscious memories and their causal significance. By analysing his dreams and free associations, Freud hoped to learn more both about himself and about the operation of the human mind.

Freud's self-analysis was episodic prior to 1897; between June and August 1897, it became systematic. It consisted largely of the application to himself of the methods and patterns of thought that he had been using with his patients. The central feature of the self-analytic process was the analysis of his own dreams, since Freud regarded dreams as the prime mode for accessing the unconscious.

A great deal of psychoanalysis has its origins in Freud's self-analysis (giving rise to the criticism that psychoanalytic theory is the unwarranted universalization of the psychology of one man). Several of Freud's works, including his paper on "screen memories" (1899a) and *The Interpretation of Dreams* (1900a), provide disguised excerpts from the self-analysis. Freud's intense, systematic self-analysis continued until 1902, although for the remainder of his life he devoted the final half-hour of each day to self-analytic reflection.

Screen memories

In the letter to Fliess retracting the seduction theory, Freud had remarked that "It seems once again arguable that only later experiences give the impetus to fantasies, which [then] hark back to childhood" (Freud, 1887–1904, p. 265). Less than a month later, in a letter to Fliess of 4 October, he noted in relation to his recovered memories of childhood seduction at the hands of his nanny, Resi Wittek, in Freiberg, that "A harsh critic might say of all this that it was retrogressively fantasied instead of progressively determined" (p. 270). He concluded that the presence of a strange and unexpected feature of such memories, in this instance the red bathwater in which he recalled being washed (apparently tinged by his nanny's menstrual blood), provided the *"experimenta crucis"* (p. 270) allowing him to decide that the memory was genuine.

Although such memories might be real memories of real events, Freud also believed that they possessed an unconscious meaning—that is, he believed that they "came to mind" at a particular moment for some special reason. Freud thought that when such memories came to mind as associations to a dream, they revealed the dream's *contemporary* meaning. When he analysed his own dream (the dream reported on 4 October 1896), the image of a pile of money—his wife's weekly housekeeping money—was associated with the childhood memory of Resi Wittek making him steal coins for her. Freud felt that the unconscious meaning of this memory concerned his *contemporary* relationship with his patients: "The dream could be summed up as 'bad treatment'. Just as the old woman got money from me for her bad treatment, so today I get money for the bad treatment of my patients" (p. 269). It is as if Freud were unconsciously saying to himself "You are abusing, exploiting and seducing your patients under the guise of caring for them. You are doing to them just what your nursemaid did to you." Freud also mentioned to Fliess that "The *whole* dream was full of the most mortifying allusions to my present impotence as a therapist" (p. 269, italics added).

In this view, it is a real contemporary *experience* that is "aligned" (p. 320) with earlier experiences and "projected back . . . into earliest infancy" (p. 338).

Freud finally published this theory in his paper "Screen Memories" (1899a), which presents a disguised autobiographical example, an analysis of that example, and a theoretical discussion. In this paper, Freud describes an early memory of being in a meadow with two of his cousins, another boy and a girl. At the top of the meadow, a peasant woman and a children's nurse stand outside a cottage. The meadow is ablaze with dandelions, which the three children are picking. The little girl has the best bunch, and the two boys snatch away her flowers. The girl bursts into tears and runs to the peasant woman, who gives her a slice of black bread. The two boys then discard their flowers and run to the peasant woman, who also provides them with bread, which is delicious. In the memory, Freud was not yet 3 years old.

This memory is set in Freud's birthplace, the town of Freiberg. The Freuds departed from Freiberg when Sigmund was 3½ years old. Freud stresses that the yellow of the dandelions and the delicious taste of the bread seemed strangely intense. He describes two occasions when this memory spontaneously emerged in his mind.

The first arrival of the memory was, to the best of Freud's recollection, in 1872 during a summer holiday in Freiberg. Freud had been there the previous year with his high-school friend Eduard Silberstein, and they had stayed with the Fluss family, old friends of the Freuds from their Freiberg days. On that occasion, Freud fell deeply in love with the 12-year-old Gisela Fluss. When he returned to Freiberg in 1872, he once again stayed with the Fluss family. After a few days Gisela went off to school, "and it was separation after such a short acquaintance that brought my longings to a really high pitch" (1899a, p. 313). Freud regretted that economic hardship had forced the family to leave Moravia, and he daydreamed about having remained and wed Gisela. For a long time afterwards, Freud was preoccupied by a particular shade of yellow: the colour of Gisela's dress when they parted.

The second appearance of the memory relates to Freud's visit, at the age of 19, to his half-brother Emanuel (Freud describes him as an "uncle") in Manchester, where he was reunited with his niece Pauline and nephew Johann ("cousins") who featured in the memory of the meadow with the yellow flowers. Freud's two half-brothers had emigrated to Manchester in 1859 when the remainder of the Freud family also left Freiberg.

Freud departed aboard the *Huddersfield* from Hamburg to Grimsby at midnight, 20 July 1895, and remained in Ardwick, Manchester, for almost two months. According to the story in "screen memories", his father and uncle had plotted that he should emigrate to England, forsake his studies for some practical occupation, and marry his cousin Pauline. Years later, when he was toiling to earn a living, Freud looked back upon this episode and felt that his father had wanted to make reparation for "the loss in which the original catastrophe has involved my whole existence" (p. 315): the earlier displacement of the family from Freiberg to Vienna. It was during this period that the memory recurred.

Freud interprets the content of the screen memory as follows. The *yellow flowers* relate to the *yellow dress* worn by Gisela, and a *yellow alpine flower* associated with his first visit to the Alps during the period when he was struggling to earn a professional niche for himself. The *delicious bread* stands for the imagined comfort and pleasure of remaining in Freiberg and marrying Gisela: "how sweet the bread would have tasted for which you had to struggle so hard in your later years" (p. 315) as well as the "bread-and-butter" occupation planned for Freud by his father and half-brother (*abandoning the flowers for the bread*). *Stealing the flowers* represents the desire to *deflower* Gisela.

Screen memories and the seduction theory

In spite of Freud's remark in the letter to Fliess on 21 September 1897, there is no evidence that he ever re-worked the seduction theory data in light of the theory of screen memories. Eissler (1978) notes that "Freud did not report retrogressive screen memories in any of his patients" (p. 468). In fact, there is no published evidence of his use of the theory outside of the context of his self-analysis until 1903.

According to the screen-memory theory, early memories that seem to spring into one's mind for no apparent reason are *unconscious portrayals of here-and-now situations*. The key to the unconscious meaning of the memory is the context in which it is recalled. The mind unconsciously selects one memory out of its vast storehouse which encodes troubling aspects of one's contemporary situation. Had Freud reconsidered his patients' "reproductions" as screen memories, he would have had to treat them as unconscious snapshots of the situation evoking them: the psychoanalytic situation. Freud would have been forced to conclude that his patients unconsciously felt that he was sexually abusing them. This is not as implausible as it might at first sound. In fact, Freud had reached a similar conclusion in his analysis of his own memory of Resi Wittek.

CHAPTER FIVE

Sweet dreams:
Freud's topographical model

I was sent from myself as a
messenger to myself
And my essence testified to
myself by my signs.

Ibn Al-Farid

Freud had a long-standing interest in dreams. Even as an adolescent, he recorded and reflected upon his dreams. The strictly psychoanalytic theory of dreams took shape in 1895—on 25 July 1895 to be precise. It was on this date, while on holiday, that Freud successfully analysed one of his own dreams, the dream of Irma's injection. Freud now had the tool that would enable him to analyse both his own dreams (in the self-analysis) and the dreams of his psychotherapy patients. It was the dream theory that, surviving the collapse of the seduction theory in 1897, gave Freud a vehicle for carrying psychoanalysis forward.

Freud presented his work on dreams in the monumental *Interpretation of Dreams* (1900a), a book that, although published late in 1899, bore the imprint of 1900 at Freud's request, in order to suggest the dawning of a new era. *The Interpretation of Dreams* executes three tasks.

1. It provides a detailed model of the mind, derived from the speculations contained in Freud's "Project for a Scientific Psychology" (1950a [1887-1902]).

2. It provides a theory of dreaming—that is, an account of how and why dreams are formed.

3. It provides a method for interpreting dreams, an activity that at the time was generally regarded as based on superstition at best and charlatanery at worst.

I briefly describe below each of these aspects of *The Interpretation of Dreams*.

A map of the mind

Although Freud's presentation of his map of the mind appears towards the end of the book, it is probably best to describe this first, as his theory of dreaming and his method of dream analysis only make sense within the context of the psychological model.

The model of the mind presented in *The Interpretation of Dreams* is conventionally described as the "topographical model" or "first topography". Topography is the discipline of map-making. Freud's model is therefore intended as a map of the mind. Maps are by definition selective: no map represents *all* of the features of the territory being mapped. The same is true of Freud's topography, which was intended to represent only certain features of the mind.

Conventional geographical maps are concerned with the spatial relationship between territories. Freud's map, however, is not concerned with spatial relationships: it is concerned with *functional* relationships. His topographical model attempts to portray mental processes and uses a spatial metaphor to describe these processes and their relationships to one another. The use of spatial metaphor to represent functional and temporal relationships is not uncommon. In a cartoon strip, for example, a frame appearing to the left of another is taken to represent events occurring before the frame on the right. When in the left-hand frame the Coyote is about to detonate a pack of TNT (in order to obliterate the Roadrunner) and in the frame to the right we see the Coyote singed and smoking, we assume that this means the plan to blow up the Roadrunner backfired and resulted in the Coyote being blown up (although miraculously not injured). Here the two frames, read from left to right, represent both the passage of time and a causal relationship. We can also use spatial relationships to represent degrees of importance ("That's at the top of my agenda") as well as many other things.

Freud's model describes the functional relationship between hypothetical systems. Systems have three fundamental characteristics. First, a system is something that fulfils some function: its purpose is to do something. Second, systems have inputs: things enter the system. Third, systems have outputs: something leaves or is discharged from the system. The mind is pictured as a system consisting of three mental subsystems: System Unconscious (*Ucs.*), System Preconscious (*Pcs.*), and System Conscious (*Cs.*). System Unconscious is a cognitive system containing mental representations and mental processes. The representations within System Unconscious are picture-like ("thing presentations"). Unconscious mental processes are therefore entirely concrete and non-logical (logical operations require representations of properties and relations, as well as logical operators such as "if–then", "and", "or", etc.). We cannot become aware of mental contents unless they pass from System Unconscious to System Preconscious. System Preconscious links mental pictures to words ("word presentations"), is linguistically structured, and conforms to logical norms and can therefore represent *thought*. Preconscious contents can, in principle, enter consciousness.

In order for a mental content to move from *Ucs.* to *Pcs.*, it must be transcribed into language. According to Freud, there are constraints upon just which thoughts can pass into *Pcs.* Items passing from *Ucs.* to *Pcs.* must pass by a "censor" (modelled on the Roman censor, who regulated entry into the Forum). The task of the censor is to determine which thoughts can be mentally put into words and therefore be available to consciousness. Freud believed that the censor's job was to prevent the outbreak of uncontrollable distress (guilt, shame, panic, etc.). The censor therefore excludes those thoughts that, if admitted to oneself, would produce these reactions. There is also a second censor between *Pcs.* and *Cs.*, which is the gatekeeper of consciousness.

Freud had definite ideas about what sort of ideas are censored—that is, repressed. We repress mental representations of *wishes.* As we all have a repressed area of our minds, it follows that we all harbour contraband wishes, the existence of which we do not even admit to ourselves. According to Freud, the only wishes that can produce the requisite degree of distress if made conscious are *childhood wishes*—that is, thoughts that would have made us intensely fearful of punishment when we were small children. Repressed wishes are therefore infantile.

If such wishes are unconscious, how is it possible to know about them? According to the theory presented in *The Interpretation of Dreams*, there are certain conditions that allow a repressed mental content to make its influence felt. This can occur either when the censorship is relatively weak or when the wish is relatively strong. Under such circumstances (which are described more fully below), the excitation ("psychical energy") attached to the unconscious idea is diverted or *displaced* onto some innocuous preconscious idea, which consequently takes on an unwarranted significance. Energy cannot flow from an unconscious idea to just any preconscious idea: there must be an associative link between the two. This process is called *transference* [*Übertragung*]. A preconscious idea standing in for an unconscious idea is called its derivative.

The formation of dreams

Freud believed that dreams are formed under conditions of lowered censorship. When we go to sleep, it is as though our censor dozes as well. While we sleep, repressed infantile wishes gather momentum in their surge towards consciousness. Although the censor is drowsy, it is not completely disabled. Repressed ideas cannot march unhindered into preconsciousness. The repressed ideas form links with suitable preconscious ideas, which are usually trivial impressions from the day before the dream ("day residues"). It is these derivatives that get woven together to form a dream. There are, however, several more processes of transformation involved. Collectively, these processes are called the "dream work" (i.e. the work performed by the mind to create a dream). The unconscious wish is the *"latent content"* of the dream. This is transformed by the creative magic of the dream work to produce the *"manifest content"*—that is, the dream itself.

The dream work consists of five processes: displacement, condensation, considerations of representability, symbolization, and secondary revision.

Displacement disguises the raw latent content by altering the emphasis of the dream. A highly significant image may, for example, be relegated to a trivial position. In this sense, displacement operates to distract the dreamer's attention.

Through the process of *condensation*, a single unconscious thought may be realized though a number of images in a single dream. Conversely, condensation may also pack multiple meanings into a single dream image. The condensation of multiple meanings is also called *"overdetermination"*.

In their transformation into the manifest dream, unconscious thoughts are constrained by *considerations of representability*. This means that they are transformed in such a way as to permit concrete (usually visual) representation. This is perhaps best grasped by considering the problems faced by a political cartoonist. The cartoonist must find a way to express ideas in concrete pictorial form. He might, for example, depict the dominance of Germany over Britain by an image of the German prime minister sitting on the British Houses of Parliament.

Symbolization is the representing of one item by another because of some resemblance between them. When an unconscious thought is symbolized in a dream, the corresponding dream element serves as a kind of metaphor. Many people mistakenly believe that Freud interpreted dreams exclusively in symbolic terms; for example, that he regarded all elongated objects as phallic symbols, all concave objects as vaginal symbols, and so on. As we shall see, this is not true.

It is important clearly to distinguish displacement from symbolization. Displacement is based on associative linkage rather than resemblance. Using displacement, I might represent my father with the image of a boat because he once owned a boat. On the other hand, the relation between a symbol and the thought that it symbolizes is an *analogue* relationship. Using symbolism, I might represent my father as the prime minister because both father and prime minister are "the man in charge".

Strictly speaking, symbolization is not part of the dream work. Freud believed that symbolism is just a natural pattern of unconscious thought and is not essentially a method for evading censorship. In fact, Freud believed that even if there were no dream censorship it would be difficult to understand the meaning of dreams because of the inevitability of symbolic forms of representation.

Secondary revision is a process of narrative construction. It is the process weaving together the fragments of dream imagery into a "story"—a relatively coherent whole.

The processes making up the dream work do not tell the entire story of how it is that unconscious wishes can find expression by means of dreams. In order to understand this, we need to examine more closely the relationship between unconscious and preconscious ideas. I have already mentioned that unconscious ideas must form links with free-floating preconscious impressions in order to find nocturnal expression. There are some constraints on how these day residues are selected. Most important for the purposes of this discussion is the principle that day residues are chosen that are themselves linked to *preconscious wishes*. Preconscious wishes are everyday desires. The best way to understand this is to imagine the mind as tending towards the convergence of streams of desire. The day residue that is selected to become part of a dream receives reinforcement from two separate tributaries, one of which is unconscious and the other preconscious. The preconscious dimension of the latent content of the dream is called the "preconscious dream wish" or the "latent dream thoughts" (an expression easily confused with the "latent content" of the dream). In light of this, any dream can be seen to possess at least three levels of meaning: the manifest level, the preconscious level, and the unconscious level.

The interpretation of dreams

To "interpret" a dream is to discover at least its preconscious and at most its unconscious meaning. According to the Freudian theory we cannot just "read off" the meaning of a dream from its surface structure. It is necessary to undo the dream work by tracing back the associative pathways between the dream images and the dreamer's other concerns with the aid of the free-association method. The dreamer is instructed to let his or her mind freely wander from each element of the dream in turn. This can lead to some surprising discoveries.

The dreamer will usually find that the trains of association eventually converge. This indicates that a layer of latent meaning has been reached. Dream elements are only interpreted symbolically if they cannot be understood in the context of the dreamer's associations.

Abandoning oneself to free-association and discovering how this results in the revelation of meaning can be an unsettling experience. It brings one face to face with the fact that there exist sophisticated mental processes that are quite beyond conscious control. To interpret a dream successfully, it is essential to relinquish conscious control of the associative process, to refrain from trying to "figure out" the dream, and to just let one's mind dance.

I will illustrate the essentials of the Freudian approach to dream interpretation through the example of one of my own dreams. The dream was brief and simple. *I dreamed that I was Ronald Reagan sitting behind a large desk. I had a vague impression that there was an American flag displayed behind me. I felt very self-confident.*

I began the analysis by free-associating to Ronald Reagan. I had in fact seen Reagan on a television newscast before going to sleep. This programme was about the upcoming American presidential election. A political analyst commented that Reagan was almost certain to win the election, and the Democratic contender had little chance of success. I had hit upon a day residue. But what preconscious wishes might this be connected with? I associated to the thought of Reagan's almost certain victory over the other candidate. I then thought of something that had been disturbing me and which I was inclined to dismiss from my awareness. A post had become vacant at an institution where I worked. I had applied for this post, which represented a considerable promotion. I was aware that a colleague had also applied for the post, and I had reason to believe that she would be the favoured candidate. I had been working in the institution for considerably longer than my rival, and I did not have a high opinion of her abilities. I was therefore facing the prospect of being humiliated and rejected. The theme of the day-residue-linked memory was that *Reagan was bound to win*. In representing myself as Reagan, then, I could be regarded as transforming this upsetting situation into one in which I was *certain to defeat my rival and get the job*. So, in spite of surface appearances, my dream of being Reagan was the fulfilment of a preconscious wish for promotion. I had magically solved my dilemma!

I next associated to the desk. This led to the memory of my father having purchased a desk for me when I was in secondary school. I was, at the time, having great difficulty keeping up with my school work and had *failed* several classes. The theme of failing, and therefore being held back, cohered with the theme of fearing that I would not get the job. In secondary school, I had the experiences of younger, *less experienced* pupils moving ahead of me academically. Associating to the flag, I was immediately reminded of the flag displayed in American classrooms. So, on the level of preconscious dream thoughts, I hypothesized that the memories of failure and humiliation in high school were displaced onto the images of the desk and the flag. In the dream, my position behind the desk *vis-à-vis* the flag corresponded to the position of a teacher, not a student. This element of the dream seemed to condense two trains of thought. On the one hand, this reintroduced the theme of *promotion* (from student to teacher). On the other, it reminded me that it was a *teaching* position that I had applied for.

While engaged in these reflections, I began to notice a second associative theme. Ronald Reagan reminded me of my father (the two had certain characteristics in common). Taken as a symbol, a president may represent a father. Similarly, the desk had been given to me by my father. It was clear that the latent (unconscious) content of the dream had something to do with my father, and that this had something to do with my fears of failure and humiliation.

If we understand Reagan as a father-figure in the dream, I had managed to replace my father with myself.

The creation of dreams

In order for Freud's approach to dream interpretation to make sense, it needed to be put into the context of a theory describing how dreams come about. I have already touched on aspects of Freud's story of dream creation, but this requires a bit more expansion.

Freud believed that dreams are driven by wishes. In particular, they are mainly brought about by wishes that are denied direct access to consciousness because of their potential to cause a special kind of anguish. Freud believed that only childhood wishes possess this potential. Furthermore, because of their freedom from the constraints of everyday reality, dreams strive to fulfil magically both the unconscious wishes and the preconscious wishes with which they become associated.

When a childhood wish is stirred during sleep, it attempts to find discharge. The wish is blocked by the censor, so it transfers its energy onto preconscious wishes and day residues. These become the raw materials that make up the manifest dream after being worked over by displacement, condensation, symbolization, and secondary revision and being brought within the constraints of pictorial representation. The final product is the dream that we remember.

Let us speculate how, according to Freudian theory, my dream might have come about. We must start by hypothesizing the existence of an unconscious wish to take the place of my father. This wish, pressing for discharge, was repelled by my censor. The "charge" connected to this wish was then transferred onto a preconscious wish to be promoted at work, with attendant anxiety about failure. My dreaming mind then required an image from the preceding day with which to express both preconscious and unconscious wishes. It selected the image of Ronald Reagan, which I had encountered shortly before going to bed, because of its unique capacity to condense the latent thoughts about getting the job and taking the place of my father. By becoming Ronald Reagan in the dream, I magically fulfilled both wishes.

Failed accomplishments

Freud's work on dreams was roughly simultaneous with and clearly related to his work on a class of events that he called *Fehlleistungen* [failed accomplishments]. In English, we call these events "Freudian slips", although the term "parapraxes" is used in the English language psychoanalytic literature. Parapraxes are essentially trivial accidents and include such phenomena as slips of the tongue, slips of the pen, misreadings, misplacing things, and botched actions. Freud's main work on this subject was *The Psychopathology of Everyday Life*, published in 1901 (Freud, 1901b).

Some slips seem immediately intelligible and may be very embarrassing. This is often the case with slips of the tongue or pen. For example, I was once discussing Freud's theory of parapraxes with a student who was both sceptical and ill-disposed to Freudian ideas. As her objections reached their crescendo, she unintentionally referred to "Freudian slips" as "Freudian shits". We both laughed. Here is a similar example, this time involving a slip of the pen: a student's dissertation on the psychoanalytic treatment of addiction containing a detailed and laborious account of Kleinian concepts. The student introduced the section on Klein with the announcement that she would first examine Melanie Klein's "chore ideas" (instead of "core ideas" as she intended).

We can understand both of these examples immediately. In the first example, the student had been restraining herself, in deference to her teacher, from saying that in her opinion Freudian psychology was a "load of shit". This suppressed intention managed to insinuate itself into what she had chosen to say. Similarly, the student who was impatiently fulfilling the academic obligation of explaining Klein's basic ideas before being able to proceed to more advanced and interesting material suppressed the opinion that this was a chore.

Freud believed that we often lose things because for some reason we want to. Sometimes it is clear why we would want to lose something. For instance, you may misplace a letter that you resent having to reply to. You may forget the date of an unpleasant appointment (I regularly do this with dental appointments). You may bungle a task that you did not want to perform, and so on. These are all relatively *transparent* examples. Freud gives the highly plausible explanation that in such cases we find (a) a state of conflict and (b) a desire to suppress the conflictual competing train of thought. So, for example, when I forget an unpleasant appointment, this is because I both wish to go to the dentist (I want to keep my teeth in good shape and believe that regular visits to the dentist will help me secure this) and I also want to avoid going to the dentist (I want to avoid pain, and I think that my visit to the dentist is likely to cause me pain). I try to dismiss the second thought and to behave responsibly, but from its marginalized position this wish to avoid the dentist manages to get its own way by causing me to forget the appointment.

Not all parapraxes are immediately intelligible. Many are more opaque. In these instances, one must assume that the processes of repression and disguise are at work, and the parapraxis must be analysed in much the same way that one would analyse a dream. *The Psychopathology of Everyday Life* contains many examples of both transparent and opaque parapraxes, many of which were taken from Freud's self-analysis.

Freud called parapraxes the "psychopathology of everyday life", because the explanation of slips has the same general structure as the explanation of neurotic symptoms and dreams—namely, the analysis of how a disavowed idea irrationally influences one's consciousness and behaviour. Freudian slips are "miniature" neurotic symptoms, just as dreams are normal psychotic states in which repressed ideas are expressed in the form of compelling hallucinations.

There are still significant dis-analogies between dreams and symptoms on the one hand, and parapraxes on the other. The meaning of a parapraxis still seems rather direct. In dreams and symptoms, the unconscious cause is not so clearly displayed. The symptom or dream image has a far less transparent, far more convoluted relationship with its unconscious cause. There does not seem to be anything equivalent to the dream work in the formation of Freudian slips.

Freud's topographical perspective provided a picture of human beings as radically and inevitably divided against themselves, struggling against wishes that have become extruded from their own subjectivity. Consciousness was henceforth to be regarded neither as co-terminous with mind nor as its executive. Consciousness was now to be seen as a passive vehicle for expressing events occurring both deeper within the apparatus and in the external world. Memory was deemed untrustworthy: what appear to be innocent recordings of events in the childish past may, in fact, be vehicles for raw perceptions of contemporary reality.

CHAPTER SIX

Sex from the inside:
Freud's theory of sexuality

By nature, men are nearly alike; by practice, they get to be wide apart.

Confucius

Even today, Freud is regarded by many as having been obsessed with sexuality. During his lifetime, this outspoken concern with the role of sexuality in human life earned him an aura of both fascination and opprobrium. Apostates like Jung and Adler broke with psychoanalysis largely on the grounds of Freud's relentless assertion that sexuality both drives a great deal of human endeavour and drives men and women to madness, both collectively and as individuals.

Sex and dread

Syphilis, the "great pox", had existed in Europe since the late fifteenth century. An accurate diagnostic test was not developed until 1906, and effective treatment was not available until just before the First World War. It has been estimated that in Freud's time 10 to 20 percent of the urban male population suffered from venereal disease (Decker, 1991). "Walking through doctors' neighbourhoods", writes Decker, "one could read on every sixth or seventh door 'specialist for Skin and Venereal Diseases'" (p. 43). According to one study, 45 percent of young German clerks and merchants, aged 19 to 45, had suffered at one time or another from syphilis or gonorrhoea. Another study indicated that, at minimum, one German man in five had at some time suffered from syphilis, and that the incidence of gonorrhoea averaged one attack for every mature male in the country (Ramas, 1980, cited in Decker, 1991). Syphilis, in its tertiary phase (which was first recorded during the nineteenth century), could attack the central nervous system, causing insanity. Passed on from mother to foetus, it was a significant cause of infant mortality (Arrizabalaga, Henderson, & French, 1997). Gonorrhoea was described as particularly painful for women.

Throughout the nineteenth century, masturbation was regarded as both a vice and a powerful pathogen, capable of producing insanity or stemming from insanity. Masturbation was regarded as a *medical* problem and retained this status until after World War Two (Bonomi, 1997). It was widely believed that "in children the most satisfactory method of prevention was the *threat of an immediate and alarming punishment*" (Hare, 1962, cited in Schatzman, 1976, p. 105). The most frequent threat was genital mutilation by parents and physicians (Bloch, 1908).

During the late nineteenth century, surgery was the most frequently recommended "treatment" for masturbation (Spitz, 1953). Treatments for men and boys included:

> Enclosing the penis in bandages; infibulation (the placement of metal wires or rings through the prepuce in order to forestall its retraction behind the glans); section of the dorsal nerves of the penis in order to prevent sensations in and erection of the penis; blistering of the prepuce; and wearing spiked or toothed metal rings on the penis at night, which would bite into the penis if it became erect.

Girls and women were likely to receive:

> Ovariotomy (i.e. cutting into an ovary); clitoridectomy (i.e. removal of the clitoris); infibulation of the prepuce and labia

majora; surgical separation of the prepuce hood from the clitoris; blistering of the prepuce, vulva and insides of the thighs;
and, before going to sleep, putting the legs in splints or tying
them one to either side of the crib or bed. [pp. 105–106]

Genital mutilation as a "treatment" for masturbation began to
disappear in Europe during the latter part of the nineteenth century, although it persisted in the United States until the Second
World War (Bonomi, 1997).

Contraception was unreliable, uncomfortable, and expensive
as well as being opposed by the Roman Catholic majority in Austria. Death in childbirth was not uncommon. Illegal abortions were
available only to the middle and upper classes (Sharaf, 1983). Birth
control was, of course, opposed by the Roman Catholic church,
and religious opposition to many forms of sexual activity provided
an additional source of guilt.

Hysteria could also be treated by means of rationalized sexual
violence. The "castration" of hysterical women (surgically remov-
ing their ovaries) was introduced by Hegar in 1872 and became
widespread after 1885. Rudolf Chrobak, Professor of Gynaecology
and Obstetrics at the University of Vienna (and also the psychoanalyst Heinz Hartmann's maternal grandfather), who was
described by Freud (1914d) as "perhaps the most eminent of our
Viennese physicians" (p. 13), performed 146 such operations
within the space of a few years. Both Freud and Breuer were opposed to this form of "treatment" (Bonomi, 1997).

Sexual "perversions" also received medical attention. Until
about 1870, perversions were regarded as caused by an abnormality of the reproductive organs. After 1870, the triumphs of
neuroscience (particularly in the area of aphasiology) led to the
belief that perversions were caused by a lesion or abnormality of
the brain. Later still, perversions were seen as purely functional
disorders of the sexual drive (Davidson, 1990).

Sex

Freud's main work on sexuality was *Three Essays on the Theory of
Sexuality* (1905d), a book that—like *The Interpretation of Dreams*—he
updated with each subsequent edition.

In the *Three Essays*, Freud describes sexuality as being composed of "drives" [*Triebe*—often mistranslated as "instincts"]. A drive is an "endosomatic, continuously flowing source of stimulation" (p. 168). Drives have no subjective, first-person aspect. They are not mental contents. They are simply a "demand made upon the mind for work". Sexual drives are drives that impel us to obtain sensuous pleasure through the stimulation of those areas of our bodies that Freud called "erotogenic zones". The major erotogenic zones are the mouth, anus, and genitals. He believed that the drives possessed the following characteristics:

- They have a *source* in some bodily organ or process. When we classify sexual drives according to their source, we refer to "oral drives", "anal drives", and so on.

- They have *force* [*Drang*]—that is, they possess causal power to drive thought and behaviour.

- They have an *aim*, which is always the discharge of tension by means of some sexual act. The mode of discharge will depend upon the source of the drive.

- They have *objects*, defined as that by means of which drives realize their aims. Sexual drives can only be satisfied by sexual acts with real objects (normally people), but may also be expressed as fantasied sexual acts with fantasied objects.

The first of Freud's essays deals with deviations from what is generally conceived to be normal sexuality. Freud wished to undermine the sharpness of the conventional distinction between sexual normality and sexual aberration. Although he sometimes uses scare-quotes around the term "perversions" and refers to heterosexual intercourse as "what is regarded as normal", Freud, too, invokes a concept of normality in this and other passages of the *Three Essays*. It would therefore seem important to identify Freud's "take" on normal sexuality.

I think that it is probably accurate to say that when Freud, a "biologist of the mind" (Sulloway, 1979), himself implicitly or explicitly endorses a concept of normality, it is essentially a concept of *biological normality*. The strictly biological concept of normality has been clarified by the philosopher Ruth Garrett Millikan (1984, 1993) as follows. All living things have been "designed" by the

process of natural selection. Natural selection is driven by reproductive success. Features of an organism are preserved from one
generation to the next because they contribute to that organism's
reproductive success. For example, a rabbit that can run quickly is
more likely to reproduce than one who does not—the latter is more
likely to be devoured by predators. *Speed* contributes to the rabbit's reproductive success. If we were to ask the child-like question
"Why are rabbits fast?", the Darwinian answer would be: "If they
weren't they would not exist", or, perhaps more simplistically, "To
get away from foxes." We can say that the "purpose" of any feature of an organism is just the way that it has, in previous generations, contributed to reproductive success. The biological purpose
of something is its biological *raison d'être*: the historical reason for
its existence. For instance, the biological purpose of hearts is to
pump blood. Hearts exist to pump blood. Pumping blood is why
we have hearts. We can say that pumping blood is the *normal* (or
"proper") *function* of hearts. Similarly, the normal function of spermatozoa is to fertilize ova. This is the reason that sperm cells exist.
However, in the case of spermatozoa we can clearly notice the
difference between what things *do* and what they are *supposed
to do*. The overwhelming majority of all the sperm generated in
all the testicles of all the men who have ever existed have *not*
fertilized eggs. In nature, not all items *perform* their proper function. The bare fact that a sperm cell does not reach an ovum does
not mean that there is anything "pathological" about that sperm
cell. By the same token, there can be pathological features of a
sperm cell that prevent it from performing its normal function.
Some things can have multiple normal functions, such as the feath-
ers of birds, that both regulate temperature and facilitate flight.
Other things can take on secondary functions (in addition to their
normal ones). For instance, beavers use trees to build dams, but
trees do not exist for the purpose of providing raw materials for
beavers.

In light of these considerations, heterosexual intercourse is biologically normal sexuality. From a Darwinian perspective, sex
exists because it sometimes culminates in reproduction. Freud
struggles in the *Three Essays* to distinguish the biological normality
of "no-frills" heterosexual intercourse from a very different claim
about normality: namely, the view that most people's sexual de-

sires naturally flow exclusively along these channels, and that any deviation from this is a sign of illness or vice.

Freud points out that all people have aspects to their sexuality unrelated to the normal aim of reproduction. An example is the kiss, which is a purely oral mode of erotic enjoyment. These modes of sexuality, then, "provide a point of contact between the perversions and normal sexual life" (1905d, p. 150). Using this "point of contact", Freud suggests that "perversions" are sexual acts involving parts of the body not designed for reproductive sex or which "linger" in forms of sexual enjoyment that are normally *preliminary* to sexual intercourse.

The intoxication of sexual desire—the "credulity of love"— does not confine itself to the genitals, but "extends to the whole body of the sexual object" (p. 150). We sometimes regard anatomical extensions of sexual activity as "perversions" because of the conventional (socially induced) attitude of *disgust*. Those forms of sexuality which "linger" over the early stages of sexual contact include voyeurism and exhibitionism (pleasure in looking and being looked at erotically) and sadomasochism (capturing and submitting to the sexual object).

Given the conventional and culturally relative inflection of the term "perversion", Freud was concerned to find some way of objectively distinguishing between pathological and non-pathological forms sexuality. He held that it is inappropriate to use "perversion" as a term of opprobrium. The sought-after criterion is suggested in the discussion of fetishism. The sexual valuation of an item of clothing is compatible with normal sexuality (certain forms of dress may be a "turn on"). The situation only becomes pathological when the sexual excitement passes beyond the point of being merely a necessary condition attached to the object and actually *takes the place* of the normal aim and, furthermore, becomes the *sole* sexual object. Many men may be sexually attracted to women with long hair; this is a simple sexual variation. If, however, he is excited by *women's hair* (rather than by women with long hair), and still more if he is excited *exclusively* by hair, then this variation has slipped over into something pathological: a perversion.

How is it possible for one strand of the rich fabric of erotic life to become preponderant in this way? Freud believed that perversion gives us insight into the composition of sexuality itself.

Freud held that sexuality is composed of a number of "component drives", and he therefore spoke of sexuality in its multiplicity: the sexual *drives* rather than *the* sexual drive. The component drives are normally classified by their source. The anal and oral drives are instinctual components generated by zones "subordinate to the genitals" (1905d, p. 168).

Sex was commonly believed to awaken first at puberty. Freud argued that sexuality has a pre-history: childhood, too, possesses its own distinctive erotic forms. The concept of infantile sexuality was by no means a Freudian novelty. It was discussed quite extensively during the last two decades of the nineteenth century (Bonomi, 1997; Sulloway, 1979), but Freud's approach to the subject was striking in its naturalistic and non-judgemental tenor.

Infantile sexuality does not involve the urge for sexual intercourse. Freud believed infantile sexuality to be "incomparably more variegated" (1906a, p. 277) than adult sexuality. Childhood sexuality is organized around the component drives—this is the source of its variegation. In a sense, then, the sexuality of children is perverse. In a turn of phrase calculated to shock, Freud referred to it as "polymorphously perverse" (1905d, p. 191).

Of course, normal children are not *literally* perverse. It is not "perverse" for a baby to crave an erect nipple in its mouth. What we call "perversions" are highly distorted expressions of infantile sexual trends strongly coloured by adult, genital sexuality. Freud called childhood sexuality "polymorphously perverse" to emphasize *continuity* rather than to make a claim of strict *identity*.

Homosexuality

Contrary to popular belief, Freud did not normally describe homosexuality as a "perversion".

By the time Freud composed the *Three Essays*, there was already a sizeable academic literature on homosexuality (e.g. Casper, 1852; Ellis, 1897, 1901; Krafft-Ebing, 1894; Schrenck-Notzing, 1895; Shaw & Ferris, 1883). Earlier in the nineteenth century, Karl Ulrichs (1898) had described *Homosexualität* as innate rather than acquired. Ulrichs, a jurist, carefully distinguished homosexuality from "pederasty":

In Ulrichs' scheme and especially in his juridical arguments, the "homosexual" supposedly cannot be responsible for his interest in other men; it is entirely innate in or natural to him. But a "pederast" . . . supposedly is responsible for *his* interests and actions and can thus properly be punished. [Davis, 1995, p. 117]

Other writers, such as Krafft-Ebing, continued to regard homosexuality as unnatural. Davis (1995) shows that those writers most inclined to describe homosexuality as an unnatural, acquired condition were involved in the "developing 'psychotherapeutic' industries" (p. 118).

The psychotherapists sought their patients among middle- and upper-class paying customers. Basically, they claimed to "cure" a man's "acquired vice" by helping him *de*acquire it— for example, by hypnotically implanting the suggestion in an "impotent" man troubled by homosexual feelings that he should go home and have sexual relations with his wife. [p. 119]

By the turn of the century, the terms *Homosexualität* and "inversion" were used to denote a conception of same-sex love as an innate disposition, while "contrary sexual feeling" was more pejorative, reflecting a view of homosexuality as a vice or acquired pathology. Other writers, such as Friedlander (1904) and Kupffer (1899) described homosexuality as a mature *choice*, using such terms as "same-sex sexual love" (Friedlander) or "chivalric love of comrades" (Kupffer).

In the *Three Essays* and elsewhere, Freud used the term "inversion" [*Inversion*] for an innate, non-pathological *disposition* towards same-sex love. He used the term "contrary sexual feelings" [*konträre Geschlechtsgefühl* or *konträre Sexualempfindung*] to describe *occurrent* sexual activities, fantasies, and attitudes. Freud's use of "homosexuality" [*Homosexualität*] includes both of these (Davis, 1995). These subtle conceptual distinctions are largely lost in translation.

Freud believed that all human beings are originally bisexual (a concept he derived from Fliess). We are born with the propensity to sexually love both men and women. During the course of development, this disposition is usually constrained, and we become heterosexuals or homosexuals. Freud emphasized that, in light of this, the development of exclusive heterosexuality is no less a problem to be scientifically explained than is exclusive homosexuality

Homosexuality is not a "perversion" because it is not appropriately described in terms of a component drive or a piece of foreplay hijacking genital sexuality. If perversion teaches us that sexuality is complex rather than unitary, homosexuality teaches us that the object of a drive is not intrinsic to it. Drive and object are "merely soldered together" (1905d, p. 148). Exclusive homosexuality may be based on purely innate factors, may be acquired, or may be brought about by the interaction between the two. In any case, it is not an illness but (like heterosexuality) can assume neurotic or perverse forms.

Perversion inside-out

Freud claimed for the first time in the *Three Essays* that neurotic symptoms—those conversions, delusions, obsessions, phobias, and compulsions that he had been attempting to treat for the previous nineteen years—were disguised and transformed expressions of perverse sexual impulses. "Thus", wrote Freud in a famous sentence, "symptoms are formed in part at the cost of *abnormal* sexuality; *neuroses are, so to say, the negative of perversions*" (p. 165). Neurotics (psychoneurotics) repress those aspects of their sexuality which would otherwise cause excessive shame or guilt. These include both the "perverse" impulses of childhood and also, in the case of heterosexuals, homosexual impulses.

It is not only "neurotics" who have a perverse unconscious. *All of us* without exception have tamed our sexuality by splitting off and repressing certain aspects of it. "Normality" is

> ... the result of the repression of certain component instincts and constituents of the infantile disposition and the subordination of the remaining constituents under the primacy of the genital zones in the service of the reproductive function. [Freud, 1906a]

Perversions are "disturbances of this coalescence" by one or another component drive, whereas neurosis is based on "excessive repression" of infantile erotic impulses.

With this formulation, the process of psychoanalytic psycho-therapy was redefined. It is the aim of the analyst to help the patient become conscious of his or her repressed perverse impulses and fantasies, to loosen the stranglehold of repression so that these impulses and fantasies would no longer have to find tortured ex-pression in the form of neurotic symptoms. Psychoanalysis became a process directed at getting to know the more disturbing aspects of one's psychosexual life. With this reformulation, psychoanalysis became even more entrenched in its inward focus. Our sexuality is, after all, essentially something that lies *inside* us.

Psychosexual stages

The concept of infantile sexuality introduced in the first edition of the *Three Essays* was both vague and diffuse. Infantile sexuality was seen as "perverse" and bisexual. After the first efflorescence of childhood sexuality comes a moratorium, the "latency period" of the primary-school-aged child, during which relative asexuality reigns. This is followed by the storms of puberty, during which mature "genital" sexuality is born.

In the two decades following the publication of the *Three Essays*, Freud refined his concept of psychosexual development, dividing the period of infantile sexuality into sub-stages. The first of these, the "oral stage", was first described in Freud's short psy-chobiography of Leonardo da Vinci (1910c). The oral stage roughly corresponds to babyhood. Like the other two stages, it is named after its leading component drive: the oral drive. The baby's sexu-ality mainly involves sucking.

The toddler period ushers in the "anal-sadistic" stage, during which the anal and sadistic components dominate. The concept of an anal-sadistic stage was introduced in 1913 (Freud, 1913i). During this period of his work, Freud used the term "sadism" to refer to the sexual pleasure derived from the active use of one's muscles—the pleasure taken in dominating and manipulating—*not* the pleasure specifically derived from inflicting pain on others.

After the anal-sadistic stage comes the "phallic stage", which is the final phase of infantile sexuality and was not introduced into psychoanalytic theory until 1923 (Freud, 1923e). During the phallic stage, the leading component drive is phallic or clitoral sexuality. Despite its genital focus, the "phallic child" does not crave sexual *intercourse* (a defining characteristic of mature sexuality). The phallic child is content to play with its genital and to exhibit it.

Freud regarded the phallic stage as the most developmentally significant of the three. I therefore need to discuss it here in considerably greater detail, but first I must introduce some auxiliary developmental concepts.

As I have already described, Freud described psychosexual development as unfolding in a series of stages. Each of these possesses a distinctive developmental "organization". A developmental organization is, roughly, what it is like to be in a certain stage. So, for instance, the "oral organization" is a term for what it is like to be a baby, the "anal-sadistic organization" is a shorthand term for what it is like to be a toddler, and the "phallic organization" names the characteristic mode of being of a pre-school child.

We can become "fixated" to one developmental organization or another. A fixation is nothing more than an especially strong attachment. For instance, a person who particularly enjoys dominating and controlling others may be said to be fixated to the anal-sadistic organization. We tend to be fixated on those organizations that give us special satisfaction or, conversely, those that are connected with experiences of conflict or deprivation. Fixation may also be explained purely biologically: the orally fixated person may just have *constitutionally* strong oral drives. Freud gave "nature" and "nurture" equal weight in his accounts of human behaviour.

In order to understand personality and psychopathology, we must introduce yet another developmental concept: *regression* (a concept that Freud derived from the work of the British neuroscientist John Hughlings Jackson and implicitly introduced in the *Three Essays*). Regression is the partial abandonment of a developmental organization in favour of a more primitive one. We tend to regress under circumstances of stress or anxiety, and when we regress we regress to points of fixation. An orally fixated person may, for example, be inclined to drink and eat excessively when subjected to stress. Regression is a way of protecting ourselves from distress.

For Freud, psychopathology (psychologically caused mental or emotional disfunction) always involves regression: that is, in circumstances where we are so riven by conflict that we cannot cope, our sexuality tends to revert to earlier fixated forms. This in turn activates "perverse" early trends which are either acted out as perversions or are suppressed and give rise to neurosis.

The "nuclear complex"

Freud did not describe infantile sexual development solely in terms of biologically rooted oral, anal-sadistic, and phallic/clitoral urges. He also described it in terms of the child's relationships with members of its immediate family. Freud believed that there is a particular pattern of relationship which all children experience in one form or another. In his earliest psychoanalytic works, he called this the "nuclear complex" or the "father complex". In 1910 he rechristened it the "Oedipus complex" (Freud, 1910h).

The term "Oedipus" derives from the ancient Greek legend of Oedipus. Freud wrote for a public that, on the whole, had received a classical *gymnasium* education and would immediately appreciate the complex and tragic resonances of the name "Oedipus". Today, however, comparatively few of the educated public have had the benefit of studying the Greek classics, so it will prove useful to review the ancient story.

Laius, the wicked ruler of the kingdom of Thebes (he was credited with the dubious distinction of having invented pederasty), had been informed by an Oracle that he would sire a son who would kill his own father and marry his mother. When his wife, Jocasta, eventually gave birth to a boy, Laius got a couple of his "heavies" to take the boy out of town and kill him, after first having them drive a spike through his feet. The henchmen agreed to do as they were told, but could not bring themselves to kill the infant. The boy was adopted by the royal family of Corinth and raised as their natural child. He was given the name "Oedipus"—meaning "swollen foot".

In response to a reference to his true origins, the adult Oedipus consults the Oracle, who confirms the original prophecy (but refrains from telling him that he was an adopted child). Oedipus responds by fleeing Corinth. He is determined to put as many miles as possible between himself and his "parents". Oedipus wants to cheat fate, to render the Oracle false, to avoid killing his father and marrying his mother.

Of course, the hapless Oedipus ends up making a beeline for Thebes. Along the way his ox-cart meets another at a crossroads, and a dispute ensues. Remonstration turns to violence as Oedipus comes to blows with and kills his rival. Unbeknownst to him, that rival was Laius, King of Thebes, his father. Having fulfilled the first part of the prophecy, Oedipus is drawn to satisfy the second. Approaching Thebes, Oedipus encounters a strange monster, the Sphinx, who sits on the outskirts of the city posing riddles to those who enter. Those who incorrectly answered were devoured by the Sphinx, while a correct answer would destroy the Sphinx. The Thebans have offered the incentive of marriage to the recently widowed Queen Jocasta for anyone who succeeds in answering the riddle of the Sphinx. Oedipus decides to try. The Sphinx asks him: "What walks on four feet in the morning, two at noon, and three at sunset." Oedipus (who was something of an expert on feet) replied correctly: "It is Man who crawls as an infant, learns to walk erect, and, when old, hobbles about on a cane." The Sphinx is vanquished and Oedipus marries his mother. The fulfilment of the prophecy is complete.

Many years later, Oedipus mounts an investigation into the murder of Laius because a pestilence has fallen upon Thebes in consequence of the murder, and he is told the truth by the blind seer Tiresias. Oedipus blinds himself and withdrawing from society becomes a sage, looked after by his daughter Antigone.

What resonances did Freud wish to elicit by naming the nuclear complex after Oedipus? First, he wished to introduce the idea of *incest*. Second, he wanted to include the themes of rivalry and patricide. And third:

> The meaning of the term "Oedipus complex" is symbolic. . . .
> If we believe, as many of my students did, that the term "Oedipus Complex" implies only that little boys want to kill the man they *know* is their father and marry the woman they *know* is their mother, then our understanding is based on an extreme simplification of the myth. After all, Oedipus did not

know what he was doing when he killed Laius and married Jocasta, and his greatest desire was to make it *impossible* for himself to harm those he thought were his parents. [Bettelheim, 1983, pp. 21–22]

Oedipus is driven by forces of which he is unaware. In attempting to distance himself from his parents, he is inexorably and paradoxically drawn within their orbit. In this sense, we are all Oedipus. We all believe that we are in charge of our lives and "free" to choose our path. In the Freudian view, these very "free" and seemingly responsible choices are determined by deeper forces beyond our ken. For the Greeks, this was the will of the gods; for Freud, it was the activity of the unconscious.

For Freud, "oedipal" sexuality has two main characteristics. First, it is normally directed to those adults with whom the child has closest contact—that is, it is "incestuous". Second, it involves elements of possessiveness and rivalry. The child wants to possess fully one or both parents and will brook no competition. Freud did *not* propound that the Oedipus complex necessarily involves exclusive desire for the parent of the *opposite* sex. The concept of the "complete Oedipus complex", introduced in *The Ego and the Id* (Freud, 1923b), invoked simultaneous heterosexual and homosexual currents: desire for exclusive possession of mother *and* father.

Freud assumed at first that boys and girls follow much the same sort of developmental trajectory. Deeper reflection gradually induced him to modify his ideas, and he eventually created two related but none the less distinct developmental templates: one for boys and the other for girls. Although Freud presented these as detailed models, it seems likely that he intended them to represent general developmental themes that might be realized in diverse forms in any given life history.

Freud's oedipal story of the little boy runs as follows. When the male child enters the phallic phase, at around the age of 3 years, his penis becomes the leading erotogenic zone. It becomes a source of pleasure and puzzlement. Of course, the little boy does not desire sexual intercourse. Instead, he enjoys manipulating his genitals (Freud, 1924d). These masturbatory activities are directed towards the boy's first object, his mother. In his passionate desire to completely possess his mother—and be fully possessed by her—he experiences urges to dispose of the chief obstacle to the realization of this project: his father. He consequently imagines his father retaliating by castrating him (the "castration complex").

As I pointed out earlier in this chapter, during Freud's lifetime small boys were, in fact, routinely threatened with castration in order to dissuade them from masturbating. Freud believed that the threat of castration was treated as bluff and by itself carried no great conviction. Conviction only arises after observing that boys and girls are differently constructed. It is the sight of the female genitals that makes credible the possibility of castration, and it is under the pressure of this threat that the boy renounces his mother as an incestuous object and identifies with his father—the real or fantasied source of prohibition (Freud, 1923e). The boy emerges from this with a fear of and contempt for those "castrated" individuals called girls and women.

Freud's story of female oedipal development begins like that of the boy. The girl enters the phallic phase with the clitoris as her leading erotogenic zone, and the yield of pleasure derived from its stimulation is associated with the girl's desire for her mother. Like the boy, she wants to establish a passionate and completely exclusive relationship with her mother and regards her father as an obstacle to the achievement of this end.

As is the case with the boy, observations of the anatomical distinction between the sexes has a decisive impact on the developmental process. In this instance, the girl responds with "penis envy" [Penisneid] when she observes male genitals. The fact that some people (e.g. the father) are lavishly endowed with something extra between their legs must explain why it is that mother prefers father as a partner. The girl's desire to possess a penis only makes sense within the context of her homosexual Oedipus complex: she wishes to obtain a penis in order to obtain her mother's desire.

The experience of penis envy has the effect of turning a girl against her mother. Her mother, after all, failed to provide her with the coveted organ. She turns her attentions towards her father—initially merely as the bearer of the desired penis. Although the girl starts out by wanting her father's penis (i.e. that thing that makes her mother desire him), this becomes converted, by means

of symbolic slippage, into a desire for her father's baby and termi-
nates in the desire for her father. The girl now finds herself in a
heterosexual oedipal position, wanting the exclusive love of her
father and situating mother as a rival. It is the hopelessness of
these aspirations that leads to her renunciation of incestuous
longings.

It is now clear why Freud called this the "phallic stage". He
believed that for both boys and girls the crucial psychological issues revolve around the meaning given by the child to the
presence or absence of the penis. In fact, Freud believed that phallic-stage children did not regard the vagina as a sexual organ at all.
For phallic-stage children, the duality of male/female has little
emotional significance, whereas the duality of phallic/castrated is
crucial.

Freud notoriously argued that the fixation of a girl in the phallic organization entails the failure to move from "clitoral" to
"vaginal" sexuality. This is probably best understood in *psychosexual* rather than anatomical terms: the erotic idea of sexually
exciting penetration of one's vagina by a penis is a post-phallic
development.

Freud also believed that the moral sensibilities of women are
less exacting than those of men, and he attributed this to the differ-
ing ways in which they resolve the Oedipus situation. Boys
abandon incest out of fear, girls abandon it out of hopelessness.
Setting aside the possibly sexist inflection of Freud's claims, they
might be reinterpreted as stating that there is a *difference* between
masculine and feminine forms of morality.

Freud was never satisfied with his story of female sexual development, although he energetically defended it against psychoanalytic critics. During the 1920s and 1930s, the topic was debated
intensively by the psychoanalytic community. Many analysts (e.g.
Ernest Jones, Melanie Klein, Karen Horney) opposed Freud's thesis that "femininity" is a developmental acquisition, arguing that
girls have a primary awareness of their vagina and its sexual function. Although none of these writers rejected the concept of penis
envy, they each gave it less developmental significance than Freud
had done. Freud responded to his critics that they were simply
presupposing the primacy of the very thing that required explanation: female heterosexuality. He objected to simple biological ex-

planations, arguing that it is illegitimate to invoke an innate attraction to the opposite sex (he had proposed years earlier in the *Three Essays* that object-choice is acquired rather than given). These debates were revived when contemporary feminists rediscovered psychoanalysis (e.g. Chodorow, 1989).

At the conclusion of the phallic stage, children of both sexes enter the latency period, during which there is no further development of the sexual drives and sexual concerns are relatively suppressed. This is the phase of the school-age child, during which boys and girls segregate themselves from one another. Puberty marks the beginning of the "genital stage", the stage of mature sexuality. Sexual maturity involves the overcoming of castration anxiety, penis envy, and incestuous desire. To the extent that these early concerns persist, one's adult sexuality is distorted and is likely to take on perverse forms which may then be neurotically inhibited.

Freud believed that oedipal issues can never be completely surmounted. All of us have at least some residual disposition towards perversity and neurosis. There is a continuum running from a mild tendency towards "kinkiness" capable of expression in wholesome forms of sexuality, through absorption in perverse fantasies (which may be pre-packaged as pornography), to the compulsive enactment of such fantasies.

As we will see in subsequent chapters, every psychoanalytic developmental theorist proposes that there is one stage that is absolutely decisive for individuals' future mental health. For Freud, it is the phallic stage that is critical. The way that we are able to deal with the oedipal crisis determines not only the form that our sexuality will take, but also the degree of our mental and emotional well-being. For Freud, all forms of psychopathology are ultimately rooted in oedipal issues.

CHAPTER SEVEN

Illusion and reality: transference and psychoanalytic technique

> Will anyone ever penetrate the secret of this disease which
> transcends ordinary experience, this reverberation of the
> shadow of the mind, which manifests itself in a state of coma
> like that between death and resurrection, when one is neither
> asleep nor awake?
>
> Sadegh Hedayat

T he Oedipus complex is a web of troubled relationships. If
the issues that we bring to therapy are all about early relationships, it might be that the *relationship* between patient
and therapist is in itself an essential element of the treatment.
Freud covered the interpersonal aspect of the psychoanalytic process by the term "transference".

Transference

Transference [*Übertragung*] was first mentioned in *Studies on Hysteria* (1895d), where Freud wrote that psychotherapy patients

70

sometimes "transferred" disturbing ideas onto himself: a "false connection" is made between the analyst and some other person. The patient then treats the analyst as if he or she were that other person.

Freud had long been aware that ideas can be displaced: that a mental image or memory can serve as a proxy for something else. "Transference onto the physician" was just a special case of this general tendency. In *The Interpretation of Dreams* (1900a), "transference" denotes the process of substituting an innocuous preconscious representation for a disturbing unconscious idea.

My dream about Ronald Reagan as a cover for my father is an example of transference: the charge (or "cathexis") of mental energy is "transferred" across an intrapsychic barrier—the censorship—onto the preconscious thought of Reagan, who inherits the "intensity" properly belonging to my unconscious thoughts about my father.

In a case of "transference onto the analyst", it is the preconscious thought of the analyst that becomes supercharged with intensity, because it substitutes for an unconscious thought about someone else. This will at minimum cause the patient to regard his or her analyst as more emotionally significant than is warranted (leading to strong feelings of love, hate, fear, and so on directed at the analyst) and may actually cause the patient to form a distorted perception of the analyst. When an unconscious idea becomes displaced onto the analyst, the therapeutic relationship becomes inappropriately intense and confusing. A particularly graphic example is found in Freud's case of the "Rat Man":

> Things soon reached a point at which, in his dreams, his waking phantasies, and his associations, he began heaping the grossest and filthiest abuse upon me and my family, though in his deliberate actions he never treated me with anything but the greatest respect. His demeanour as he repeated these insults to me was that of a man in despair. "How can a gentleman like you, sir," he used to ask, "let yourself be abused in this way by a low, good-for-nothing fellow like me? You ought to turn me out; that's all I deserve." While he talked like this he would get up from the sofa and roam about the room,—a habit which he explained at first as being due to delicacy of feeling: he could not bring himself, he said, to utter

such horrible things while he was lying there so comfortably. But soon he himself found a more cogent explanation, namely, that he was avoiding my proximity for fear of my giving him a beating. If he stayed on the sofa he behaved like someone in desperate terror trying to save himself from castigations of terrific violence; he would bury his head in his hands, cover his face with his arm, jump up and suddenly rush away, his features distorted with pain. [Freud, 1909d, p. 209]

By 1905, Freud had come to the conclusion that transference is an "inevitable necessity", that "there is no means of avoiding it", and that the analysis of transference is "by far the hardest part of the whole task" of psychotherapy (Freud, 1905e, pp. 116–117). From this point onwards, the term "transference" was used as a shorthand term for transference to the analyst.

It is clear in the passage from *The Interpretation of Dreams* quoted above that the general psychological concept of transference played a central theoretical role in Freud's model of the mind: it was only by virtue of the (hypothetical) process of transference that the unconscious can have any impact on conscious mental life. By the same token, it is only by virtue of transference, in the broad sense of the word, that we can know anything at all about unconscious mental life.

In its more narrow, clinical sense, transference—the displacement of unconscious attitudes onto the analyst—was used to explain the passionate and sometimes bizarre attachments that patients formed with their analysts. From 1905 onwards, Freud was more and more inclined to fudge the distinction between transference as a hypothesized unconscious process (which is, in principle, unobservable) and the phenomena that it is invoked to *explain*. Freud began to speak of patients' falling in love with their analysts as an *example* of transference rather than as a phenomenon *caused* by transference. This confusion has persisted in psychoanalytic discourse to this day.

In his early writings, Freud described transference as episodic, occurring at those points when an unconscious content is powerfully pressing against the constraints of repression. Transference was described as a form of resistance. It occurred as an alternative to remembering our childhood wishes. In transference, we blindly live out our past rather than being conscious of it. One of the main tasks of the psychoanalyst was seen to be the interpretation of transference: the transformation of this compulsive living-out into insight and understanding leading to personal growth.

Freud (1916–17) held that the patient's "positive" transference (his or her affection, admiration, or devotion to the analyst) provided the motive power for the psychoanalytic process. In other words, it is the patient's unconscious childish love, and the hope to gain the love of the psychoanalyst, that keeps him or her in therapy. According to this thesis, there is something deeply irrational at the very heart of psychotherapy. Patients come to therapy not merely for cure, but for *salvation*. Freud recognized that the psychoanalytic process was, to a great extent, driven by suggestion (positive transference). Although he granted that psychoanalytic patients were moved by their suggestibility, Freud denied that psychoanalytic cure was *based* on suggestion. He believed that all varieties of psychotherapy are empowered by transference. In cures through suggestion, the therapist manipulates the transference, acting into the role of "father" or "mother" and exercising benign (or not so benign) authority over the patient's life. The psychoanalyst must ultimately analyse the positive transference—that is, show the patient how his or her affection is ultimately based upon repressed childhood longings.

Although in one sense an obstacle to the work, in another sense transference proved to be a therapeutic boon. Transference causes all of the patient's unconscious "issues"—the very things that are at the root of his or her distress—to become concentrated upon the analyst and to come to life in the immediacy of their interaction.

A few years later, Freud propounded that an artificial neurosis is created by the psychoanalytic situation itself and that this replaces the original neurosis. He called this the "transference neurosis". All of the patient's unconscious wishes and defences become "locked on" to features of the analyst and the analytic situation. Ideas about the analytic situation become the main derivatives of pathogenic ideas. Thus, free associations are not really free (in the sense of being undetermined or random). They are determined not only by forces *internal* to the patient but also by the analytic *situation* in which the patient, is embedded. Freud held that the causal impact of the analytic situation is so pervasive that all of the patient's associations refer to it in some way (Freud, 1925d).

Transference and internalism

The theory of transference makes the relationship between analyst and patient central to the psychoanalytic process. However, it also presents a particular *theorization* of that relationship. In essence, the transference concept involves the notion that the patient's internal world is unconsciously and inappropriately imposed upon the psychoanalytic situation. The patient's vision of the analyst is believed to be clouded by a fog of unconscious phantasies, wishes, and memories. In short, the theory of transference is strongly internalistic. Of course, if we emphasize the role of internal factors to this extent, we run the risk of neglecting the role of the external world. A number of psychoanalysts have pointed this out and have expressed the need to redress the balance (e.g., Ferenczi, 1933; Laing, 1959; Langs, 1976a; Little, 1951; Smith, 1991; Szasz, 1963).

The extreme internalism of Freud's theory of transference directly contradicts his early theory of screen memories. In the earlier theory, memories were unconsciously selected in order to represent some contemporary event or situation, whereas the theory of transference views the present relationship as a metaphor for a much earlier one. As we shall also see, Freud's approach to psychoanalytic listening also sits poorly with the transference thesis.

Countertransference

In Freud's philosophy, all human beings suffer from neurotic conflict. None of us is fully reconciled to reality. Each of us views the world through spectacles coloured by our deep, inextinguishable, and yet unattainable infantile desires. In Freud's philosophy, all of us are essentially divided beings, permanently out of touch with some of the most vital aspects of our being. No amount of psycho-analysis can eliminate these features of human life. They are part of the package of being human.

Psychoanalysis deals with extremely widespread if not universal human conflicts. According to Freud, all of us have Oedipus complexes, all of us hate those whom we love, and all of us grapple with anti-social impulses and the danger situations of infancy. If this is the case, than psychoanalytic work has a paradoxical—or at least a self-undermining—quality; it involves two people striving to know things that *neither* of them wants to know. The contents of the unconscious are "bad news" for analyst and patient alike. Working with the repressed is like working with radioactivity: it can burn you (Freud, 1937c).

Freud coined a special term for the analyst's own tendency to obstruct the psychoanalytic process. He called it "counter-transference". Although the terms "transference" and "counter-transference" are similar, and are often mentioned in the same breath by those who should know better, they refer to very different things. As we have seen, the term "transference" denotes a hypothetical intrapsychic process in which a preconscious mental representation of another person functions as a substitute for an unconscious mental representation of an archaic figure, normally mother or father. In short, transference is a form of displacement. Countertransference is a much broader term for all of those forces in the analyst that are antagonistic to the psychoanalytic process. Countertransference subsumes the analyst's transference onto the patient, but includes a great deal more as well. For Freud, counter-transference was the analyst's *problem*, and he made no effort to put a positive gloss on it. This perspective was clear from the start.

Freud (1910d) described countertransference as the analyst's inappropriate reaction to the patient's transference. Counter-transference is a result of the patient's unconscious influence on the psychoanalyst. It is the patient who takes the psychopathologi-cal initiative: the analyst merely responds. Freud uses the term in the same general way to refer to sexual desire aroused in the analyst by patients in states of positive transference (Freud, 1915a). Freud did not have any term describing analyst's propensity for *initiating* defensive or otherwise anti-analytical engagements. He had no language to describe the seductiveness, perversity, sadism or repressiveness introduced *by the analyst* into the psychoanalytic situation. More recently, analysts have expanded the notion of countertransference and have come to regard it as an analytical tool rather than as an obstacle (see Smith, 1991, for a description and critique of this position).

Taken together, the notions of transference and countertransference present a skewed conception of the psychoanalytic relationship. The analyst is idealized (for any inputs on his or her part are responses to the patient's material) while the patient is said to engage with the analyst largely, if not mainly, by means of illusory displacements from earlier figures. The analyst was expected to "completely overcome" countertransference in order to become "master of the psychoanalytic situation" (Freud, in Nunberg & Federn, 1962–1975, Vol. 2). The Quixotic quest for complete transcendence of countertransference was rarely challenged during Freud's lifetime. Indeed, it was apparently not until 1956 that an analyst wrote that countertransference is inevitable (Tower, 1956, but see also Winnicott, 1956a).

Evenly suspended attention and unconscious perception

I have discussed the method of and rationale for free association in chapter three, but I have not yet mentioned that Freud recommended that the analyst adopt a corresponding listening attitude. He named this listening attitude *gleichschwebende Aufmerksamkeit*— "evenly suspended attention"—and described it as the counterpart to the fundamental rule of free association.

> The technique . . . is a very simple one. . . . It consists simply in not directing one's notice to anything in particular and in maintaining the same "evenly-suspended attention" (as I have called it) in the face of all that one hears. [1912e, pp. 111–112]

The attitude of evenly suspended attention has several functions. First, it prevents the analyst from succumbing to mental fatigue arising from "the strain on our attention which could not in any case be kept up for several hours daily" (p. 112). Second, it discourages the analyst from selecting and censoring what he or she hears from the patient:

> For as soon as anyone deliberately concentrates his attention to a certain degree, he begins to select from the material before him; one point will be fixed in his mind with particular clearness and some other will be correspondingly disregarded, and in making this selection he will be following his expectations or inclinations. This, however, is precisely what must not be done. In making the selection, if he follows his expectations he is in danger of never finding anything but what he already knows; and if he follows his inclinations he will certainly falsify what he may perceive. [p. 112]

The attitude of passive attentiveness makes it more likely that the analyst will escape the closed circle of his or her beliefs and be more receptive to novelty: Freud wanted psychoanalysts to be creative listeners. Freud also believed that evenly gliding attention provides a measure of protection against the analyst's counter-transference-based selection from the patient's material:

> Just as the patient must relate everything that his self-observation can detect, and keep back all the logical and affective objections that seek to induce him to make a selection from among them, so the doctor must put himself in a position to make use of everything he is told for the purposes of interpretation and of recognising the concealed unconscious material without substituting a censorship of his own for the selection that the patient has foregone. [p. 115]

Finally, Freud believed that his recommended listening stance allowed analysts to listen to themselves—that is, to become aware of their own stream of consciousness. But why should this be either necessary or desirable for the performance of the psycho-analytic task? Freud believed that the analyst must

> ... turn his own unconscious like a receptive organ towards the transmitting unconscious of the patient. He must adjust himself to the patient as a telephone receiver is adjusted to the transmitting microphone. Just as the receiver converts back into sound waves the electric oscillations in the telephone line which were set up by sound waves, so the doctor's unconscious is able, from the derivatives of the unconscious which

are communicated to him, to reconstruct that unconscious, which has determined the patient's free associations. [pp. 115–116]

In other words, he hoped that openness to one's own passing thoughts and fantasies, which he believed to be derivatives of unconscious processes, would allow the psychoanalyst access to his or her own *unconscious understanding* of the patient's unconscious. The analyst's unconscious mind is therefore "an instrument" for the work (p. 116). This conception of unconscious insightfulness bears a good deal in common with Freud's original theory of screen memories; it is inconsistent with the theory of transference, according to which the unconscious part of the mind exercises a predominantly distorting influence on interpersonal perception.

In characterizing the unconscious dimension of the therapeutic relationship as irrational and disruptive, Freud was ignoring a phenomenon that had troubled him for years: unconscious perception and rationality. The topographical model of the mind, which presented the unconscious as dominated by the pleasure principle and therefore completely cut off from reason and reality, could not accommodate the possibility of sophisticated and yet unconscious cognitive acts. And yet, Freud was well aware that such things occurred. This tension was one of several factors that drove him to abandon the original topographical model and, in 1923, to put a new topography in its place.

CHAPTER EIGHT

The psychology of the "I": Freud's ego psychology

Art begins at the point where resistance is overcome.

André Gide

I have described in chapter one how psychoanalysis began as a radical revision of an age-old conception of our place in the natural world. At bottom, Freud offered a deeply naturalistic view of the mind. The mind, he believed, is a function of the brain. It is therefore, in essence, a material mind subject to the laws governing macroscopic physical objects. The mind is, at bottom, a physical entity and is in no way set apart from the rest of the physical universe.

Freud's view of the mind ran against many prejudices. Scientists and laymen alike were inclined to view the mind as something standing outside the great web of causation. The philosophical doctrine of "agent causation"—the view that human choices are entirely autonomous and uncaused—was and is very popular. As Freud wrote in his polemic against Alfred Adler:

The ego is here playing the ludicrous part of the clown in a circus who by his gestures tries to convince the audience that every change in the circus ring is being carried out under his orders. But only the youngest of the spectators is deceived by him. [1914d, p. 53]

Developments in psychoanalytic research eventually forced Freud to reconsider his conception of the ego. This reconsideration culminated in the publication of *The Ego and the Id* in 1923 (Freud, 1923b).

An intelligent unconscious?

Freud's 1923 revision was brought about by the identification of various incoherencies, tensions, and explanatory lacunae in his first topographical model. One of the most important of these was the problem of unconscious cognition. Freud (e.g. 1915e) made it quite clear that *Ucs.*, the unconscious, is fundamentally irrational and, being dominated by the pleasure principle, is out of touch with reality. "We might say," wrote the British philosopher Israel Levine (1923), "that the unconscious system has no *logic*" (p. 127).

Freud was aware from the outset that certain well-known phenomena did not agree with this picture of the unconscious mind, and he occasionally voiced his disquiet about the matter in his writings. The earliest expression of concern with the issue is found in *The Interpretation of Dreams*. Freud notes that it is beyond dispute that dreams can carry on intellectual work begun during the day, resolve problems, and provide artistic inspiration, but he regarded the theoretical implications of this as uncertain. Freud could conclude either that there was something wrong with his theory of dreaming or that there was something wrong with his conception of unconscious mental life. By 1913, he seems to have settled on the latter and asserted that "everyone possesses in his own unconscious an instrument with which he can interpret the utterances of the unconscious in other people" (1913i, p. 320). The same general point is made in *Totem and Taboo* (1912-13), where he wrote that "psychoanalysis has shown us that everyone possesses in his unconscious mental activity an apparatus which enables him to interpret other peoples' reactions, that is, to undo the distortions which other people have imposed upon the expression of their feelings" (p. 159). By 1915, Freud was more equivocal, suggesting that such processes might, after all, prove to be preconscious rather than unconscious (1915a).

It was in response to these and other difficulties that Freud decided to jettison the old topographical model. The old map depicting the mind as composed of the three functional systems *Ucs.*, *Pcs.*, and *Cs.* was abandoned in favour of the "structural model", or "second topography".

The second topography

The second topography makes use of a sociopolitical metaphor to picture the human personality. The personality is described as being composed of three "agencies", which should be understood in the sense of "government agencies". The government of the mind is the upshot of a system of checks and balances worked out between these three agencies. Freud christened these agencies the "It", the "I", and the "Over-I", which in English translations of Freud appear as the Latin terms "id", "ego", and "superego".

The most primitive of the three agencies is the "id". Freud took the term from Nietzsche by means of the eccentric psychoanalyst Georg Groddeck, whose *Book of the It* was published by the Psychoanalytischer Verlag in 1923, the same year as Freud's *The Ego and the Id*.

> I hold the view that man is animated by the Unknown, that there is within him . . . an "It", some wondrous force which directs both what he himself does and what happens to him. The affirmation "I live" is only conditionally correct, it expresses only a small and superficial part of the fundamental principle, "Man is lived by the It". [Groddeck, 1923, p. 11]

In Freud's version, the id has many of the same characteristics as the old System Unconscious. It is constituted by the mental representations of the drives, both destructive and sexual. The id is wet and hot, as well as being somewhat menacing. The very name conjures up memories of horror films: "*It* Came from Outer Space" or "The Thing". The id is an alien within oneself: that impersonal something within us all. The id is completely governed by the pleasure principle. It is a "seething cauldron", a lusting apparatus blindly striving for discharge and completely dissociated from reason and reality.

According to Freud, we are born "all id". One of the problems with being all id is that this has very little survival value. Craving food and merely hallucinating its presence does not fill one's belly. The pain and frustration experienced by the infant bring about a metamorphosis of the id. A new structure, the "ego", differentiates out of it.

The ego is, as Heinz Hartmann would say many years later, an organ of adaptation. That is, the ego is that part of ourselves the task of which is to reconcile the strivings of the id with the opportunities and constraints of reality. Consciousness is one function of the ego, as is the control over motility. The ego is capable of self-reflection (accessing its own processes). The ego goes to sleep at night, censors dreams, and renders distressing thoughts unconscious. It is the seat of logic, reason, language, and perception. The ego must manage the id, and it (functionally) lies at the interface between the inner core of the self (the id) and the external world. The ego has no energy of its own. All human motivation ultimately comes from the id, and it is this reservoir that the ego must parasitize in order to carry out its programme of survival:

> In its relation to the id it is like a man on horseback, who has to hold in check the superior strength of the horse; with this difference, that the rider tries to do so with his own strength while the ego uses borrowed forces. The analogy may be carried a little further. Often a rider, if he is not to be parted from his horse, is obliged to guide it where it wants to go; so in the same way the ego is in the habit of transforming the id's will into action, as if it were its own. [Freud, 1923b, p. 25]

Our lives are largely run by this mighty animal held only tenuously in rein. We are all Oedipus, striding towards Thebes thinking to ourselves that we have *chosen* this fate, whereas in fact we are propelled by forces beyond our awareness and beyond our control.

The superego differentiates out of the ego. The German term "over I" suggests something towering over and above one: something to which one must subordinate oneself. In fact, the superego is an outpost of society within the mind: it is an internalization of the taboos and ideals of one's culture. The superego constrains the ego, which must satisfy the demands of the id in a manner in accord with the requirements of the superego. The superego is therefore that mental organ responsible for morality.

Freud believed that the superego formed at the moment of the collapse of the Oedipus situation. The child *internalizes* his parents in their role of lawgivers, as prohibitors. Once this happens, an inner sense of guilt replaces the fear of punishment. It is important to realize that Freud did not believe that the superego is created by internalizing one's parents. Rather, he thought that we internalize our parents' superegos. On this account, culture is a Dawkinsian "meme" using individual human beings as vehicles for its long journey down the generations (Dawkins, 1976).

Without superegos, we could not exist in culture. Each of us would be "looking out for Number One" with no real commitment to the collective. This does not mean that the superego operates by primarily rational means towards primarily rational ends. The superego is also a device for disposing of destructive impulses. Freud believed that each of us possesses the inclination towards cruelty and destructiveness, a tendency that runs counter to the interests of social life. The superego helps us get along with our neighbours by re-routing the aggressive tendencies onto *ourselves*. In the anthropomorphic jargon of the structural model, we can say that the superego *punishes* the ego. The superego therefore drives self-destructive behaviour and can, paradoxically, cause people to commit criminal acts *in order* to court punishment.

The unholy alliance between id and superego can be illustrated by the case of Adolf Hitler. Hitler's sexuality was perverse: he was sexually aroused by having women urinate and defecate on his body. And yet, in his invective against the Jews, he raged against their "uncleanness" and "revolting sexual ways" (Bromberg & Small, 1984). Arguably, the aggression that Hitler's superego directed against his ego, to punish it for sexual deviance, was redirected against the Jews. Hitler could vicariously punish himself and thereby satisfy his superego, and simultaneously engage in an orgy of destruction and thereby satisfy his id.

The reader should bear in mind that this example is purely for illustrative purposes. I do not mean to imply that it is the best explanation (or even a valid explanation) of Hitler's persecution of the Jews.

Where Is System Unconscious?

Freud *replaced* his earlier topographical model with the tripartite model of 1923. Strictly speaking, "System Unconscious" was removed from psychoanalytic theory at this point. From this point onwards, when Freud spoke of *das Unbewusste*—"the unconscious"—he meant something like "that which is unconscious". "Unconsciousness" became a mere quality or property of mental events.

In the 1923 model, id, ego, and superego are all mostly unconscious. That is, we are unconscious not only of rampant infantile wishes and drives (the id), but also of rational cognitive processes (the ego) and guilt-inducing moral imperatives (the superego). It is clear how this formulation solves the problem with which this chapter began: unconscious problem-solving is an ego function. There is no contradiction between the existence of unconscious rationality and the theory of unconscious irrationality, because these two phenomena represent the activity to two distinct mental agencies.

The idea of the ego being mainly unconscious was an extremely novel idea. Wilhelm Reich, who was present when Freud delivered *The Ego and the Id* at the 1922 Berlin Congress, recalled:

> It was beautiful. . . . It was very beautiful, awfully beautiful. That was the last time he spoke at a Congress. He meant something very important there, something very deep, very deep. The Ego is just as unconscious as the Id. Prächtig! Wunderbar! It takes a genius to think that way. [Reich, 1967]

The theory of radically unconscious ego functions threw light on an important clinical problem. If resistance and defence are the processes that cause mental states to become or remain unconscious, why are resistance and defence in themselves unconscious? When a person is repressing something, he or she does not (directly) *know* that they are doing this. When patients are transferring an unconscious representation onto their analysts, they are not *aware* that this is going on. Within the purview of the second topography, resistance and defence proceed from the unconscious parts of the ego. These processes are structurally unconscious rather than repressed.

Anguish

Freud's new ego psychology provided a new psychoanalytic approach to anxiety. Freud's use of the word *Angst* is not well served by its translation as "anxiety". "Anxiety" is too delimited, whereas Freud's use of *Angst* includes anxiety, shame, and guilt but is not simply a term for all unpleasant emotions. I shall continue here to use "anxiety", as this term is well established, but the reader should bear in mind the wider meaning.

Freud's first theory of anxiety arose in his study of anxiety neurosis during the 1890s. As I have described in chapter three, Freud believed anxiety neurosis to be caused by sexual abstinence. He reasoned that when sexual energy is prevented from discharge it becomes transformed into anxiety, like wine turning into vinegar. From this view, anxiety is more a neurotic consequence than a cause and is physiological rather than psychological in nature.

Wilhelm Reich revived Freud's thesis during the 1920s and passed it on to humanistic psychotherapy via Fritz Perls, his analysand, who invented Gestalt Therapy. Perls's dictum that "anxiety is blocked excitement" thus has a lineage extending right back to early Freud.

This account is really an oversimplification of a sequence of complex theoretical transformations; for a more detailed account, see Macmillan (1991).

Freud's final revision of the theory of anxiety, which appeared in the 1926 book *Inhibitions, Symptoms and Anxiety* (1926d), described anxiety as a motive for repression: we push an idea out of awareness because it would otherwise give rise to excruciating anxiety. The question of the ultimate origin of anxiety lost interest for Freud. It was sufficient to say that anxiety is a response of the ego to perceived danger. Neurotic anxiety is caused by the unconscious awareness of an intense, unmanageable repressed need before which the ego feels helpless.

Freud (1926d) distinguished between various forms of anxiety. *Automatic anxiety* is the consequence of being immersed in an uncontrollable situation of danger. As infants, we often experience automatic anxiety in consequence of our helplessness and our incapacity for anticipating danger. *Signal anxiety* is a milder form of anxiety that occurs when a contemporary situation resembles an earlier traumatic situation. Signal anxiety is an inner warning that danger is at hand. A danger situation, in the strict Freudian sense, is "a recognised, remembered, expected situation of helplessness" (1926d, p. 166). The signal of anxiety announces an impending helplessness. Signal anxiety activates protective measures.

Freud (1926d) also believed that there were forms of anxiety typical of each of the stages of psychosexual development. Separation anxiety—the dread of loss—is characteristic of the oral stage; during the anal stage, we experience the fear of the loss of love, while the typical form of anxiety during the phallic stage is, of course, castration anxiety. Moral anxiety (guilt) can only be experienced once the superego has been established at the conclusion of the phallic stage.

The mechanisms of protection

From the time of his collaboration with Josef Breuer onwards, Freud was keenly interested in the ways in which human beings protect themselves from an awareness of their own mental activity. Freud used the term "defence" [*Abwehr*] for the ways that we keep our own thoughts out of awareness. The development of his new ego psychology gave impetus to the study, classification, and interpretation of defences.

Freud's choice of the term "defence *mechanisms*" is significant. Defences occur automatically in response to inner situations of danger. The Freudian concept must therefore be distinguished from more voluntaristic conceptions of "self deception", such as that promoted by Sartre (1943).

Defences are evoked by signal anxiety. Their purpose is to pre-empt automatic anxiety. Defences are ultimately designed to avert an external catastrophe. Comparing a repressed instinctual drive with a wolf, Freud (1926d) wrote that:

> A wolf would probably attack us irrespective of our behaviour towards it; but the loved person would not cease to love us nor should we be threatened with castration if we did not entertain certain feelings and intentions within us. Thus such instinctual impulses are determinants of external dangers and so become dangerous in themselves; and we can now proceed against the external danger by taking measures against the internal ones. [p. 145]

Like a person who shoots an attacking wolf, the ego "joins issue with the threatening instinctual process and somehow suppresses it or deflects it from its aims and thus renders it innocuous" (p. 146).

Freud and others identified and named a number of discrete defence mechanisms. Two of these have a special status because of their global and far-reaching effects: these are repression and disavowal.

The term "repression" [*Verdrängung*] was established in German-language psychology before Freud. Repression has been defined as "forgetting and then forgetting that you have forgotten", a *bon mot* attributed to R. D. Laing. Repression is thus motivated forgetting. According to Freud (1915d), repression involves three moments. Primal repression is a simple turning away from the offending thought. Repression proper (or "after pressure") involves setting up innocuous ideas in place of the repressed ones. Finally, the "return of the repressed" is the tendency for repressed ideas to re-assert themselves in the form of derivatives: dreams, slips, symptoms, and so on.

Disavowal [*Verleugnung*] is sometimes called "denial". Disavowal is the repudiation of belief in some aspect of external reality. It is well described by the joke of the man who, having been accused of returning a rare Chinese vase that he had borrowed in a damaged state, said in his defence: "In the first place, I never borrowed the vase, in the second place, it was cracked when I borrowed it, and in the third place, I returned it in perfect condition."

Repression is a subtle and sophisticated defence whereas disavowal is more primitive and potentially disruptive. Disavowal is particularly associated with the psychoses, although this is not invariably the case. Freud believed that disavowal played an important role in fetishism (1927e) and religious belief (1927c).

"Projection" [*Projektion*] is a term that Freud adapted from neuroscience. In neuroscientific discourse, an event occurring in the brain (e.g. pain) is "projected" onto the body.

When we engage in projection, we attribute some feature of ourselves onto others rather than correctly recognizing it as our own. Projection has a special connection with paranoia.

The term "introjection" [*Introjektion*] was introduced into the psychoanalytic lexicon by Sándor Ferenczi in 1909. The term was coined by the nineteenth-century Swiss philosopher Richard Avenarius (Ward, 1896–1898). It is one of a group of similar terms, including "identification", "incorporation", and "internalization", that are accorded fine shades of meaning by different authors, although there is no agreement on usage across the board. I therefore confine myself here to one term. Introjection is best understood as the counterpart of projection. It is the mis-attribution of some feature of another person to oneself. In introjection, we "take on" features of others, whereas in projection we offload aspects of ourselves onto others. Introjection plays a special role in depressive states.

Displacement [*Verschiebung*] played an important role in the theory of dreams and the concept of transference. In displacement, we use one idea as a proxy for another (in much the same way that when someone makes me angry, I may respond by punching the door). Displacement is said to play an important role in the phobias ("anxiety hysteria", in the older psychoanalytical terminology), where the feared object or situation is a substitute for something else.

Turning round upon the self [*Wendung gegen die eigene Person*] is the process of substituting oneself for an object: hating oneself instead of hating the object, or loving oneself instead of loving the object. It is said to play a role in some depressive, masochistic, and narcissistic conditions. Anna Freud's (1936) concept of "turning against the self" is a special case of this defence.

Reaction-formation [*Reactionsbildung*] is the transformation of an attitude into its opposite: hate becomes concern, lasciviousness becomes disgust, and so on.

Undoing [*Ungeschehenmachen*] is diachronic reaction-formation. An offending thought or action is "cancelled out" by a subsequent thought or action. Undoing is the process of magically destroying the existence of a prior thought or action.

Negation [*Verneinung*] is simply allowing oneself to think a threatening thought in its negative form. Negation is betrayed by locutions such as "I wouldn't dream of . . .", "The last thing in the world I would want to do is . . .", and so on. Freud (1925h) believed that when a thought is released from repression, it makes its first appearance in consciousness in the form of a negation. Negation is often confused with denial (disavowal).

Isolation [*Isolieren*] is the detachment of thought from emotion. Using isolation one can think and discuss things in a completely detached manner that would otherwise have given rise to intense emotion. Isolation normally goes hand-in-hand with displacement, as the emotions are siphoned-off by means of substitute ideas to which they become attached. Isolation, negation, reaction-formation, and undoing are all especially associated with obsessional neurosis.

Acting out [*Agieren*] is the process of repeating something rather than remembering it. As we have seen, the notion of acting out was vital to Freud's theory of transference. Acting out is particularly associated with the perversions and impulse disorders.

The term "rationalization" was coined by the Welsh psychoanalyst Ernest Jones. Rationalization is the act of concocting a false reason for some action or attitude. It is thus an act of self-justification.

It is doubtful whether processes like regression, conversion, and sublimation can reasonably be described as defences. Regression and conversion are best understood as mechanisms of symptom formation. Sublimation, a term derived from chemistry and used in a psychological sense by Nietzsche (1878–80), is the use of sexual motives to realize non-sexual aims. It is the very relaxation of defences that makes sublimation possible.

Implications for technique

Freud's articulation of the structural model fundamentally altered his conception of the psychoanalytic process. According to the new model, psychopathology can best be understood as the ego being torn asunder by its conflicting loyalties to the id, to the superego, and to the need to survive in the world. Unable to effect a skilful compromise between competing agencies with conflicting interests, the ego must resort to desperate and maladaptive moves. Civil war has broken out within the soul. The aim of psychoanalytic treatment is to give aid to a beleaguered ego, and to enhance its power and scope in relation to the id and the superego. Psychoanalysis forms an alliance with the small voice of reason over and against the clamour of the lust for pleasure and the lust for righteousness.

The new model also had important implications for the method of work at the psychical coal face: the rules of psychoanalytic technique. During the first portion of Freud's career as a psychoanalyst, his concept of psychotherapeutic technique ran something like this. By dint of careful listening and observation, the psychoanalyst makes true inferences about those pathogenic ideas that the patient has repressed into the unconscious. The analyst's interventions are geared towards *convincing* the patient to accept consciously these interpretations as true. This can only be accomplished by getting the patient to *override* his or her resistances.

The new formulation changed all that. Once it became clear that the defences themselves are unconscious, the whole conception of psychoanalytic technique was radically altered. In attempting to *persuade* the patient to "overcome" his or her resistances, Freud and his colleagues were both making the mistake of treating a basically unconscious process as though it were a conscious strategy and committing the additional error of attempting to *induce* patients to abandon their resistances. Through such efforts, which extended from the "hammer it home" approach to less aggressive and more seductive strategies, Freud was employing the very *suggestive* influence, the manipulation of the positive transference, that he otherwise decried.

Once it was clear that defences (and therefore the resistances that they support) are essentially unconscious, it became obvious that the appropriate and consistently psychoanalytic clinical approach to resistance is to *analyse* it. Analysts began to recognize the need to help patients become aware of just how and for what reason they were excluding certain thoughts from conscious awareness. It became important to *interpret* defences and resistances. If we compare the unconscious part of the mind to a locked room, we can say that in the early days of psychoanalysis practitioners attempted to guess what was in the room and persuade or coerce the patient into agreeing with them. Once the clinical ramifications of the structural model began to be recognized and disseminated, analysts were more likely to call their patients' attention to the fact that the door is locked and offer them a key. It was left to Wilhelm Reich, the *enfant terrible* of the Vienna Psycho-Analytical Society, to elaborate this new dispensation systematically.

PART TWO

PSYCHOANALYSIS
AFTER FREUD

CHAPTER NINE

Enfant terrible:
Wilhelm Reich in Vienna

> He was like a man who was standing on top of the world
> looking over into a new world. That is what Daddy was like.
> He had lifted himself so that he was looking over the horizon
> to a new world, a free and happy world. He stood there on the
> edge of the universe looking into the future, and when he
> turned around to say, "Come on, let's go," they pulled the
> ladder out from under him and killed him.
>
> Peter Reich

One day in the winter of 1918, three impoverished Jewish students sat next to each other in the cold classroom of the University of Vienna medical school. The two young men, fresh from service in the Great War, and huddled in their well-worn army coats, were named Wilhelm and Edward. The beautiful, vivacious young woman was named Greta. As the lecturer droned on, a fourth student, Otto, wrote a note on a piece of paper and passed it around the class.

Wilhelm Reich, Edward Bibring, Greta Bibring, and Otto Fenichel were soon to become major players in the psychoanalytic movement, building international reputations as scholars and psychotherapists. All would later suffer exile in the United States of America. The note that the young Otto Fenichel passed around the class was a petition for a seminar on sexology, a subject that was not covered by the existing medical curriculum. A group of enterprising students, including the four friends, resolved to organize these seminars themselves. Eventually, a lecture series on sexology was arranged. Of course, amongst those in Vienna with interesting things to say about sex were the psychoanalysts, and the series therefore included a presentation on psychoanalysis. Although Reich found the psychoanalytic presentation bizarre, it clearly kindled his interest. Within two years, at the age of 22, Reich was a practising analyst and an active member of the Vienna Psycho-Analytical Society. A few years later, he would be making major contributions to psychoanalytic theory and technique, but by 1934 he was *persona non grata* within the movement and in 1957 he died of heart failure in an American prison.

Reich's background

Wilhelm Reich was born in Dobrzynika, Galicia, on 24 March 1897. He was brought up in Jujinetz, Bukovina, a different province of the Austro-Hungarian empire. His parents were well-off Jewish cattle-farmers and were snobbishly devoted to high German culture. They forbade Wilhelm and his brother Robert from attending local schools and associating with the local Ukrainian- and Yiddish-speaking youngsters. Wilhelm and his brother were educated by tutors who would visit the farm.

Reich's early environment was unhappy, isolated, and suffused with violence. His father would sometimes physically abuse his wife and was known to hit her for as little as the failure to have dinner ready on time. He was intensely jealous of his wife and would sometimes berate her for being a "whore".

One day, when Reich was 12 years old, he discovered his mother having sexual intercourse with his tutor. The details of this crucial experience were spelled out in Reich's very first psychoanalytic publication, a disguised autobiographical account entitled "The Breakthrough of the Incest Taboo in Puberty" (Reich, 1920).

Reich hinted at the affair to his father, who eventually dragged the whole story out of him. After about a year of intense marital discord, Reich's mother committed suicide by drinking a bottle of bleach, enduring a slow, agonizing death. After the death, Reich went away to boarding school, returning to Jujinitz during holidays. His father, a broken man, committed suicide in 1915 by standing in a pond in the middle of winter. He successfully contracted pneumonia, a mode of death that protected the life-insurance payment to his sons.

Reich and his brother had now to take over the running of the farm, but this was short-lived. World War One was in full swing, and in the summer of 1915 Russian troops marched onto the fields. The two boys fled to Vienna, and Reich joined the army. He fought in Italy and made the rank of lieutenant. In 1918, an impoverished and displaced Wilhelm Reich returned to Vienna and enrolled at university. Like Freud, he began in the faculty of law, but soon switched to medicine.

Becoming a psychoanalyst

It was the little note scrawled by Otto Fenichel that led Reich eventually to meet Sigmund Freud in 1919. Freud was at the height of his powers, and the psychoanalytic movement was a growing enterprise. The four friends visited Freud in order to obtain information on sexuality. Reich later recalled of their initial meeting that:

> Freud's personality made the strongest and most lasting impression. . . . To begin with, he was simple and straightforward in his attitude. . . . Freud spoke to me like an ordinary human being. He had piercingly intelligent eyes; they did not try to penetrate the listener's eyes in a visionary pose; they simply looked into the world straight and honest. . . . His manner of speaking was quick, to the point and lively. The move-

ments of his hands were natural. Everything he did and said
was shot through with tints of irony. [Reich, 1942a, cited in
Sharaf, 1983, p. 57]

Freud knelt down in front of a bookcase and pulled out various
offprints and books to lend to Reich and his fellow students, which
included *The Interpretation of Dreams*, "Instincts and Their Vicissitudes", "The Unconscious", and *The Psychopathology of Everyday
Life*. In the face of such hospitality, it is hardly surprising that
Reich recalled that he "had come there in a state of trepidation and
left with a feeling of pleasure and friendliness".

Reich, who had studied psychiatry during the course of his
medical training, undertook postgraduate studies in neuropsy-
chiatry under Julius Wagner-Jauregg. Reich was profoundly impressed and inspired by Freud's intelligent and humane attitude
towards the mentally ill.

I was deeply moved by the earnestness with which Freud
sought to comprehend mental patients. His views were head
and shoulders above the "priggishly conceited" opinions
which the psychiatrists of the old school expressed about mental illness. As they saw it, some things were simply "crazy".
. . . For instance, there are catatonics with stereotypies who sit
for hours with their fingers pressed against their forehead as if
in deep thought. Think of the deep, self estranged, searching
far-roving look of these mental patients. And what does the
psychiatrist ask them? "How old are you?" "What's your
name?" "How much is three times six?" "What's the difference between a child and a dwarf?". He diagnoses the patient
as being disoriented, schizophrenic and megalomanic, period!
There were some twenty-thousand such persons in the Vienna
"Steinhof". Each and every one of them had experienced the
inner collapse of his world. [Reich, 1942b, pp. 35–36]

Reich began practising psychoanalysis in late 1919 or early
1920, while still a medical student, when Freud began referring
patients to him. He gained membership to the Vienna Psycho-
Analytical Society in the autumn of 1920. He underwent two brief
analyses himself, the first with Isidor Sadger, whom even Freud
regarded as excessively zealous, and the second, during the early
1920s, with Paul Federn, one of the earliest members of Freud's
circle.

The impulsive character

In 1908 Freud expressed the view that the entire personality can be coloured by a component drive. The "anal character" is marked by the traits of stubbornness, stinginess, and orderliness (Freud, 1908b), a thesis that was elaborated by Sadger (1910), Abraham (1921), and Jones (1918). Abraham went on to contribute papers on the "oral character" (1924a) and the "genital character" (1925). With the publication of *The Ego and the Id* (1923b) in 1923, psycho-analytic characterology took a new turn. Freud conjectured that the "character of the ego"—that is, the personality—was largely forged from *defences* against instinctual impulses. He singled out three of these for special attention, claiming that we acquire traits of personality by (1) *identifying* with persons who have caused us frustration, (2) building *reaction formations* against our sexual im-pulses, and finally (3) *turning against ourselves* our own aggression. So constituted, character structure itself might be considered as "neurotic". But was it possible to alter the structure of the entire personality by means of psychoanalytic treatment? This was the new frontier confronting the psychoanalysts of the 1920s.

Reich's first psychoanalytic book dealt with a form of character pathology that is now called the "borderline personality organiza-tion" (see chapter twelve) but which Reich (1925) called the "impulsive character". Like later writers on the borderline syn-drome, Reich described the impulsive character as transitional between the psychoneuroses and the psychoses, and possessing characteristics of both.

Reich provides a detailed description of the dynamics of this character type and relates its aetiology to experiences of having been treated cruelly or sexually abused during childhood. The paradoxical early environment of the future impulsive character is characterized both by poor impulse control and brutal punishment for instinctual expression.

Reich had obtained his clinical experiences of the treatment of impulsive characters at the Vienna Psycho-Analytical Policlinic. Although analysts in Vienna commonly devoted two hours a week of their working time to providing free treatment for those who could not afford to pay, this was clearly insufficient for meeting the needs of the Viennese proletariat. One of Freud's dreams had been to open psychoanalytic clinics where the poor could be treated on a larger scale. He induced Anton von Freund, a wealthy brewer and benefactor of the frequently impoverished International Psycho-Analytical Association, to fund such a clinic in Berlin in 1920, and he wanted to open a second one in Vienna. There was strong opposition from the local medical authorities and the department of health:

> The psychiatrists were flatly against it and advanced all sorts of quibbling excuses, while the doctors' union feared that the medical profession would suffer pecuniary damages. In short, the founding of a clinic was considered altogether useless. Eventually, however, the necessary authorization was received. We moved into a few rooms in the cardiac ward of Kaufmann and Meyer. Six months later an injunction was issued against our continuation. And so it went, back and forth, because the medical authorities did not know what to make of it. [Reich, 1942b, p. 65]

Reich worked for eight years at the Policlinic, eventually becoming Assistant Director. It was during Reich's stint at the Policlinic that he was first confronted with the experience of work with impulsive characters. Many of these patients were highly disturbed and must have been a considerable challenge for the brilliant young analyst. The flavour of this work is well captured by the clinical accounts included in Reich's 1925 monograph on "The Impulsive Character" (Reich, 1925).

> A twenty-six year old single female came to the psychoanalytic clinic because of continuous sexual excitation. She longed for satisfaction but could feel nothing during intercourse, not even the entry of the penis. . . . The slightest bodily movement would dispel every upcoming pleasure sensation. She also suffered from insomnia, anxiety states, and compulsive masturbation. She would masturbate with a knife handle up to ten times a day, reach a high pitch of excitement, then stop the friction to avoid consummation. She would do this to exhaustion until, finally, she would have no climax at all or she would deliberately make her vagina bleed and derive satisfaction from the accompanying masochistic fantasies. . . . During masturbation she fantasied that her vagina, that she called "Lotte", was a little girl. She would carry on a continuous

dialogue with it while playing both roles: "Now, my dear, you
will be satisfied—look [during analysis] the doctor is with
you. He has a beautiful long penis, but it has to hurt you".
Lotte: "No, I don't want it to hurt me!" (she would cry). "You
have to suffer, this is the punishment for your lewdness, you
are a slut. It must hurt even more—the knife must come out
through your back". [pp. 49–50]

The patient believed herself to be the illegitimate child of "the
count"—her mother's lover:

She had fantasies of being raped by the count with the other's
help (It was not clear whether this was fantasy or reality—
consider her masturbatory fantasies!) She would feel a big
penis enter her vagina, and this would cause her great pain.
The room was dark and someone was nearby shouting to her
to be still and not cry out. [p. 51]

The patient's childhood was chaotic. Reich believed that such his-
tories were typical of impulsive characters.

Analysis later uncovered a similar fantasy (or dark memory?)
from her fourth year of life. Two men, tenants of her parents,
carry her into their rented room. One is holding her and the
other forces his oversized penis into her vagina. She wants to
scream but cannot. . . . At age ten, she had coitus with an older
brother. At age six, while playing with her two-year-old
brother, she saw his penis and tried to insert a knitting needle
into it. The penis bled, and the patient pulled it. The boy cried,
and the mother beat the girl and pulled her hair. At age twelve
she got a job as a baby-sitter. Every night for two years, her
employer stimulated her but did not consummate. At age fifteen she believed herself pregnant; menses ceased for two
years and returned after she broke off her first analysis. At this
time she conceived the idea of tying a piece of wood to her
vagina. Subsequently she often came to analysis with a knife
in her vagina. Obviously this was possible only through vaginal spasm. She was unable to fall asleep without having a
knife stuck in her vagina. [p. 51]

This deeply troubled young woman became involved with
paedophilic activities as well as with a sadistic lover who beat her
with whips and got her to procure him young girls. Reich com-
pelled his patient on the threat of termination to separate herself

from him. She immediately formed an intense transference onto Reich.

> She immediately transferred the masochistic attitude to the therapist, brought a whip to the analytic hour, and started to undress to be beaten. Only the strictest intervention could keep her from doing so. She would run after me in the streets and look for me in my home at ten o'clock at night. She could not bear it any longer; I would have to have intercourse with her or beat her up. She had to have a child of mine because only I could satisfy her. So it went for about eight months. [p. 52]

In the eighth month of analysis the patient attempted to murder her husband and sister and took to bringing rat poison to her sessions.

Reich's detailed analysis of the psychodynamics of this and similar cases anticipated and perhaps influenced the work of other analysts (such as Klein and Kernberg) on primitive mental states. Reich analysed the case largely in terms of pathological superego development. The patient suffered from an intensely cruel superego which was "isolated" from the rest of her personality and introjected from her mother. Much of the patient's behaviour amounted to the sadistic expression of this persecutory superego or the patient's reaction to it.

Orgasm

Although classical psychoanalytic theory was largely about sexuality, very little of this was devoted to the sexuality of adults. The psychoanalytic literature was devoted mainly to the sexuality of children and the *deformations* of adult sexuality induced by infantile fixations: inhibitions, neuroses, and perversions. There was virtually no attention paid to that defining aspect of mature sexuality: the orgasm.

From the outset, Reich's interest in psychoanalysis rode piggyback on his interest in sexuality. He held that Freud was one of the very few people who had anything worthwhile to say about sexuality and, in addition, who offered therapeutic and, by implication, prophylactic measures against sexual misery.

During the early 1920s, Reich began to study adult sexual behaviour psychoanalytically. Using the Vienna Policlinic as his data source, Reich interviewed and examined the case records of over two hundred patients. He drew several conclusions from this research: that psychopathology is always accompanied by some disturbance in sexual functioning, that the severity of psychopathology is directly proportional to the severity of sexual disturbance, and that the restoration or establishment of the capacity for sexual gratification is strongly correlated with successful psychoanalytic treatment.

Reich's views were strongly criticized by the other Viennese analysts, who believed that neurotic or psychotic patients could have a completely healthy sex life. These criticisms were inspired by confusing superficial sexual performance with real sexual gratification.

Reich believed that ostensibly "very potent" men were often highly disturbed and that they "experienced little or no pleasure at the moment of ejaculation, or they experienced the exact opposite, disgust and unpleasure" (Reich, 1942b, p. 89). The same was true of apparently hypersexual women. In all such cases, sexual functioning is underpinned by carefully concealed pathological phantasies and conflicts.

Reich clearly needed to develop a refined conception of healthy sexual functioning. His account centred on the experience of orgasm, hence he referred to undisturbed functioning as "orgastic potency". Reich produced a highly detailed account of the orgastically potent sexual act, which was described as involving tenderness; the absence of violence, sadomasochism, or other forms of perversity; mutuality; surrender to slow, gentle, and spontaneous movements; and the absence of talk or laughter with the exception of terms of endearment. At the height of orgasm, the entire body and personality are caught up in the sexual act. There is an involuntary convulsion of the entire body and a clouding of consciousness. Sexual excitation is *completely* discharged. After orgasm, partners feel satisfied, tender, and sleepy. "It's not just to fuck . . .", Reich later reported to Kurt Eissler, "It is the real emotional experience of the loss of your ego, of your whole spiritual self" (Higgins & Raphael, 1967, p. 24).

If contemporary sexual behaviour is disturbed in every case of psychopathology, this implies that psychopathology must always involve an element of what Freud had called "actual neurosis": the toxic effect of dammed-up or "static" sexual energy. Reich believed that such "libidinal stasis" provided the energy source for all psychopathological conditions. Psychological conflicts cause a disturbance in one's sexual life which in turn causes an accumulation of undischarged sexual tension. The accumulated tension not only supports symptoms (conversions, obsessions, hallucinations, and so on), but also reactivates and exacerbates infantile sexual conflicts.

Reich's thesis had important ramifications for psychoanalytic treatment. Becoming *conscious* of repressed infantile sexual trends is not sufficient for cure. The patient must become capable of orgastic potency and must exercise this capacity. If this does not occur, dammed-up sexual tension will once again give rise to neurotic symptoms.

Reich published his orgasm theory in *Die Funktion des Orgasmus* (1927), which he dedicated to Sigmund Freud. (It is a convention of Reich scholarship to refer to this work under its German title so as not to confuse it with Reich's *The Function of the Orgasm*, 1942b.) Prior to publication, he gave Freud a copy of the manuscript for his 70th birthday. Freud was cautiously supportive. After two months, he wrote to Reich that the manuscript was "valuable, rich in observation and thought".

Sexual politics

During 1927, the year that Reich published *Die Funktion des Orgasmus*, Austria was seething with social unrest. In January, a group of World War One veterans fired into a crowd of Social Democratic protesters, killing a man and a child. The trial took place on 14 July, and the veterans were acquitted. On 15 July, one of Reich's patients, freely associating on the couch, mentioned that

Viennese workers were occupying the inner city in protest against the verdict. The police were armed, and several people had already been killed. Reich left the session to join the workers on the street.

When Reich arrived, protesters had set fire to the Palace of Justice and were attempting to obstruct the arrival of firemen. Mounted police rode into the crowd. Later that day, Reich returned with his wife, Annie, and the two narrowly escaped the ensuing carnage as the streets of "Red Vienna" flowed with blood. Hiding behind a tree, they witnessed the police cordon firing on the angry crowd. Eighty-nine people were killed and over a thousand were wounded. That same day, Reich joined the *Arbeiterhilfe*, a medical wing of the Austrian Communist Party.

Of course, Reich wanted to combine psychoanalytic insights with left-wing politics. In addition to providing medical aid to protesters injured in clashes with the police, Reich

> ... engaged in a kind of "community psychiatry", or at least his version of it. Reich, together with a paediatrician, a gynaecologist, and his friend Lia Laszky (who had become a nursery-school teacher), would go out several days a week into the suburbs and rural areas around Vienna. They would arrive in a van, announcing their visits in advance. Interested persons gathered at a local park and Reich's group spoke to them about sexual matters. Reich would talk with the adolescents and men, the gynaecologist with the women, and Lia with the children. Upon request, the gynaecologist would also prescribe and fit contraceptive devices. [Sharaf, 1983, p. 130]

The team also printed and distributed pamphlets. In the evenings they held political meetings at which Reich spoke. He founded a Socialist Association for Sex Hygiene and Sexological Research which opened six free clinics in Vienna staffed by physicians and psychoanalysts and provided advice, counselling, and information on sexual matters for all who needed it. The association was particularly concerned with the legalizing of abortion and contraception (subversive ideas in Roman Catholic Austria), the elimination of venereal disease by means of education, and the sexual welfare of young people. Reich also attempted to develop a theoretical synthesis of psychoanalysis and Marxism (Reich, 1929).

Reich's experiences in the Vienna Psycho-Analytical Policlinic and his political concerns converged with his orgasm theory. In Reich's view, psychopathology was *inevitable* in so far as social conditions did not make it possible for the vast majority of citizens to enjoy a gratifying sexual life. Psychoanalysis was therefore implicated in the movements for social change. Reich later came to realize that social change must proceed hand-in-hand with psychological change: to the extent that we are neurotic, we will inevitably undermine any movement towards social change and cling to retrograde or even fascistic social systems (Reich, 1933b).

Psychoanalytic chaos

During the late 1920s, the psychoanalytic world was buzzing with the new ego psychology. This intellectual ferment gained momentum over the decade to follow and did not really subside until subsequent developments in the 1960s. A number of analysts made contributions to the new ego psychology, including Anna Freud, Robert Waelder, Hermann Nunberg, Heinz Hartmann, and Paul Federn. With the exception of Federn, whose psychoanalytic phenomenology of ego feeling was highly original (and to which we will return in chapter twelve), all of these writers confined themselves to developing strands of theory implicit in Freud's published work. In general, the ego psychologists played down the theoretical role of sexuality and the unconscious in favour of the ego and consciousness, unbalancing Freud's delicate conceptual dialectic. Reich felt that the psychoanalysts themselves were betraying psychoanalysis and were seizing on ego psychology in order to evade the more disturbing aspects of Freud's brain-child.

> It was a very disturbing situation. ... The vivid and fluid description of facts was replaced by a mechanical schema which seemed to make further thinking unnecessary. Clinical discussions drifted more and more into the background and speculation began. Soon strangers who had never analysed came along and delivered "brilliant" lectures on the ego and superego or on schizophrenics they had never seen. ... Clinical investigation stagnated. Sexuality became something

shadowy; the "libido" concept was deprived of every trace of sexual content and became a figure of speech. Seriousness in psychoanalytic communication disappeared. It was more and more replaced by a pathos reminiscent of moral philosophers. [Reich, 1942b, p. 110]

None of the psychoanalysts used Freud's ego psychology to rework systematically the principles of psychoanalytic technique. In fact, during the 1920s there was barely any new literature on technique at all apart from the published case studies by Freud and a series of rather anecdotal papers that he had written between 1911 and 1914 which, although useful, were already considerably out of date.

There was hardly any discussion of psychoanalytic technique, a lack which I felt very keenly in my work with patients. There was neither a training institute nor an organised curriculum. The counsel to be had from older colleagues was meagre. "Just go on analysing patiently," they would say, "it'll come." What would come, and how, one did not quite know. . . . Later analysts have never experienced this desolate being at sea in matters of technique. [Reich, 1942a, cited in Sharaf, 1983, pp. 72–73]

Reich turned to Freud for help, but he merely counselled patience. In fact, Reich felt that the analysts were becoming increasingly unconcerned with the mechanisms of psychotherapeutic cure.

At the 1922 congress of the International Psycho-Analytical Association in Berlin, Freud called for an investigation of the relationship between psychoanalytic theory and technique. A cash prize was offered to the person making the best contribution to this investigation. On the train back to Vienna, Reich suggested to some of his younger colleagues that the Vienna society establish a seminar on psychoanalytic technique in order to study systematically the problems of psychotherapy. Furthermore, this was to be a *kinderseminar* restricted to young analysts, who would have an arena to "discuss their theoretical troubles and doubts and, above all, to learn to speak freely" (Reich, 1942b, p. 53). Reich turned to Freud with the idea, and Freud gave it his blessing. The project of establishing a seminar on technique was soon formally proposed and accepted by the Vienna Society. The Vienna Technical Seminar was led by Hermann Nunberg from 1922 to 1923 and then by Edward Hitschmann from 1923 to 1924. Reich took over the leadership in 1924 and continued in this capacity until 1930. A similar seminar was established in Berlin.

When Reich assumed leadership of the Seminar, he established a new set of ground rules. Cases were to be presented systematically, and the focus of presentations was to be on resistance. Reich set out to develop empirically a sound, scientific approach to psychoanalytic technique. Order gradually emerged from the chaos. The new approach was christened "character analysis". Reich's experiences in the Vienna Technical Seminar confirmed his impression that a great deal of psychoanalytic work was quite chaotic.

> The remembrances and actions are quite numerous, but they follow one another in great confusion; the analyst learns a great deal; the patient produces abundant material from all layers of his unconscious, from all periods of his life; everything is there in large chunks, as it were. Yet nothing has been worked through in accordance with the therapeutic goal; notwithstanding the wealth of material, the patient has not gained any conviction of its importance. The analyst has done a good deal of interpreting, but the interpretations have not deepened the analysis one way or another. It is clear that everything the patient has offered serves a secret, unrecognised resistance. Such a chaotic analysis is dangerous inasmuch as, for a long time, the analyst believes that it is going very well, simply because the patient is "coming up with material." . . . In this way the patient is able, for years on end, to use up his analytic hour without the slightest change taking place. [Reich, 1933a, pp. 25–26]

Freud's work implied that it was the ego's unconscious defences that maintained a neurosis. It followed that the main task of the psychoanalyst should be the analysis of these very defences. In the psychoanalytic situation, the defences make themselves felt in the form of resistance: the patient's unconscious failure to comply with the psychoanalytic process. It seemed to follow, then, that psychoanalysts should single-mindedly concentrate on interpreting patients' resistances. But this was not in fact what was being done. Analysts were inclined to *avoid* interpreting resistances, often preferring to deal with them, if at all, by means of exhortations or threats of termination. This approach was out of kilter with psychoanalytic theory, which held that it is only through insightfully undermining the defences that the structure of a neurosis can be dismantled.

Reich identified a set of "typical errors" leading to chaotic situations in analysis, and he openly illustrated these with clinical examples drawn from his own work. For instance, psychoanalysts sometimes accused their patients of resisting, while failing to interpret the resistance. They exhorted patients to "give up" their resistances and sometimes accused them of not wanting to get well, instead of pursuing the Freudian goal of cure through understanding. Reich, on the other hand, emphasized that "a stagnation in an analysis which remains unclear is the fault of the analyst" (Reich, 1933a, p. 23, emphasis added).

Another common error was the *failure to recognize the absence of emotion as a resistance.* Although the recovery of early memories is essential to cure in Freudian analysis, these must be accompanied by their corresponding emotions in order to produce sound therapeutic results. Many analysts failed to recognize this and therefore failed to treat the absence of emotion as a resistance.

Analysts often interpreted indiscriminately. The unconscious content of the patient's material should not be interpreted until the resistances have been eliminated. If resistances are left intact, the effects of interpretations will be neutralized.

Reich also found that there was a widespread tendency to avoid dealing with negative transference (the patient's fear or hatred of the psychoanalyst). Nunberg, the first leader of the Technical Seminar, believed that the best way to deal with negative transference was to foster a powerful positive transference and then to use the suggestive advantage acquired to eliminate the negative transference. Reich pointed out that this approach merely avoids patients' aggression and anxiety, and hence the deeper sources of their difficulties. He believed that it was particularly important to interpret the negative transference.

Of course, one reason why analysts were inclined to avoid exploring negative transference was simply that it was unpleasant.

Negative transference was a collective blind spot of the analytic community.

> Failure to recognise the negative transference appears to be a general occurrence. Undoubtedly, this can be traced back to our narcissism, which makes us highly receptive to compliments but quite blind to all negative tendencies in the patient unless they are crudely expressed. [Reich, 1933a, p. 25]

Having identified these and other common errors of technique, Reich subsumed them under four headings.

1. *Premature interpretation.* The analyst interprets material before eliminating the resistances, "and only too late the analyst notices that the patient is going around in circles, completely untouched" (Reich, 1933a, p. 27).

2. *Unsystematic interpretation of meaning.* The analyst interprets the unconscious meaning of material as it "comes up" instead of adjusting interpretations to the structure of the patient's psychopathology.

3. *Unsystematic interpretation of resistance.* The analyst fails to focus consistently on the patient's main resistance and interprets meaning before this has been worked through.

4. *Inconsistent and unsystematic interpretation of transference.* The analyst fails to notice the degree to which the patient conceals his or her resistance by means of "sterile accomplishments and acute reaction formations" (Reich, 1933a, p. 27) and overlooks or fails to pursue concealed transference resistances.

Character analysis

Reich's technique of character analysis was intended to replace the older approach of "symptom analysis". He believed that true psychoanalytic cure must involve a modification of the whole personality or "character".

During the 1920s, the majority of psychoanalysts regarded resistance as an episodic phenomenon. Resistance was thought to occur now and then (for instance, when a patient is silent for a protracted period of time). Reich came to disagree with this view. He held that some resistances are *chronic*, because they are embedded in the very structure of the patient's personality (as Freud had theoretically implied in *The Ego and the Id*). For instance, a patient with a "paranoid" personality will be deeply suspicious of every interpretation offered to him. His suspiciousness is an aspect of his character: it is a *character resistance*. Because the character resistances can be difficult to detect, Reich also called them "latent resistances".

Latent resistances are most clearly expressed in the patient's *bearing*:

> The way the patient speaks, looks at and greets the analyst, lies on the couch, the inflection of voice, the degree of conventional politeness which is maintained, etc., are valuable clues in assessing the secret resistances. ... And once they have been understood, they can be eliminated through interpretation. It is not only *what* the patient says but *how* he says it that has to be interpreted. [Reich, 1933a, p. 49]

The very fact that a patient devoutly reports his dreams in each session because he feels that this is what the analyst expects of him is more therapeutically important than the content of the dreams themselves. In this instance, the analyst should focus his interpretations on the patient's obsequious attitude rather than on the content of the dreams. Reich's approach enjoined the analyst to identify the principal latent resistance, the mainstay of the patient's defensive armour, and to one-pointedly interpret it. The analyst should avoid all temptations to diverge from this path. The work of character analysis is gradual, focused, and unrelenting, for unless the main resistance is eliminated, true radical psychoanalytic cure cannot be achieved. The elimination of the character resistance *is* the successful completion of the analysis.

Reich held that some degree of negativity is always present from the beginning of treatment, although this often remains concealed (Reich, 1933a, pp. 32–33). Reich admits that this early "resistance" cannot really be considered neurotic, as it is warranted by the situation. It is nonetheless essential for the patient to learn that he or she can freely voice his or her concerns. Before long, true transference resistances enter the picture. According to Reich, these stem from negative transference. Many patients conceal their negative feelings towards their analyst.

Reich was the first analyst to insist that all interpretations of resistance should be made "in the transference"—that is, that interpretations should primarily explain how and why the patient is attempting to obstruct the analyst's efforts. According to Freud's ego psychology, defences are layered. The interpretation of defence must respect this layering: the psychoanalyst must work, as it were, from the surface downwards. Interpretations of the main character resistance deepen incrementally during the course of analysis. Reich argued that the analyst should at first interpret only the *contemporary* significance of the resistance and should completely avoid attempting to specify its childhood origins. It is essential for the analyst to establish clearly the here-and-now meaning of the resistance before delving into the past. Relating all interpretations to what is going on in the relationship gave Reich's technique a sense of immediacy and emotional intensity.

Reich compared the character resistances to a suit of armour, which is simultaneously protective and restrictive. Whereas the patient initially experiences his or her neurotic character structure as "me", the systematic, painstaking analysis of the character resistance brings about a change. The patient comes to realize that he or she is more than their resistances. When patients are able to experience their character structure as something that limits them, as something imposed upon their core self, the analytic process enters its final phase. Once the main resistance begins to give way, numerous infantile memories emerge of their own accord or in the face of minimal resistance. It is at this point that the analyst is able to interpret the infantile origins of the transference and to help the patient reconstruct his or her childhood biography. The recovery of childhood memories (and the emotions that go with them) is made possible only by the analytical removal of the psychological strait-jacket of resistance. This process of freeing-up simultaneously restores to the patient the capacity for sexual gratification. As we have seen, Reich believed that it was essential that the patient take advantage of this new-found freedom if the cure is to be sustained.

After 1929

During 1929, Reich travelled to the USSR, where he spoke on psychoanalysis and society and consulted with like-minded colleagues; his *Psychoanalysis and Dialectical Materialism* (1929) was also published there. Later in the year, on 12 December, a meeting of the inner circle of the Vienna Psycho-Analytical Society, one of the usual series of fortnightly meetings, was held in Freud's home, during which Reich outlined his views on the importance of social and economic reform. Freud had only recently completed writing *Civilization and Its Discontents* (1930a), a work that came to far more pessimistic conclusions about the possibility of eliminating neurotic conflict. Freud believed that neurotic conflict was the price extracted by social existence, and that no amount of social reform could alter this. His reasoning was largely based on his belief in an innate tendency towards destructiveness: the "death instinct" (see chapter ten). He held that people cannot peacefully co-exist in society unless this tendency is curbed. Human aggression is (imperfectly) curbed by its redeployment against the self by means of the superego. Instead of hurting others, we hurt ourselves and are therefore doomed to neurotic conflict.

Reich was able to disagree with this view, because he did not believe in the primacy of the death instinct. Instead, Reich held that our primary sexual and self-preservative drives become twisted and malformed by oppressive child-rearing practices and a culture that unnecessarily and irrationally restricts sexual expression and gratification. Both human destructiveness and Freud's "polymorphous perversity" (which Reich called "pornographic" sexuality) are artefacts of cultural practices and are normally concealed behind a mask of restraint and politeness. Reich believed that Freud had penetrated behind the mask of civilization to reveal the twisted middle layer of the personality but had failed to realize that there was something decent and loving beyond this.

Freud was not opposed to the principle of social reform. As Reich later recalled:

> I went to him and told him that I wanted to work on a social basis. I wanted to get away from the clinics, from individual treatment, and get onto the social scene. Freud was very much

for it. It is complete nonsense . . . [to say that] Freud refused to consider sociology. He never did. There is no trace of such a thing. I want to make that very clear. He knew exactly how things were in the world. But before he could go outside, he first had to know what was inside. He was very happy that somebody who knew the inside so well went out and tried to do something about it. [Reich, cited in Higgins & Raphael, 1967]

Freud's objections apparently stemmed from his disagreement with the thesis that neurotic conflict can be prevented by means of social engineering, and his disagreement with Reich's revolutionary antagonism to established cultural institutions.

Freud was certainly disturbed by Reich's presentation. Richard Sterba, who was present on the occasion, reports that this was the only occasion when he observed Freud behaving in an angry and authoritarian manner (Sterba, 1978, cited in Jacoby, 1983). Reich's views were discussed in subsequent meetings of the Society and in private with Freud.

In 1930, Reich moved from Vienna to Berlin, which he hoped would be a more intellectually hospitable environment for him. The Berlin Psycho-Analytic Institute was the first and perhaps the most brilliant psychoanalytic institute in the world. In Berlin, Reich joined an active group of Freudian Marxists which included Otto Fenichel (his friend from university days), Karen Horney, Edith Jacobson, George Gerö, and Erich Fromm.

On the political front, with Freud's enthusiastic backing, Reich attempted to create an umbrella organization for various groups devoted to the issue of sexual reform. He called this the German Association for Proletarian Sex-Politics (Sex-Pol) which, at its height, numbered at least 40,000 members (Sharaf, 1983). Reich resumed his programme for sexual education and counselling on a larger scale than had been possible in Vienna, and he established a small publishing house, the Verlag für Sexualpolitik. He was deeply concerned about the rise of National Socialism and wrote and spoke against the Nazi movement.

The Communist Party took exception to Reich's views on sexual reform, and in 1933, shortly before Hitler was appointed chancellor, Reich was expelled from the party. At the same time, Nazi attacks on his work began appearing in the press, inducing

Reich to return to Vienna. Reich was not alone in this. Between 1932 and 1934, three-quarters of the members of the Berlin Institute had fled Germany (Cocks, 1985).

Vienna was also full of political unrest, and Reich was a political liability for the mainly Jewish psychoanalytic movement. Although the Nazis were by no means opposed to psychotherapy, they strongly disapproved of the Freudian school, and Freud's works were included in the book-burnings. Psychoanalysis was described as striving to

> . . . *remove the last ethical support* from the patient's soul in its battle over control of its instinctual life, and cast it down before the Asiatic world view, "Eat, drink and be merry for tomorrow you die!" And that was Freud's *aim* or perhaps his *assignment*, for he lined up dutifully with other Jewish endeavours *to strike the Nordic race at its most sensitive spot, its sex life*. [Cocks, 1985, p. 88]

On the psychotherapeutic front, Jung (1933) was arguing that "the difference between Germanic and Jewish psychology should no longer be effaced, something that can only be beneficial to science" (pp. 533–534). Nazi attacks on psychoanalysis typically zeroed in on the issue of sexuality. Reich's high profile as a sexual reformer, combined with his anti-Nazi activities, made him a dangerous man for the psychoanalytic movement to remain associated with. The Internationale Psychoanalytische Verlag, which had agreed to publish Reich's (1933a) book *Character Analysis*, now rescinded their contract. The Psychoanalytische Verlag covertly published the volume, but it bore the official imprint of Reich's Verlag für Sexualpolitik. Reich had to pay the printing costs himself. In May, he fled to Denmark. In 1934, he was excluded from the International Psycho-Analytical Association, an act that Anna Freud evidently described as "a great injustice" (Sharaf, 1983, p. 102). Although promised, no public statement was ever made to explain the reasons for Reich's expulsion. According to Fenichel (cited in Jacoby, 1983), the unpublishable real reason was that many felt that Reich was too psychologically disturbed. Later, when Reich emigrated to the United States, he clearly had delusional beliefs (Sharaf, 1983). However, as Jacoby (1983, p. 84) notes: given the pressures upon him, "If Reich lost his mental equilibrium, he had sufficient cause".

Reich was hounded out of Denmark, Sweden, and Norway in rapid succession, and he emigrated to the United States in 1939. By this point, his research interests had spiralled far away from psychoanalysis (those interested in these aspects of his work can consult the excellent 1983 biography by Sharaf). True to form, Reich attracted unfavourable attention in America, was pursued by the press and the FDA, and eventually died of heart failure in a state penitentiary at the age of 59. By 1932, even Freud had placed Reich in the same category as Jung, Rank, Adler, and Stekel and effectively excommunicated him from the psychoanalytic movement (Freud, 1933a, p. 144).

The *Wunderkind* of the Vienna society, was completely ignored by the psychoanalytic community. Freud refused to help Reich when he was excluded from the International Psycho-Analytical Association and was being pressured to leave Denmark. "It was", R. D. Laing reflected, "as though he had never existed" (cited in Boadella, 1973, p. 130).

In spite of his rejection by and subsequent rejection of psychoanalysis, Reich never wavered in his admiration for Freud, although he had little but contempt for most of Freud's heirs.

> I left behind me an age which had finally got hold of a little corner of the Freudian thought system, but had completely thrown overboard Freud's courage to stand alone, his adherence to some basic truth, his penetrating sense of what is right regardless—in other words, the complete abandonment of basic research of human emotions to petty little nuisance considerations such as career, easy money, easy recognition by institutions which owed their very existence to the evasion of the very facts of life they pretend, falsely, to disclose. [Reich, epigraph in Higgins & Raphael, 1967]

Reich's legacy

The issue of Reich's legacy is a complex one. Features of Reich's theory of technique were incorporated into mainstream psychoanalysis. However, after 1933, Reich himself left the psychoanalytic fold to develop other forms of psychotherapy such as character-analytic vegetotherapy and medical orgonomy (Sharaf, 1983). Both of these modalities had a strong impact on the development of the various neo-Reichian therapies, such as Alexander Lowen's "Bioenergetics" (Boadella, 1973). Reich's analysand Fritz Perls also incorporated Reichian ideas into Gestalt Therapy (Boadella, 1973). Reich also originated several key ideas that are normally attributed to Klein and Kernberg, as I demonstrate in subsequent chapters.

CHAPTER TEN

New positions:
Kleinian psychoanalysis

Limbs shall trample, hit and kick; lips fingers and hands shall
suck, twist, pinch; teeth shall bite gnaw mangle and cut;
mouth shall devour, swallow and "kill"... eyes kill by a look,
pierce and penetrate; breath and mouth hurt by noise, as the
child's own sensitive ears have experienced. One may suppose
that before an infant is many months old it will not only *feel*
itself performing these actions, but will have some kind of
ideas of doing so.

Joan Riviere

W riting from his eyrie in remote Oslo in 1936, in a tribute
to Freud on his 80th birthday, Reich, now a fully-
fledged outsider, bleakly surveyed the contemporary
psychoanalytic scene:

And what do things look like in the psychoanalytic movement
itself? The English school is a sectarian circle completely
divorced from life as it is. The Berlin Society attempted *Gleich-
schaltung* and thus perished. The Hungarian group consists
almost exclusively of the house-analysts of rich people, with-

out either scientific development or serious perspective. The Vienna Society is under the pressure of political reaction and ruled by some death-instinct theorists who no longer can be taken seriously from a scientific point of view. The French group looks desolate. [Reich, 1936, p. 264]

As we shall see, Reich's terse condemnation of the "English school", a psychoanalytic code-word for the movement initiated by psychoanalyst Melanie Klein, is in fact a clever conceptual pun: Klein's theory centres on the concept of a psychotically organized "internal world" cut off from incursions of reality.

Melanie Klein was a massively influential psychoanalytic figure. Her influence has been a dominant one in Great Britain and Latin America. Since the 1970s, the work of ecumenics like Otto Kernberg (see chapter twelve) have expanded her influence to North America. Whatever one's opinion of Klein's theories and methods, her influence and originality are undeniable.

Klein's background

Melanie Klein (*née* Reizes) was born in Vienna on 30 March 1882. Her father, Moritz, was a Galician Jew. Initially a Talmudic scholar, Moritz defied his religious parents' wishes by studying medicine. Moritz divorced his first wife, with whom he had been united in an arranged marriage as was customary in the Jewish *stetl*, when he was in middle age. It was while staying in a Viennese *pension* that Moritz met Libussa Deutch, a beautiful Slovakian Jewess half his age, who became his second wife.

The couple settled in the little Austrian town of Deutsch Kreutz, where Moritz maintained a medical practice. After the birth of three children, the family moved to Vienna, evidently because of financial difficulties, where Moritz became a dentist and worked as a medical consultant to a vaudeville theatre (Grosskurth, 1986). Libussa took the unusual step of supplementing the family income by starting her own business: she opened a shop that sold exotic plants and animals. Eventually, the Reizes were able to move out of the poor neighbourhood of Borsegasse, where Melanie was born, to the more fashionable Martinstrasse, although later the family would once again fall on hard times.

Melanie was a bright student and entered *gymnasium* early. She soon formulated the resolution to become a psychiatrist. At the age of 17, she was introduced to Arthur Klein, a Hungarian chemistry student studying in Switzerland. Arthur proposed to her, and she accepted. Marriage was delayed for four years while Arthur completed his professional training as a chemical engineer. During the next few years Melanie, bore two children, Hans and Melitta. In 1910, the Klein family moved to Budapest. In 1914, Klein's third child, Erich, was born. The years between the marriage and her discovery of psychoanalysis were lonely ones in which she experienced bouts of depression. Klein appears to have begun an extramarital affair around 1914, when Arthur was required to undertake military service.

Becoming a psychoanalyst

It was also in 1914 that Melanie Klein encountered psychoanalysis, through the vehicle of Freud's (1901a) book *On Dreams*, which was a popularization of *The Interpretation of Dreams*. Klein was "hooked", and she apparently entered analysis with Sándor Ferenczi the same year. She sought treatment for her "acute depression" and remained with him until 1919 or 1920 (Grosskurth, 1986).

Sándor Ferenczi [1873–1933] was the pioneer of psychoanalysis in Hungary and one of Freud's most prominent psychoanalytic colleagues (I return to his work in chapter eleven). Ferenczi had a reputation as both a brilliant theorist and a therapeutic innovator, and he maintained a close if tempestuous friendship with Freud for many years. Organized psychoanalysis had only begun in Hungary in 1913, with the establishment of the Budapest Psycho-Analytical Society. The headquarters for the Budapest Society was heavily funded by Anton von Freund, who would later subsidize the Vienna Polyclinic and the International Psychoanalytic Press. Klein's inaugural paper to the Budapest Society, delivered in the summer of 1919 and published in 1920, was a case study of her treatment of her own 5-year-old son, Erich. In 1921, it was republished with the identity of the patient suppressed. Ferenczi appears to have thought well of Klein. He encouraged her to explore psychoanalytic work with children and appointed her to a post in his Budapest clinic, where she worked with children. Ferenczi himself had a long-standing interest in how psychoanalytic knowledge might contribute to the education of children (Appignanesi & Forrester, 1992).

At the time, child psychoanalysis, or "early analysis", as Klein called it, was only just being developed. The psychoanalytic investigation of childhood was regarded as possessing both research and therapeutic significance. Psychoanalytic scrutiny of children's minds could confirm or disconfirm claims *reconstructively* made by Freud and others. Furthermore, as adult disorders were supposed to be based on the "infantile neurosis", the psychoanalytic treatment of children might eradicate neurosis before it became stubbornly entrenched in the personality.

The pioneer in this field was indisputably Hermine Hug-Hellmuth (Maclean & Rappen, 1991). Hug-Hellmuth entered the University of Vienna in 1897, the first year that women were permitted, and emerged in 1909 at the age of 38 with a teaching qualification and a PhD in physics. Her initial contact with psychoanalysis was through Isidor Sadger (Reich's first analyst), who was her half-sister's physician. She became a member of the Vienna Psycho-Analytical Society in 1913. Hug-Hellmuth's first psychoanalytic papers were based on accounts of her nephew, Rolf. Later, she wrote on the psychoanalytic treatment of children. Hug-Hellmuth was murdered by her nephew in 1924. After completing his prison sentence, Rolf approached Paul Federn demanding financial compensation for having been a victim of psychoanalytic experimentation (Appignanesi & Forrester, 1992).

The other major pioneer in child analysis was Anna Freud, Sigmund's youngest daughter. Anna began attending meetings of the Vienna Psycho-Analytical Society while still a teenager. She was trained as a nursery-school teacher and began practising child analysis in Vienna just prior to Hug-Hellmuth's death. She established a seminar on the technique of child analysis in Vienna, at which the first wave of child psychoanalysts were trained. She was also involved in two psychoanalytic educational experiments in Vienna: Siegfried Bernfeld's Baumgarten Nursery, an enlightened if short-lived school for Jewish orphans of World War One, which was run along psychoanalytic lines, and the Hitzig School founded by Dorothy Tiffany Burlingham in her own back garden. Later, in London, Burlingham ran the Hampstead Nursery for orphans of World War Two.

During the 1920s, the world capital for psychoanalytic work with young people was certainly Vienna. Concern with children and young people was widespread within the movement. In addition to the work of Hermine Hug-Hellmuth and Anna Freud, the charismatic August Aichhorn, something of a delinquent himself, specialized in work with juvenile delinquents and established a string of child guidance clinics. Siegfried Bernfeld was deeply interested in adolescence, and established an Archive for Youth in Vienna. Reich campaigned for the sexual rights of adolescents and published psychoanalytically informed books on sex education for children, as well as investigating how children might be raised in a "sex-affirmative" manner. Margaret Mahler, a young paediatrician training as a psychoanalyst, established the Abulatorium Rauscherstrasse, the first psychoanalytically orientated well-baby clinic, which was the primary source for referrals to the Viennese child analysts (Stepansky, 1988). Tucked away in Budapest, Klein was in something of a psychoanalytic backwater as far as child analysis was concerned. This probably proved advantageous, as it allowed her to develop her ideas independently, away from Anna Freud's overpowering influence.

In developing her technique of child analysis, Klein was confronted with the problem of how to access a small child's unconscious mind. The "fundamental rule" of free association on the couch is not practical when dealing with young children. Klein drew upon and considerably developed Hug-Hellmuth's practice of *playing* with her child patients. She believed that imaginative play is the functional equivalent of free association and that, in play, children display derivatives of their deepest phantasies, fears, and desires. Klein called her approach "psychoanalytic play technique".

Klein used a standard set of toys, which included small wooden figures of both genders and in two sizes, automobiles, wheelbarrows, swings, trains, aeroplanes, animals, trees, fences, houses, bricks, balls, marbles. The consulting-room was also equipped with scissors, knife, paper, pencils, paints, chalks, clay, and running water. Each child patient had his or her own set of toys, which was kept in a drawer, and was also allowed to bring toys along to sessions. Klein allowed the child to play with the toys and would participate in the game if she was assigned a role. During the course of play, she would interpret what she believed the child was unconsciously enacting. Whereas in the analysis of adults "acting out" was regarded as a defence and was discouraged in favour of pure verbalization, the analysis of children took acting out as its raw material. Klein initially believed that children's play was saturated with sexual phantasy, revolving around the Oedipus complex, penis envy, and castration anxiety. The bulk of her clinical material evidently came from Klein's analysis of her own children, Erich ("Fritz"), Hans ("Felix"), and Melitta ("Lisa"). Klein's analysis of her children thus played a similar role in her psychoanalytic thinking to that played by self-analysis in Freud's.

Berlin

In 1919 political upheaval overtook Hungary. Belá Kun, a former Russian revolutionary and friend of Vladimir Lenin, established a communist government, during which time Ferenczi was appointed Professor of Psychoanalysis, in response to a student petition. After Kun's invasion of Slovakia, Rumania invaded Hungary, and a new anti-Communist regime was established by Miklós Horthy. In the process, five thousand people were killed. The new government was actively anti-Semitic, forcing Jews out of the professions and barring them from higher education. Ferenczi was expelled both from his professorial post and from the Hungarian Medical Association. Klein fled to Slovakia, and her husband fled to Sweden, initiating a separation that would culminate in divorce five or six years later.

On the invitation of Karl Abraham, Klein moved from Rosenberg in Slovakia to Berlin. Abraham, the founder and head of the Berlin Psycho-Analytic Institute, was one of the most stalwart of Freud's followers. Abraham was a good organizer. Under his directorship the Berlin Psycho-Analytic Society and Institute flourished and in many ways eclipsed the more *laissez-faire* operations in Vienna and Budapest. Abraham was a "big shot" in the psychoanalytic movement, of the same rank as Ferenczi. Unlike Ferenczi, whose main interest had always been in therapeutic technique, Abraham's focus was on psychopathology, especially the puzzle of psychotic depression. It was Freud's ongoing theoretical dialogue with Abraham that led him to write his main contribution to the psychology of depression, "Mourning and Melancholia" (Freud, 1917e). In this paper, Freud argued that depression is a pathological form of mourning. Like a bereaved person, the depressive is responding to a loss. The depressed person has lost something or someone who was intensely *hated* as well as loved, and he or she deals with the loss by unconsciously *identifying* with the lost object. In consequence, the depressed person's hatred is turned against himself or herself, giving rise to self-reproach. Abraham (1924b) made use of Ferenczi's concept of introjection to elaborate this notion, arguing that the depressed person unconsciously experiences the process of identification as a concrete *incorporation*. In unconscious phantasy the lost object has actually been taken inside the body (Hinshelwood, 1994). The depressed person relates to the object in an oral mode.

Klein continued her child analytic work in Berlin, becoming a full member of the Berlin Society in 1923. Abraham was strongly supportive of her work, not least because he believed that it corroborated his own thesis about depression. In 1924, Abraham reluctantly took Klein into analysis, which was truncated by his death fifteen months later at the age of 48.

From 1924 onwards, Klein was catapulted into psychoanalytic prominence. Under Abraham's patronage, she began to develop her ideas more freely and delivered several conference papers on her work. The following example, which was presented at the, international psychoanalytic conference at Salzburg in 1924, conveys something of the flavour of Klein's work with children. It concerns Peter, a 3¾-year-old boy.

> In Peter's second session my interpretation of the material that he had brought had been that he and his brother practised mutual masturbation. Seven months later, when he was four years and four months old, he brought forward a long dream, rich in associative material, from which the following is an extract. "Two pigs were in a pig-sty and in my bed. There

were also two boys in my bed in a boat; but they were quite big, like uncle G- (a grown-up brother of his mother's) and E- (an older girl friend whom he thought almost grown-up)." Most of the associations I got from this dream were verbal ones. They showed that the pigs represented himself and his brother and their eating meant mutual *fellatio*. But they also stood for his parents copulating together. It turned out that his sexual relations with his brother were based on an identification with his father and mother, in which Peter took the role of each in turn. After I had interpreted this material Peter started his next session by playing round the wash-basin. He put two pencils on a sponge and said: "This is the boat that Fritz (his younger brother) and I got in." He then put on a deep voice— as he often did when his super-ego came into action—and shouted at the two pencils: "You're not to go about together all the time and do piggish things." This scolding on the part of his super-ego at his brother and himself was also aimed at his parents (as represented by his uncle G- and his grown-up friend E-) and set free in him affects of the same kind as he had felt towards them when he had witnessed the primal scene. [Klein, 1932, p. 23]

It was during the Berlin period that Klein began to argue against accepted psychoanalytic ideas. In particular, she disputed Freud's chronology of the Oedipus conflict, arguing that the heterosexual triangular drama of incest and parricide dated back to the period of weaning. Many of the Berlin analysts raised objections to Klein's work. Some objected to Klein's very direct, sexual interpretations of her child patients and felt that the child's naturally weak ego would be overwhelmed. Klein's rejoinder was that such ideas are intolerable not because of a weak ego, but because of a strong, persecutory superego that *forbids* the child to think consciously about sexual matters. Other analysts pointed out that psychoanalysis diminishes the authority of the superego, and that this procedure might therefore be destructive to the child, who has not yet fully developed a superego. Should not the analyst guide and support the development of the superego rather than undermine it? Klein responded with the claim that even very young children can have very powerful and oppressive superegos. Finally, some analysts denied that small children possessed sufficient intellectual sophistication to comprehend and make use of interpretations of unconscious phantasies. Klein countered that clinical material from early analyses clearly demonstrates that even very young children are able to understand and make use of psychoanalytic interpretations (Strachey, 1925).

Klein had many psychoanalytic enemies in Vienna and Berlin. Helene Deutsch, for example, called her "confused" and a "housewife with fantasies" (Roazen, 1985, p. 155). Writing from Berlin to her husband early in 1925, Alix Strachey wrote of Klein that "there's no doubt she's hated by a large section (all male) of the ψas ... but I can't make out whether they hate her because of frightful affective resistances against her Frühanalyse; or whether they have those f.a.r.'s because they hate her" (Meisel and Kendrick, 1986, p. 188). These analysts regarded her as "feeble-minded about theory" (p. 180). Opposition to Klein was fed from several tributaries. She was one of only three child analysts in Berlin at the time and was in direct competition with the Viennese approach pioneered by Anna Freud. As I have already noted, many of Klein's colleagues had strong reservations about her practice of offering very direct interpretations of what she took to be children's unconscious sexual phantasies. These concerns were exacerbated in the autumn of 1924 by the murder of Hermine Hug-Hellmuth by Rolf, her psychoanalytic guinea-pig, leading analysts to question the advisability of tampering with children's unconscious minds.

Klein's intellectual style also had something to do with the opposition that she engendered. Even at this early stage in her career, Klein conducted herself like a woman with a mission. Her own (at least apparent) self-confidence contrasted sharply with her lack of scientific training and a penchant for sweeping generalizations (Grosskurth, 1986).

Sensing which way the wind was blowing, Klein had made enquiries about visiting the United Kingdom to give some lectures promulgating her ideas. The issue of child analysis was, at the time, being rather chaotically debated at the British Psycho-Analytical Society, which was the largest in the world.

Klein had an important supporter in England, the redoubtable Welshman Ernest Jones. After a spell in Toronto, which he left in the wake of a sexual scandal involving a patient, Jones returned to

London to establish what became the British Psycho-Analytical Society. Jones had contributed a great deal to the psychoanalytic literature and was a skilful psychoanalytic politician and organizer, as well as an expert figure-skater and chess player.

Jones had heard Klein speak at the 1924 Salzburg Congress and was impressed with her work, whereas Klein herself was "all agog to capture England for her cause" (Meisel & Kendrick, 1986). She spent a very successful three weeks in London in July and was deeply appreciated by her British audience.

After Abraham's death on Christmas Day 1925, opposition to Klein in Berlin became more overt. Klein accepted Jones's invitation to emigrate to England, and she arrived there in September 1926. She immediately took Ernest Jones's wife and two children into analysis, a gesture from Jones symbolizing his endorsement of her work. In fact, the British took up Klein's work so avidly that by 1927 Ferenczi could report to Freud on her "domineering influence" in England (Grosskurth, 1986). Klein's theories and methods took root and flowered on British soil, and her distinctive approach to psychoanalysis became known as the "English" or, later, the "Kleinian" school.

The paranoid–schizoid position

From the time of her induction into psychoanalysis until 1946, Klein gradually elaborated a distinctive approach, including a model of infantile development, a theory of psychodynamics and psychopathology, and an approach to psychoanalytic technique. Klein changed her terminology over the course of these years, although her fundamental concepts remained quite stable. I do not rehearse these changes here but instead present Klein's definitive model.

As I mentioned in chapter nine, the theory of the death instinct had been propounded by Freud in 1920. The concept of a death instinct had been much discussed by the Viennese analysts for many years before Freud came round to endorsing a version of it (Kerr, 1994). Freud's concern with the pervasiveness of psychological conflict led him to postulate two classes of drives (or "instincts"). In his first theory of the drives, the sexual drives were juxtaposed with the self-preservative drives (or "ego instincts"), thus neatly capturing the twin Darwinian imperatives of reproduction and survival.

Isidor Sadger introduced the concept of narcissism into psychoanalysis in 1909 (Nunberg & Federn, 1962–1975, Vol. 2). Both Sadger and Freud unhesitatingly described narcissism as a form of sexuality. Narcissism is the state of being in love with one's own image—a sexual attachment to oneself. In 1911, Otto Rank pointed out that if we strive to avoid danger because we care for ourselves, and if self-regard is an expression of our narcissism, than it follows that the Freudian self-preservative drives can be *reduced* to sexuality (Rank, 1911). Taken to its logical conclusion, Freud's own theory seemed to be undercutting his dualism. At around the same time, Carl Jung, who was well on his way to becoming a psychoanalytic apostate, was arguing for a unitary, non-dualistic concept of psychic energy. Freud was clearly troubled by all of this and mounted a somewhat baroque defence of his theory in 1915 (Freud, 1915c). By 1920, he had capitulated to Rank's reasoning ("psychoanalysis has not enabled us hitherto to point to any [ego] instincts other than the libidinal ones": 1920g, p. 53) and resolved the difficulty by advancing a new dualism.

In *Beyond the Pleasure Principle* (1920g), Freud advanced a new instinctual antithesis to replace his earlier, untenable version. This seems to have arisen out of investigations into sadomasochism undertaken between 1915 and 1920 (Bibring, 1934). Freud concluded that there are in human beings impulses to inflict harm (including self-harm) that have nothing to do with sexual gratification, and he postulated a primary urge to self-destruction which he termed the "death instinct", which is opposed by the life instincts of sexuality and self-preservation. In order to preserve ourselves, we deflect the death instinct outwards, where it appears as the "aggressive drive": the urge to harm or destroy others. The superego harnesses some of this destructive energy and turns it once again against the self. Freud believed that the existence of the death instinct posed grave problems for social existence: human beings are faced with the stark alternatives of harming themselves or harming others. The majority of psychoanalysts immediately rejected the notion of the death instinct, whereas Freud became more and more convinced of its utility.

During the years after her move to London, Klein came to emphasize the dynamic and pathogenic role of aggression in human behaviour. Like Freud, she attributed the problem of aggression to the operation of the death instinct (Klein, 1932). According to this view, we are saddled, from birth, with urges to harm others. Human beings are

> ... creatures among whose instinctual endowments is to be reckoned a powerful share of aggressiveness. As a result their neighbour is for them not only a potential helper or sexual object, but also someone who tempts them to satisfy their aggressiveness on him, to exploit his capacity for work without compensation, to use him sexually without his consent, to seize his possessions, to humiliate him, to cause him pain, to torture and kill him. [Freud, 1930a, p. 111]

Freud's examples of cruelty and exploitation aptly describe the behaviour of grown men. What about children? How does the death instinct express itself in the infant? Klein believed, with Freud, that the infant deflects the death instinct outwards as destructive aggression, which becomes manifest as the emotion of *hate*. However, the infant has such a limited cognitive grasp of reality, and is under the sway of its drives and emotions to such a degree, that it *projects* these feelings outward. That is, at those times when the activation of the death instinct causes hatred to well up in the infant, this is subjectively experienced not as hatred but rather as *persecution* by the world outside. By the same token, loving feelings (envoys of the life instincts) are experienced as nurturance from the world outside.

I have used the term "nurturance" because, as Klein believed that these processes were activated from the earliest days of extra-uterine life, they must, according to psychoanalytic theory, be bound up with *orality*. During the oral stage, the main sexual object for the baby is the breast, so it follows that the infant alternates between states of feeling persecuted by its mother's breast and being nurtured by it. Klein referred to the process of cleaving the world into "good" and "bad" as *splitting*. The idea of being persecuted by a breast can be difficult to grasp. Consider the experience of hunger pangs. For an adult or older child, such pangs mean "I'm hungry". According to Kleinian writers, a tiny baby experiences such pains differently. They are felt to emanate from a persecutory breast that has somehow managed to get inside the baby, where it is inflicting damage. Horror films such as *Alien* graphically portray this idea.

According to Klein, the tiny infant does not have a concept of its mother as a whole person. In the first place, the infant relates only to her breast. In the second place, even the breast is experienced as two distinct entities: the bad (persecutory) breast and the good (nurturing) breast. In Kleinian jargon, one says that the tiny infant relates only to *"part* objects". Klein believed that the infant struggles to get the "good" part objects inside of itself and to expel or fend off the "bad" part objects. When the baby imagines that it has taken a part object inside itself ("introjected" it), this is called an *"internal* object". According to Klein, as we develop and grow, we build up an "internal world" populated with internal objects. The notion of an internal world is a distinctively Kleinian conception.

When the baby feels that it is interacting with a "bad", persecutory breast, it feels itself to be "bad" as well. By the same token, when the baby interacts in phantasy with a "good", nurturing breast, it feels itself to be "good". The baby's image of itself is thus split along with its objects. There is a good part-self and a bad part-self. Klein referred to this fragmented and sometimes nightmarish situation as the *paranoid–schizoid position*. It is paranoid, because the baby feels persecuted. It is schizoid because it involves splitting. Klein eventually concluded that babies occupy the paranoid–schizoid position during approximately the first three months of life outside the womb.

The depressive position

According to Klein, infants pass from the paranoid–schizoid to the *depressive* position. She introduced this concept in "Contribution to the Psychogenesis of Manic-Depressive States" (1935), which was written during a period of depression following the death of her son Hans in a mountaineering accident, which many suspected was suicidal. In Klein's system, the depressive position is crucial for psychological development. The degree to which we are able to negotiate the depressive position determines the degree of our mental health. The less we have been able to progress to the depressive position, the crazier we are.

Klein's theory states that at around the age of 3 months the infant begins to become capable of (a) recognizing that it relates to a whole person—the mother—and not just a body-part—the breast—and (b) recognizing that the "good" and "bad" breasts are in fact attributes of one and the same person—the mother. We can say that the infant starts to become capable of relating to "*whole objects*".

Entry into the depressive position is momentous and emotionally agonizing. The reason for this is not far to seek. On entering the depressive position, one realizes that the very person whom one has savagely attacked and destroyed in phantasy is she upon whose goodness one has depended. According to Klein, the depressive position entails the sense that one has destroyed what one loves and values: the infant's inner world is filled with death and destruction. Whereas the paranoid–schizoid position is characterized by "persecutory anxiety"—the fear of being attacked by something external to oneself—the depressive position opens up the possibility of experiencing "depressive anxiety"—a sense of deep sadness that one had destroyed what one values as good.

Depressive anxiety can be fended off by paranoid defences: a regression to the paranoid–schizoid mode of splitting and projection. It can also be defended against by means of what Klein (1935) called the "manic defence". The manic defence is an *attitude* that denies dependence, guilt, and concern. It is characterized by the "manic triad" of triumph, control, and contempt.

The depressive crisis can ultimately only be negotiated to the extent that one has established an enduring sense of inner goodness, based on identifying with a "good" internal object, capable of withstanding the ravages of depressive remorse. From this flows *reparation*, which is the phantasied attempt to make good the damage that one has inflicted upon one's objects. In the absence of this, entrenchment in manic or paranoid defences is inevitable.

The superego and the Oedipus complex

Klein was in the audience when Reich delivered a paper on the impulsive character at the Berlin Psycho-Analytic Society on 10 January 1925. Alix Strachey, who was also present, wrote to her husband that Reich was "trying to fiddle with the arrangements between the Ich & Ichideal . . . and was rather smartly set upon. But the room re-echoed with the boom of his voice till the last" (Meisel & Kendrick, 1986, p. 180).

Reich argued in the paper that, rather than being the heir to the Oedipus complex, forms of the superego are present from soon after birth. In 1926, Klein published "Psychological Principles of Early Analysis" in which she argued that primitive, persecutory forms of the superego are present from earliest infancy and therefore that the superego does not emerge, as Freud would have it, at the conclusion of the phallic stage (Klein, 1926). She did not cite Reich's work in this and most of her subsequent papers on the subject. As well as discussing early stages of superego development, Reich also remarked on early object-relations. "The first objects in the infant's environment", he said, "are not people as entities but merely their organs. . . . From the mother's breast the libido proceeds to encompass the mother herself as the supplier of nourishment, love and tranquillity" (Reich, 1925, p. 277).

Reich's remarks on object relations clearly anticipated and plausibly influenced Klein's later account of the transition from part- to whole-object relations during the depressive position. Klein's sole reference to Reich's theory of early superego development appears to be a passing remark in *The Psycho-Analysis of Children* (Klein, 1932).

Klein believed that the superego originates in the "bad" internal objects of the paranoid–schizoid position.

> But in the small child we come across a superego of the most incredible and phantastic character. And the younger the child is, or the deeper the mental level we penetrate to, the more this is the case. We get to look upon the child's fear of being devoured, or cut up, or torn to pieces, or its terror of being surrounded and pursued by menacing figures, as a regular component of its mental life; and we know that the man-eat-

ing wolf, the fire-spewing dragon, and all the evil monsters out of myths and fairy-stories flourish and exert their unconscious influence in the phantasy of each individual child, and it feels itself persecuted and threatened by those evil shapes. [Klein, 1933, p. 249]

For Klein, these "evil monsters" are, in the final analysis, introjections of parts of the infant's parents (its mother's breast), into which destructive impulses had previously been projected. Rather than being an embodiment of morality and cultural ideals, the earliest form of the superego is nothing less than a vehicle for the baby's unbridled hatred and cruelty. If follows that the advent of the depressive position must involve a modification of the superego. The infant now sees the mother as a whole person and is able to identify with her, feeling remorse for his earlier phantasied attacks upon her body. With the coming of the depressive position, and its working through, the superego undergoes transformation into something more closely resembling the agency described by Freud.

At this stage the super-ego makes itself felt as conscience. It forbids murderous and destructive tendencies and links with the child's need for guidance and some restraint from his actual parents. ... However, even in normal adults, under strong internal and external pressure, the split-off impulses and split-off dangerous and persecutory figures reappear temporarily and influence the super-ego. The anxieties then experienced approximate to the terrors of the infant, though in a different form. [Klein, 1963, p. 279]

In the paranoid–schizoid position, the superego is a wholly destructive and predatory embodiment of the death instinct. After its successful depressive reorganization, "the individual is supported and helped by its influence, for it strengthens the loving impulses and furthers the tendency towards reparation" (p. 279).

We have seen how, in Freud's vision, the Oedipus complex is *replaced* by the superego at the conclusion of the phallic phase. What is the relationship between the two in Klein's system? For Klein, the depressive position is a precondition for the emergence of the Oedipus complex. The emotion of jealousy, so central to the Oedipus situation, assumes relations between whole objects.

Klein assumes both that genital sexual desire makes its *début* during the first year and that infants have an innate knowledge of the existence of the genital apparatus. The inevitable experience of oral frustration leads infants of both sexes to turn in phantasy towards the father's penis for oral gratification. The earliest relationship to the paternal phallus is fractured along the same emotional fault-line as the relationship to the breast: the baby seeks to incorporate orally the "good" penis and fend off the malignant "bad" penis. During the depressive position, this early situation is transformed as follows:

> Genital desires in the infant of either sex coalesce with oral desires and therefore an oral, as well as a genital, relation with the father's penis ensues. Genital desires are also directed towards the mother. The infant's desires for the father's penis are bound up with jealousy of the mother because he feels she receives this desired object. [Klein, 1952b, p. 78]

Klein believes that the sexually frustrated baby imagines that father and mother perpetually enjoy with one another the very thing that he or she lacks (the mother's breast or the father's penis). Mother and father are phantasied as existing in a constant state of mutual oral, anal, or genital gratification. This, in turn, gives rise to phantasy images of the mother containing the father's penis or the whole father inside her body, or the father containing the mother's breast or the whole mother inside his body. Envious attacks on the parents in phantasy may exacerbate primitive persecutory or depressive anxieties.

For Klein, the Oedipus complex arises during the depressive position and diminishes as depressive issues are worked through and resolved. The Oedipus complex thus *coexists with* rather than being replaced by the superego (the earliest forms of the superego actually precede the Oedipus complex). Whereas for Freud, the superego is essentially a function of human culture, which maintains itself by forbidding incest and parricide, for Klein the superego is primarily a matter of early object relations and only secondarily takes on a cultural role.

Envy and projective identification

After 1946, Klein concentrated on fine-tuning her ideas and made relatively few theoretical innovations. The most important of these are undoubtedly Klein's conception of the role of envy and her concept of projective identification.

Klein regarded envy as a pervasive and especially malignant expression of the death instinct, operative from the very beginning of extra-uterine life. Constitutionally powerful envy can in itself be pathogenic:

> My work has taught me that the first object to be envied is the feeding breast, for the infant feels that it possesses everything he desires and that it has an unlimited flow of milk, and love which the breast keeps for its own gratification. This feeling adds to his sense of grievance and hate, and the result is a disturbed relation to the mother. If envy is excessive, this, in my view, indicates that paranoid and schizoid features are abnormally strong and that such an infant can be regarded as ill. [Klein, 1957, p. 183]

The concept of the defence mechanism projective identification is poorly articulated in Klein's own writings, and has come to take on a different meaning to that which Klein herself intended. In Klein's (1946) account, projective identification is the process of projecting parts of oneself into another with the unconscious intention of hijacking them. Projective identification can result either in the sense that the object has *acquired* the characteristics of the projected part of the self, or that one is in some sense *merged* with the object. The excessive use of projective identification has the effect of depleting the sense of self. More recent, neo-Kleinian accounts of projective identification describe it as an interactional defence, in which one projects a disowned aspect of oneself into another person and then behaves in such a way as to induce that other person to take on board the projected features. To use a banal example, I might get rid of a sense of my own ineptitude as a scholar by getting one of my students to feel stupid. If, in response to my patronizing behaviour she ends up actually feeling herself to be stupid, then I have successfully projectively identified my own split-off self-image into her. Langs (1976a) terms this process "interactional projection".

Mental health and psychoanalytic technique

Although Kleinian methods began with the analysis of children (often very disturbed children), Kleinian technique has been used extensively with adults, including psychotic adults whom Freud believed could not be helped by psychoanalysis. Klein herself wrote no systematic account of her therapeutic technique, although illustrations are scattered throughout her *oeuvre*.

Klein conceived of mental health as based on the successful negotiation of the depressive position, and hence the elimination of extensive splitting and its attendant persecutory anxieties. The role of the psychoanalysis is thus not primarily to make the unconscious conscious, or to extend the ego at the expense of the id, although both of these processes are entailed by it. The Kleinian conception of psychoanalytic cure could be captured in the slogan: "Where part-objects were, there whole objects shall be." The analyst strives to restore integrity to a split—or, in extreme cases, fragmented—inner world.

Classical Freudian psychoanalytic practitioners tended to regard transference as an episodic phenomenon, occurring now and again and marked by either manifest comments about the analyst or the presence of resistance. It was Reich who, in the 1920s, first emphasized the existence and importance of chronic, latent transference attitudes. This was yet another aspect of Reich's work which Klein took up, although she gave it her own unique stamp. For Klein, transference is nothing less than the way that we organize our relations with others in accord with unconscious phantasies stemming from the first year of life. In the Kleinian view, such unconscious phantasies are always present and are not pathological *per se*. In the famous words of Betty Joseph, transference is a relationship in which "something is always going on" (Joseph, 1985, p. 61). Transference encompasses the whole of the patient's relationship to the analyst (Klein, 1952a). Transference is usually unconscious, expressed through the patient's behaviour (as Reich had emphasized) or in verbally encoded form.

> For many years—and this is up to a point still true today—transference was understood in terms of direct references to the analyst in the patient's material. My conception of trans-

ference as rooted in the earliest stages of development and in deep layers of the unconscious is much wider and entails a technique by which from the whole material presented the *unconscious elements* of the transference are deduced. For instance, reports of patients about their everyday life, relations and activities not only give an insight into the functioning of the ego, but also reveal—if we explore their unconscious content—the defences against the anxieties stirred up in the transference situation. [Klein, 1952a, p. 55]

In the Kleinian view, patients may covertly express transferences onto the analyst by talking about manifestly unrelated matters. A virtually paradigmatic example of this is provided by Segal (1967), who describes a trainee who, during the first session, described his desire to qualify as a psychoanalyst as quickly as possible and and then went on to mention his digestive problems and, later still, cows. Segal interpreted to him that she was the cow, like his mother's breast, and that he wanted to greedily devour all of her "analysis milk". Kleinian analysts try as much as possible to focus their interpretations on the immediate transference relationship. Segal's illustration demonstrates yet another Kleinian innovation: the analyst can represent a part object (e.g. the breast or penis) as well as a whole object in the transference. For example, patients' disparagements of the analyst or of the analytic process may be interpreted in terms of primitive envious attacks on the nurturing breast.

Another striking feature of Segal's vignette is her use of such a "deep" interpretation at such an early stage of the analysis. In contrast to the ego-psychological principle of gradually working through the defences, Kleinians adhere to the principle of interpreting the most primitive unconscious phantasies and anxieties active at any given moment. The rationale for this procedure is the belief that psychological healing comes about only through the resolution of fundamental psychotic defences and anxieties.

Because of the important conceptual role of projective identification, Kleinian analysts pay particular importance to their own countertransferences. By studying the states arising in them during the psychoanalytic hour, these analysts try to make inferences about the disowned states that their patients are "projecting into" them. Somewhat ironically, this approach was first advanced by

Paula Heimann (1950), in a paper that was published as a gesture of defiance at Klein's domineering influence (Heimann was Klein's secretary and, simultaneously, her patient). Klein herself rejected Heimann's proposals, but they were taken up, subsumed under the concept of projective identification, and incorporated into Kleinian theory by her followers, notably Bion.

Politics of psychoanalysis

It should be clear from this summary of Klein's position that her conception of the mind and of human development was in many respects different from and contradictory to that proposed by Freud. Not surprisingly, the Kleinian movement aroused opposition from both British and continental Freudians. A particularly significant bone of contention was Klein's emphasis on the importance of phantasy over and above reality (King & Steiner, 1990).

This situation was exacerbated by Klein's long-standing rivalry with Anna Freud, who was by the 1930s Freud's heir to the psychoanalytic papacy. Melanie Klein and Anna Freud were the two leading exponents of child analysis. Whereas Klein believed that child analysis should, in essence, be conducted in much the same way as the psychoanalysis of adults, and developed her own innovative conception of human development and psychic structure, Anna Freud argued that the analyst should take a more authoritarian, educative stance. She also denied that children form a transference to the analyst, and she remained loyal to her father's developmental and topographical conceptions.

Another player in the conflict between Freud's loyal daughter and Melanie Klein was Klein's disloyal daughter, the psychoanalyst Melitta Schmideberg, who publicly attacked her mother with the backing of her analyst Edward Glover, a one-time supporter of Klein's ideas. In order to diffuse the situation, a series of exchange lectures were arranged between London and Vienna. With the steady rise of National Socialism during the 1930s, many analysts became refugees and some of these found asylum in England. By 1938, these made up one-third of the British Psycho-Analytical

Society (Grosskurth, 1986). In June, the Freuds arrived as well, an event that Klein described to D. W. Winnicott, then a member of Klein's circle, as "a disaster" (Grosskurth, 1986, p. 241). As World War Two loomed, the British Psycho-Analytical Society was engaged in a civil war of its own. Intense ideologically driven infighting continued into the 1940s. In 1942, a series of debates was organized by the British Psychoanalytical Society which were euphemistically called the "Controversial Discussions". These meetings were devoted to an examination of the beliefs responsible for the rift between the (Anna) Freudians and the Kleinians, with a third group—the non-aligned "middle" group, represented by Sylvia Payne—watching by the sidelines. After years of internecine conflict, a compromise was finally reached whereby psychoanalytic training in Britain would be divided into two streams in the hands of the Kleinian "A" group and the Freudian "B" group.

Klein's influence and reputation waxed ever brighter during the post-war period. This continued until her death in 1960 from complications following a fractured hip suffered just after surgery for colonic cancer.

Klein's legacy

It is impossible to overestimate the impact of Klein's work on psychoanalysis. The Kleinian tradition has been continued by a host of practitioners centred mainly in the United Kingdom and Latin America. It has also given rise to the post-Kleinian tradition exemplified by the work of Bion and Meltzer (Hinshelwood, 1994). Finally, as I describe in later chapters, Klein's influence was brought to bear on North American psychoanalysis mainly through the work of Kernberg and Langs.

Klein's work opened up the psychoanalytic study of earliest infancy, an area that Freud regarded as beyond the reach of his own method of enquiry. As this chapter has shown, Klein's approach to these issues was strongly internalistic and innatist, with scant attention to environmental contingencies and adaptation, and a tremendous emphasis on the hypothesis of an innate, self-destructive trend—the death instinct. The historical dialectic of the development of psychoanalytic theory demanded a counterpoint to Klein's perspective on earliest infancy. The most articulate representative of this trend was D. W. Winnicott, to whom we now turn.

CHAPTER ELEVEN

Winnicott in transition:
a British Independent

> Behind your thoughts and feelings, my brother, there stands a
> mighty ruler, an unknown sage—whose name is self. In your
> body he dwells; he is your body.
>
> Friedrich Nietzsche

On 21 February 1952, an apostate Kleinian wrote impatiently to Klein's protégé Hannah Segal about the political
conflicts that continued to plague the British Psycho-
Analytical Society years after the conclusion of the Controversial
Discussions:

> I am very genuinely concerned about Melanie Klein's contri-
> bution to psychoanalysis. ... This contribution of hers is
> steadily being made unacceptable because of the propaganda
> indulged in at every meeting, by Dr Heimann and yourself in
> particular. There is a saying that good wine needs no blush. In
> a similar way the good in Melanie's contribution need not be
> pushed forward in Scientific Meetings. It can be expressed and
> discussed. At present it is put forward aggressively and then
> defended in a way that can only be called paranoid. In other

words ... the Kleinian psychology is organising itself into something which the Klein disciples will preach until it is hated ... and in any case the way all the sub-Kleinians pop up in defence every time one of them reads a paper gives the impression, which it will take a long time to eradicate, that there is a paranoid organisation amongst the custodians of the good internalised breast. [Rodman, 1987, pp. 26–27]

The author of this letter was D. W. (Donald Woods) Winnicott, the unofficial leader of the "Independent" group of British psychoanalysts, who refused to genuflect either to Anna Freud or to Melanie Klein.

Winnicott's background

Winnicott was born in 1896 in Plymouth, Devon, where his father Frederick, a successful local businessman, eventually became mayor. Frederick was very active in the Methodist Church and later in life was knighted. As befitted their standing, the Winnicotts lived in an imposing home set in spacious grounds complete with croquet lawn, orchard, and vegetable garden (Kahr, 1996). Frederick was a traditional Victorian father, who spent little time with his children. Donald was surrounded by women: his mother Elizabeth, his two sisters Violet and Kathleen, his aunt Delia, his nanny Allie, his sisters' governess, the cook, and several maids. Winnicott's later psychoanalytic writing was almost exclusively concerned with the relationship between mothers and infants, and the role of the father or the phallic dimension is notable in its absence. Winnicott himself had marked feminine characteristics as an adult, including a very high-pitched voice.

Such was the Winnicott sense of decorum that when the 12-year old Donald uttered the word "drat!" at the dinner table, his father resolved to send him to boarding-school so as to ensure that he mixed only with "decent" friends. At the age of 14, Winnicott was sent to Leys School for Boys in Cambridge, a highly respectable Methodist establishment. In 1914, he began his medical studies at Jesus College, Cambridge. In 1917, he enlisted in the Royal

Navy and became Medical Officer aboard a destroyer. After the war, Winnicott completed his medical studies at St Bartholomew's Hospital in London. He obtained his medical qualification in 1920 and decided to specialize in paediatrics. In 1923, he was appointed to posts at the Queens Hospital for Children and Paddington Green Children's Hospital. Winnicott opened his private medical practice in London's West End in 1924.

There was a yawning cultural gap separating Winnicott from Freud (and also, although somewhat less so, from Klein and Reich). Winnicott came from a background of social and economic security. His family were part of what Freud called the "compact majority", who never had to face or perhaps even think about racial discrimination. Freud's family were wanderers, with memories of the pogroms only recently behind them. They were members of what was then considered a racial minority, and, later, four of Freud's siblings would be exterminated in the Nazi death camps because of this. Freud himself grew up in poverty, without access to the civil rights of the gentile majority. Such cultural differences breed different sensibilities. As we will see, Winnicott's vision of human nature is far less riven with conflict and tragedy than that of his continental forebears. Winnicott grew up with a sense of *entitlement* that would forever elude more anguished theorists like Freud, Klein, and Reich. Equally, it might be argued that his very security debarred Winnicott from empathic access to certain tormenting aspects of the human condition.

Becoming a psychoanalyst

Winnicott first encountered psychoanalysis in 1918, through Oskar Pfister's book on *The Psychoanalytic Method* (Pfister, 1913), and shortly afterwards he read Freud's *Interpretation of Dreams*. He decided to enter analysis himself and was referred by Ernest Jones to James Strachey.

Quite apart from an intellectual interest in psychoanalysis, Winnicott sought analysis because of personal difficulties, most probably involving sexual impotence (Kahr, 1996). The analysis lasted ten years. Winnicott entered formal psychoanalytic training in 1927, obtained his qualification as an adult psychoanalyst in 1934, and was certified as a child psychoanalyst in 1935.

The start of Winnicott's psychoanalytic training coincided with Melanie Klein's emigration from Berlin to London. Furthermore, his analyst, James Strachey, had been involved with Klein at one remove through the activities of his wife, Alix, who had befriended her in Berlin. Strachey suggested to Winnicott that he meet Melanie Klein.

As a trainee psychoanalyst with a large paediatric practice, Winnicott had his own reasons for being interested in Klein's work. He was well aware from direct experience that the roots of at least some forms of psychopathology are lodged further back in earliest infancy, and Klein was at the time the only psychoanalyst who was attempting to investigate these matters in any detail. Winnicott took Klein's newly published book *The Psycho-Analysis of Children* (Klein, 1932) on holiday with him in 1932. He was sufficiently impressed to enter supervision with Klein in 1934 and to continue with her for six years. Winnicott had the highest regard for Klein as a supervisor, stating that she remembered his clinical work better than he did himself (Winnicott, 1962a). He thus "changed from being a pioneer to being a student with a pioneer teacher" (p. 173).

Winnicott sought analysis with Klein, who refused him on the grounds that she wanted him to analyse her son. He then turned to Joan Riviere, a vigorous and by many accounts aggressive proponent of Klein's doctrines. The five years he spent with Riviere were not a happy experience, and after the termination of the analysis she publicly attacked and humiliated him at public meetings (Kahr, 1996).

The facilitating environment

In 1939 Winnicott was appointed Consultant Psychiatrist for the Government Evacuation Scheme for Oxfordshire, a post that he held for the duration of the Second World War. Winnicott was clinically responsible for over 250 children who had been evacuated from their homes in London and placed in foster homes in the country to avoid the threat posed by German bombing. A number of these children developed psychological and psychosomatic symptoms as a consequence of the trauma of evacuation, or they became delinquent, engaging in such activities as arson, train wrecking, truancy, and robbery. Winnicott (1963) believed that such anti-social children have experienced emotional *deprivation*, by which he meant the experience of support being withdrawn:

> Where failure is not mended within the requisite time, seconds, minutes, hours, then we use the term deprivation. A deprived child is one who, after knowing about failures mended, comes to know about failure unmended. It is then the lifework of the child, to provoke conditions in which failures mended once more give the pattern to life. [Winnicott, cited in Davis & Wallbridge, 1981, p. 116]

Winnicott's attitude towards anti-social behaviour typified his concern with the real relationship between a real child and its real environment. Issues pertaining to the inner world (Klein) or self- and object-representations (Freud) were important for him but were subordinate to the issue of adaptation to reality. Winnicott developed his ideas about the role of environmental provision in two distinct yet interrelated directions: in relation to child development and in relation to psychoanalytic technique.

Omnipotence and reality

From the beginning of his psychoanalytic career, Freud was sensitive to the disjunction between fantasy and reality. How, he wondered, do we learn to distinguish between something out there in the world and a wishful apparition conjured up by our own mind? How does the pleasure principle give way to the reality principle?

After his analysis of the Rat Man (Freud, 1909d), Freud took to calling the maladaptive incursion of the pleasure principle into adult thought "the omnipotence of thought", a term supplied by the Rat Man himself. The omnipotence of thought is quite obvious in certain neurotic conditions. An obsessional neurotic may, for example, harbour the belief that a disaster may be brought about merely by virtue of his thinking about it. Freud believed that there were pockets of such magical thinking in all psychopathological states.

In *Totem and Taboo* (1912–13), Freud claimed that the preservation of infantile omnipotence was a by-product of the preservation of narcissism. The concept of narcissism was imported into psychoanalysis from sexology in 1909 by Isidor Sadger, a man whom even Freud regarded as being obsessed with sex. Freud first discussed the concept of narcissism in the second edition of the *Three Essays on the Theory of Sexuality*, published in 1910, and developed it in several other publications (Smith, 1985). Freud postulated that the first person whom we love is ourself, and that the earliest self representation contains everything in the baby's experiential world that is "good". As he would put it many years later: "To begin with the child does not distinguish between the breast and his own body. . . . The breast has to be separated from the body and shifted to the '*outside*' because the child so often finds it absent" (Freud, 1940a, p. 188). Gradually we learn that there is goodness outside ourself and badness inside ourself, and in this way we learn to love others and to recognize our dependence upon them (Freud, 1915c). Even when we learn to love, we do not renounce our narcissism fully. We also set up an *ideal* of personal perfection to which we aspire. We then love ourselves (experience self-esteem) to the extent that our real self approximates to this *ego-ideal* (Freud, 1914c). The concept of the ego-ideal was later developed into the theory of the superego.

Freud believed that the degree to which we remain arrested in the narcissistic phase of development, or the extent that we regress to it, determines the degree to which we believe in our own omnipotence. His argument was based on the idea that primitive narcissism involves self-idealization, and that attributing magical powers to oneself is a manifestation of this.

In 1913, Sándor Ferenczi published a paper entitled "Stages in the Development of the Sense of Reality", which proposed a radically different theory of omnipotence. Ferenczi's developmental model posits that during the intra-uterine phase of life the infant does not experience drive frustration, because its needs are supplied by homeostatic mechanisms within the mother–infant unit. Ferenczi suggests that this is experienced by the foetus as a state of omnipotence. "It is a state", write Glatzer and Evans (1977), "in which one does not *even need to need*. It is self-sufficiency" (p. 89). Ferenczi called this the stage of "unconditional omnipotence". According to Ferenczi, then, the original feeling of omnipotence is justified by the real environmental circumstances in which it finds itself. The foetus is given the "impression" that it is omnipotent, and this sense of omnipotence is therefore "no empty delusion" (Ferenczi, 1913, p. 219).

After birth, the newborn baby gives us the impression that "he is far from pleased at the rude disturbance of the wish-less tranquillity he had enjoyed in the womb, and indeed that *he longs to regain this situation*" (p. 220). This is normally "instinctively" recognized by the infant's caretakers, and they

> ... deliberately bring him into a situation that resembles as closely as possible the one that he has just left. . . . They lay him down by the warm body of the mother, or wrap him up in soft, warm coverings, evidently so as to give him the illusion of the mother's warm protection. They guard his eye from light stimuli, and his ear from noise, and give him the possibility of further enjoying the intra-uterine absence of irritation, or, by rocking the child and crooning to him monotonously rhythmical lullabies, they reproduce the slight and monotonously rhythmical stimuli that the child is not spared even in utero. [pp. 220–221]

Ferenczi assumes with Freud (1900a) that the small infant deals with its needs by means of the pleasure principle—that is, that as soon as the baby begins to desire something it *hallucinates* its fulfilment. Adding this to his first premise that the newborn infant longs to return to the nirvana of the womb, Ferenczi (1913) deduces that after an infant is born, it *hallucinates* being back in the womb: "The first wish-impulse of the child cannot be any other than to regain this situation" (p. 221). And yet, at the very moment that the distressed baby is hallucinating being in the womb, its care-taker is recreating in reality something resembling that very experience! The infant must, from its own perspective, experience this as a kind of omnipotence:

> Since the child certainly has no knowledge of the real concatenation of cause and effect, or the nurse's existence and activity, he must feel himself in possession of a magical capacity that can actually realise all his wishes by simply imagining the satisfaction of them. [p. 222]

The physiological symbiosis of the womb has been replaced by an intentional choreography, but the effect is similar. By providing what the infant desires at the very moment that these desires are being hallucinated, the infant is given the impression that the pleasure principle actually works and that he or she can bring about real satisfaction by means of wishful fantasy. Ferenczi calls this the period of "magical-hallucinatory omnipotence" (p. 222).

As an infant develops and its needs become more complex, the environment ceases to be so perfectly coordinated with its needs. The development of motor coordination allows the baby to signal its needs in a more explicit manner than the uncoordinated motor discharges of the previous phase. When the child signals a need by performing a gesture (e.g. reaching for mother when it desires to be held), this, too, is subjectively experienced as a form of omnipotence. Speaking of coordinated gestures, Ferenczi writes that:

> These are now made use of by the child as magic signals, at the dictation of which the satisfaction promptly arrives (naturally with external help, of which the child, however, has no idea). The subjective feeling of the child at all this may be compared to that of a real magician, who has only to perform a given gesture to bring about in the outer world according to his will the most complicated of occurrences. [p. 224]

This "period of omnipotence by the help of magic gestures" (p. 225) is followed by the "period of magic thoughts and magic words" (p. 230), during which the sense of omnipotence is yet again gained more conditionally than during its predecessor. Memesis gives way to true symbolization, and "From this accrues the great progress: there is no longer a necessity for the cumbrous figurative imagination and the still more cumbrous dramatic representation" (p. 230). Not only does the development of speech make it possible to think consciously, but it provides a new, more conditional preserve for infantile omnipotence in a harsh and hostile world:

> . . . for his wishes that can be set forth in thoughts are so few and comparatively uncomplicated that the attentive *entourage* concerned with the child's welfare easily manages to guess most of these thoughts. The mimic expressions that continually accompany thinking (peculiarly so with children) make this kind of thought reading especially easy for the adults; and when the child actually formulates his wishes in words the *entourage*, ever ready to help, hastens to fulfil them as soon as possible. [p. 230]

Naturally, Ferenczi proposes that from the infant's point of view, its thoughts and incantations have directly brought about the desired state of affairs. Ferenczi neither names nor exhaustively discusses the further diminution of the sense of omnipotence during the course of psychological development, although he argues that the psychological trait of optimism (and philosophical doctrines such as the theory of "free will") result from the preservation of a residue of infantile omnipotence, whilst the trait of pessimism reflects the incapacity to reconcile oneself to the loss of this illusion. It is in scientific reasoning that the reality sense reaches its apogee and omnipotence "experiences its greatest humiliation" (p. 232).

Ferenczi was apparently the first analyst to publish a radically interactional account of omnipotence, and the simultaneous development of the reality sense. These concerns were also central to Winnicott's thinking. Indeed, Winnicott's ideas about these matters arguably form the backbone of his developmental theory.

Basing his ideas on his extensive paediatric experience, Winnicott argued that normal mothers enter an altered state of consciousness during the advanced stages of pregnancy and remain in this condition for some weeks after the baby's birth. He termed this the "primary maternal preoccupation". The primary maternal preoccupation is a state of exquisite sensitivity to the baby. After birth, this allows her to start off her relationship with the newborn "with an almost complete adaptation to her infant's needs" (1951, p. 238), which is a continuation of "the physiological provision that characterises the pre-natal state" (Winnicott, cited in Davis & Wallbridge, 1981, p. 99). For healthy psychological development, the baby has an absolute need for "a *perfect* environment" (Winnicott, 1949, italics in original)—that is, a perfect adaptation from its mother.

This adaptation to the newborn infant is operationalized through an attitude and a style of activity that Winnicott calls "holding". Holding protects the junior baby from what Winnicott calls the "impingements" of the external world. Holding secures *continuity* between intra- and extra-uterine life.

The mother's adaptation to the baby's needs produces a unique intermeshing of the external world with the infant's imagination. This evolved reciprocity develops into a very special kind of interaction from the infant's point of view:

> ... the infant comes to the breast when excited, and ready to hallucinate something fit to be attacked. At that moment the actual nipple appears and he is able to feel that it was that nipple that he hallucinated. So his ideas are enriched by actual details of sight, feel, smell and next time this material is used in the hallucination. [Winnicott, 1951, pp. 152–153]

This *"experience of omnipotence"* (Winnicott, 1962b, p. 57) creates an *illusion* of having created the breast by means of one's own imagination: *"the object is created, not found"* (Winnicott, 1963, p. 181). In Winnicott's writing, the term "illusion" always bears this particular conceptual inflection. A Winnicottian "illusion" is the harmonious mixture of fantasy and reality.

In the earliest scenario, the breast and mother are what Winnicott calls "subjective objects"—that is, objects not yet distinguished by the baby as separate from itself. During the earliest stages of extra-uterine life, when the baby does not distinguish objects from itself, it exists in a state of *absolute dependence*. The infant who is absolutely dependent is not at all aware of its dependence.

Transition

The mother's collusion with her baby's omnipotence, her adaptation to its needs, is one moment in a bi-phasic task which Winnicott calls "good-enough mothering". The second phase of good-enough mothering is the mother's gradual de-adaptation to her infant's needs. It is this process that gradually constrains the experience of omnipotence. This entails a transition from absolute to *relative* dependence, during which the infant has the unsettling experience of realizing that it is dependent.

In order to facilitate the journey from absolute to relative dependence, infants often adopt a "transitional object". What is a transitional object? It is the "first possession" (Winnicott, 1951, p. 232), the "security blanket". It is some special object, such as a piece of cloth or a soft toy, that becomes extraordinarily significant to the infant. The transitional object appears to have magical soothing powers. It helps the infant fall asleep at bedtime and provides balm for the narcissistic wounds inflicted by an unyielding world (Winnicott, 1951).

The transitional object is heir to the moment of illusion in earliest infancy. It is transitional in the sense of being *in-between* the inner world of imagination and the outer world of material reality: the transitional object is a real, material object while simultaneously being, from the infant's point of view, an imaginative creation. It is also transitional in the sense of being a piece of equipment designed to assist the infant in its painful transition from absolute dependence to independence, a pocket of symbiosis carried through an increasingly objective world. When in need, the infant can "top up" on fusion without compromising its new-found autonomy.

Transitional objects are made necessary by the mother's de-adaptation to the baby: the second phase of good-enough mothering. Experience of frustration, of failure of empathy, "has value in educating the infant in respect of the existence of a not-me world" (Winnicott, 1963, p. 181). Just as Ferenczi's baby was forced to resort to the magic of gestures and later of words, so Winnicott's baby is forced to resort to explicit communication *"as the object changes over from being subjective to being objectively perceived, in so far as the child gradually leaves the area of omnipotence as a living experience"* (p. 182). Once it has moved out of the stage of absolute dependence, the infant has to signal its desires to a separate object. Although he does not develop the idea as explicitly as Ferenczi, Winnicott seems to hold that the infant's communicative efforts are in the service of an (eroded) omnipotence. The baby

... begins to enjoy experiences based on a "marriage" of the omnipotence of intrapsychic processes with the baby's control of the actual. Confidence in the mother makes an intermediate playground here, where the idea of magic originates, since the baby does to some extent *experience* omnipotence. [Winnicott, 1971, p. 55]

The next incarnation of the magical world of illusion is imaginative play. Play is a transitional phenomenon because it takes place neither "inside" the child nor "outside" but partakes of both. The child "manipulates external phenomena in the service of the dream and infests chosen external phenomena with dream meaning and feeling" (p. 60). Play renders omnipotence fully adaptive by confining it to certain channels.

According to Winnicott, the play of children is continuous with the play of adults, and with creativity and cultural experience. Although widely credited to Winnicott by psychoanalysts, the idea that creativity is a manifestation of the need to play was introduced into aesthetics by the eighteenth-century German philosopher/poet Schiller (1795). Schiller's thesis was presented to psychoanalytic readers by Otto Rank (1932). I am not aware of any evidence that Winnicott was aware either of Schiller's thesis or of Rank's elaboration of it.

Psychopathology and psychotherapy

Like Ferenczi, Winnicott provided a model of normal development of the sense of reality and, additionally, of the capacity for play and creativity. He also provided a model of the pathological consequences that ensue when this process goes awry.

Winnicott was more concerned with disturbances in the sense of self than with the disorders caused by intrapsychic conflict studied and treated by Freud. A Freudian psychoneurotic, who represses threatening sexual wishes, must possess an ego that is sufficiently coherent to repress instinctual drives. But what about people who have not achieved this level of integration? How can they be psychoanalytically understood? More importantly, how can they be psychoanalytically helped? Freud's technique of making the unconscious conscious, and extending the reach of the ego at the expense of the id, was based on his model of psychoneurosis. The technique of interpretation, as classically conceived, makes little sense in relation to those suffering from a lack of personal integration. If you are not "together" enough to repress things, then no amount of interpretation of the unconscious will be of help.

In investigating these matters, Winnicott had the work of Klein and her followers to draw on. Although profoundly influenced by Klein, there was a fundamental issue that divided them: Klein's neglect of the formative role of the infant's real environment (Winnicott, 1962a). For Klein, it is the life and death instincts that are the most significant causal factors. In Klein's view, the structure and development of the personality is ultimately to be explained with reference to features internal to the baby. For Winnicott, on the other hand, the baby's personality is radically shaped by the environment, and the fate of the drives—which are no longer invoked as fundamental units of explanation—are subordinate to this. Klein and Winnicott occupy extreme positions on a psychoanalytic continuum between emphasis on the environment and emphasis on the internal make-up of the individual when explaining psychopathology.

Winnicott (1956b) distinguished between those who suffer from repressed oedipal conflicts and those who suffer from pre-self disorders. The latter have suffered some form of environmental privation. In light of the concept of good-enough mothering, this leaves two basic options: either the child has suffered excessive impingement during the period of absolute dependence, or the mother has failed to de-adapt to the child during the phase of relative dependency.

Because the child's sense of self is extremely tenuous during earliest infancy, it is readily disrupted by environmental impingement. The most important function of the mother is to provide an experience of omnipotence by means of keeping such impingements at bay.

> At the stage which is being discussed it is necessary not to think of the baby as a person who gets hungry, and whose instinctual drives may be met or frustrated, but to think of the

baby as an immature being who is all the time *on the brink of unthinkable anxiety.* Unthinkable anxiety is kept at bay by this vitally important function of the mother at this stage. [Winnicott, 1962b, p. 57]

Winnicott's "unthinkable anxieties" are psychotic anxieties. They include the terror of going to pieces, of falling forever, of having no relationship with one's body, of having no orientation (1962b), and of being totally isolated (Winnicott, 1968). Excessive impingement can give way to infantile schizophrenia or autism, latent schizophrenia, schizoid personality, or the False Self defence (Winnicott, 1962).

Of these, the concept of the False Self defence was Winnicott's most original contribution, and it came to dominate his thinking about psychological disorders. A false or "caretaker" self is created when the infant is forced to comply with impingement. Because we tend to master impingements by thinking about them, a person of high intelligence may use his or her intellect in the service of the False Self (Winnicott, 1960). Those who use the False Self defence may also suffer from depersonalization because of the divorce of the False Self from somatic experience.

> In extreme examples of False Self development, the True Self is so well hidden that spontaneity is not a feature in the infant's living experiences. Compliance is then the main feature, with imitation as a speciality. When the degree in the split in the infant's experience is not too great there may be some almost personal living through imitation, and it may even be possible for the child to act a special role, that of the True Self *as it would be if it had had existence.* [Winnicott, 1960, p. 147]

Although in many ways disadvantageous and impoverishing, the False Self is specifically adapted to perform a vital function: it protects the True Self from exploitation.

The False Self defence (and other "pre-self" disorders) pose special problems for psychoanalytic technique. The False Self personality does not require the lifting of repressions to unveil hitherto disowned drives and wishes. Instead, he or she needs to come into being. The traditional psychoanalytic tool of interpretation seems quite inadequate to this task: no amount of information can call forth a spontaneous, living self. Furthermore, there is a danger that the False Self personality will simply adapt to the analyst's interpretations: a false analysis of a false self.

Winnicott dealt with these problems by redefining the process and goal of analysis. The aim of analysis in cases of primitive mental disorders is the actualization of a hidden or potential self. The means by which this is reached is therapeutic regression, which is promoted by the appropriate management of the analytic setting.

I have already discussed Freud's views on regression in chapter six and noted that Freud saw regression as an attempt to evade an anxiety situation or developmental task. Reich held that regression in adults was promoted by the damming-up of contemporary sexual impulses which then reactivated infantile forms of sexual expression. Klein held that we regress to the paranoid–schizoid position in order to avoid the agonies of the depressive position.

These writers did not regard regression as *intrinsically* helpful to the patient. For them, it is only when successfully interpreted (and thus resolved) that regression participates in the healing process.

Although most of the psychoanalytic community took a dim view of regression in the analytic situation (Balint, 1968), there were some exceptions—notably the ubiquitous Sándor Ferenczi. Ferenczi encouraged regression in his more highly disturbed patients (Balint, 1968). His technique involved providing patients with those experiences of which (he believed) they had been pathogenically deprived during infancy (affection, cuddles, etc.). Freud commented that "we cannot make a whorehouse out of the psychoanalytic situation" (Roazen & Swerdloff, 1995, p. 108) and was worried that the psychoanalytic method would be brought into disrepute by these experiments. Ferenczi's work was continued, in a more moderate form, by his protégé Michael Balint (e.g. Balint, 1932, 1968), who eventually became a member of the British Independent Group.

In Winnicott's view, the main function of regression is the giving-up of the False or "caretaker" Self. Because the pre-self disorders are the product of early impingements, regression is to a state of appalling dependency—that is, to the point of early environmental failure.

Winnicott believed that the psychoanalytic setting possesses a maternal function, that it "reproduces the early and earliest mothering techniques" (Winnicott, 1954, p. 286). Regression is fostered by providing a safe, reliable "holding" analytic setting which induces an "unfreezing" of the environmental failure situation (p. 287).

Winnicott's emphasis on the gratifying, maternal function of the setting was decisively new. Before this, the analytic environment had been described, when described at all, as fundamentally restrictive and frustrating: a symbolic embodiment of the incest taboo. Later, Bleger (1967), an Argentinian analyst, extended Winnicott's view by arguing that it is precisely because of its primitive maternal function that the setting has the power to evoke "unthinkable" psychotic anxieties.

Winnicott as analyst

Although Winnicott emphasized the secure "holding" that the setting can and should provide for deeply disturbed patients, in practice his behaviour was often of the kind that many contemporary practitioners would see as promoting *insecurity*.

Margaret Little's (1985) personal record of her analysis with Winnicott gives an interesting snapshot of his clinical approach. Little began analysis with Winnicott when she was already a qualified analyst. She had met him on several occasions at the British Psycho-Analytical Society prior to seeking analysis with him.

During the first session, Little lay curled up on the couch, completely covered by a blanket, "shutting myself in, taking up the smallest possible amount of space and being as unobtrusive as I could; hiding in the womb, but not safe even there" (p. 21). She was completely silent. In another early session, she smashed a vase in his consulting-room. Winnicott left the room, coming back only at the end of the session.

> Some weeks after this, throughout the whole session I was seized with recurring spasms of terror. Again and again I felt a tension begin to build up in my whole body, reach a climax,

and subside, only to come again a few seconds later. I grabbed his hands and clung tightly till the spasms passed. He said at the end he thought I was reliving the experience of being born; he held my head for a few minutes, saying that immediately after birth an infant's head could ache and feel heavy for a time. [Little, 1985, p. 20]

From a Freudian perspective, it is striking that Winnicott made no reference to the possible sexual significance of waves of tension building to a climax coupled with her initiating physical contact. Winnicott had presumably already decided that Little was suffering from an impingement-related disorder and hence did not regard it as appropriate to interpret the enactment as a disguised expression of an unconscious sexual wish. It is also striking that there is no apparent consideration of Little's *grasping* him possibly having anything to do with his having *left* the room not long before. Winnicott then *initiates* physical contact and explains the episode as a repetition of the process of being born. This explanation effectively excluded a consideration of what was going on between them there and then in the consulting-room.

Literally, through many long hours he held my two hands clasped between his, almost like an umbilical cord, while I lay, often hidden beneath the blanket, silent, inert, withdrawn, in panic, rage or tears, asleep and sometimes dreaming. Sometimes he would become drowsy, fall asleep and wake with a jerk, to which I would react with anger, terrified and feeling as if I had been hit. [p. 21]

In addition to the physical "holding", Winnicott would feed Little, providing her with coffee and biscuits at the end of sessions. Further physical contact was provided by his medical interest in his patient: "he kept stethoscope, sphygmomanometer and clinical thermometer handy, and used them" (p. 27). Winnicott also sometimes managed holiday breaks in a manner that was, to say the least, unusual. On one occasion, he went behind Little's back to arrange that she be invited by a friend to join her on holiday. On another occasion, he had her hospitalized during the break.

Little's analysis was very stormy, involving periods of profound depression, hospitalization, psychotic acting-out, and an accident that could be understood as an unconscious suicide attempt. She clearly felt that the analysis with Winnicott was extraordinarily helpful to her, and Winnicott's own modifications of standard technique could be justified in light of his clinical theories as "holding" interventions required to facilitate the necessary regression to dependence. However, Winnicott's clinical approach might alternatively be seen as an expression of his own need to transgress interpersonal boundaries, to engage seductively with his patients (he once told Little that he joined the Royal Navy because the uniform matched the blue of his eyes), and to undermine their autonomy. In light of these considerations, we might consider the possibility that the regression endured by Winnicott's patients was to a significant degree an artefact of his clinical setting, an adaptation to Winnicott's own emotional need to have others depend upon him.

Winnicott died of heart failure in 1971. Although he did not live to a great age, his life was fruitful and, on the whole, a happy one. Such was Winnicott's impish nature that even as an elderly man he could be reproached by a policeman for riding his bicycle down a hill at high speed with his feet on the handlebars (Kahr, 1996)! Although highly innovative in his work, Winnicott found a secure niche in the psychoanalytic establishment and served two terms as president of the British Psycho-Analytical Society.

Winnicott's legacy

As the most prominent member of the British Independent Group, Winnicott's work has had a huge impact on contemporary psychoanalysis. A number of contemporary practitioners such as Rycroft, Coltart, Bollas, and Phillips have clearly worked along lines initially set out by Winnicott (Rayner, 1990). Winnicott's emphasis on environmental management also had a decisive effect on the work of Robert Langs (chapter fourteen).

British psychoanalysis developed a unique intellectual culture based on the work of Klein, Winnicott, and others. North American analysts operated within a very different frame of reference and were, on the whole, ignorant of or actively hostile towards British psychoanalytic thought. When Winnicott presented a paper at the New York Psychoanalytic Society in 1969, he received such strong criticism that, muttering that he could now understand how the Americans had got involved in Vietnam, he returned to his hotel room and suffered a massive coronary (Kahr, 1996). This situation was soon to change, as American analysts were forced by new clinical problems to import Kleinian ideas. The chief architect of the American assimilation of Klein was Otto Kernberg. At about the same time as this, America's own version of Winnicott appeared. His name was Heinz Kohut.

CHAPTER TWELVE

Self and object in America:
the American Object Relations School
and self psychology

> After the destruction of the Temple in Jerusalem by Titus,
> Rabbi Jochanan ben Sakkai asked for permission to open a
> school at Jabnet for the study of the Torah. We are going to do
> the same.
>
> Sigmund Freud (on the occasion of the dissolution of
> the Vienna Psycho-Analytical Society, March 1938)

We have already seen how the diaspora of Central European analysts during the years preceding the Second World War affected the psychoanalytic culture of the United Kingdom. It also affected the United States. Whereas the refugees entering Britain entered a Klein-dominated psychoanalytic scene, the immigrants to America entered a psychoanalytic culture that was recognizably Freudian but distant in spirit from the societies that they had reluctantly fled. The flight to freedom was itself fraught with difficulty. The American Psychoanalytic Association formed a committee on relief and immigration to assist the refugees. One hundred and forty-nine refugees were brought into the United States by this committee.

Psychoanalytic culture in the United States was dominated by medicine. The American analysts had successfully defied Freud's (1926e) edict that the psychoanalytic profession should remain separate from that of medicine. Furthermore, even during the Depression years of the 1930s, psychoanalysts were an affluent medical elite (Hale, 1995) and European medical qualifications were not honoured. Some of the most prominent figures in psychoanalysis—men like Siegfried Bernfeld, Otto Fenichel, and Theodor Reich—were treated with condescension by their American colleagues and forbidden to practice. The American scene drew adherents from a more affluent, less bohemian social stratum. It included far fewer women than European psychoanalysis (Fermi, 1968).

The new psychoanalytic mainstream that arose in the United States was a transformation of the ego psychology movement that had been developing in Europe since the 1920s. The chief architect of the new, American ego psychology was Heinz Hartmann.

Heinz Hartmann

Heinz Hartmann's family had produced distinguished academics and statesmen for generations. As befitted this background, Hartmann rubbed shoulders with many of the prominent Viennese intellectuals of the day and, like Freud, studied far more widely than the medical curriculum of the University of Vienna required.

Hartmann's psychoanalytic writings focused on the role of the ego in human life. This emphasis stemmed in part from his belief that the ego concept provided common ground between psychoanalysis and the adjacent scientific disciplines of academic psychology, neuroscience, and developmental psychology. After the *Anschluss* of Austria, Hartmann fled to France, Switzerland, and finally, with the aid of the APA committee, arrived in the United States in 1941. He had been analysed by Freud in Vienna, at Freud's request (Roazen & Swerdloff, 1995).

Hartmann's first major work, *Ego Psychology and the Problem of Adaptation* (1939), announced his life-long concern with the psychoanalytic theory of adaptation. Hartmann used the term "adaptation" in its biological sense (he is sometimes wrongly accused of promoting social adaptation or conformity). Biological adaptation is the "fit" between some feature of an organism and its environment. The ego is an "organ of adaptation" because it is governed by the reality principle: the capacity to come to grips psychologically with the real world.

Perhaps because of his interest in the philosophy of the Vienna Circle, Hartmann was concerned with terminological precision. In a landmark review of Freud's use of the term "ego", Hartmann (1950) argued that it had been used in two distinct senses. In works like *The Ego and the Id* (1923b), Freud defined the ego as a hypothetical structure mediating between the id, the superego, and the external world, the seat of the reality principle, and so forth. However, in other contexts this definition does not make sense. For instance, in "On Narcissism: An Introduction" (1914c), Freud described narcissism as the state of being in love with one's own ego. But how can one be in love with a hypothetical mental structure, a theoretical entity? Hartmann solved this problem by deftly arguing that, in some contexts, Freud used the term *das Ich* ["the ego"] to denote the "self representation" [*Ichvorstellung*]: our *image* of ourselves.

Edith Jacobson

Edith Jacobson was a German analyst and a member of Fenichel's Marxist circle at the Berlin Institute. She was incarcerated by the Nazis for two and a half years, following the arrest and murder of one of her parents by the Gestapo (Hale, 1995). One of Jacobson's patients was a government official, and the Gestapo wanted her to divulge information revealed during analytic sessions (Blanck & Blanck, 1994). Jacobson refused. Feigning illness, she was temporarily released and was smuggled across the Czech border by psychoanalytic colleagues from Prague (Jacoby, 1983). She then made her way to New York.

Once established in the United States, Jacobson attempted to investigate systematically Hartmann's notion of a representational world within a developmental context. She created a maturational topography of the representational world, drawing conclusions about the composition of self and object relations and their relationship with one another during each stage of development. Jacobson's main discussion of these topics is her slender but turgid book *The Self and the Object World* (1964). She was not a profuse writer, and, like Hartmann, her writings are often heavy, Germanic, and convoluted.

Because of her specific interests, Jacobson is classed as a representative of what has come to be called the American Object Relations School, an approach that grew out of Hartmannian ego psychology. The trailblazer of this movement was a brilliant Hungarian psychoanalyst/paediatrician whom Jacobson analysed in the United States. Her name was Margaret Mahler.

Margaret Mahler

Margaret Schönberger Mahler was born in the Hungarian town of Sopron, on the Austro-Hungarian borders, in 1897. During her adolescence, the family moved to Budapest, where she came into the orbit of Sándor Ferenczi and his circle. As a 16-year-old high-school student, she was already clandestinely reading Freud's "Five Lectures on Psychoanalysis" (1910a [1909]) in class. At the time of her death, at the age of 88, in the United States, Mahler would be widely regarded as one of the major figures in the history of psychoanalysis.

Although the period that she was in Budapest was just before the Horthy government, which excluded Jews from the professions and from university studies, it was clear which way the wind was blowing. Mahler had resolved to become a paediatrician, and so she continued her studies in Munich, Heidelberg, and Jena, where she was part of the intellectual circle surrounding Karl Jaspers and Karl Mannheim; she was also selected by Rudolf von Degkwitz to assist him in developing a vaccine for measles. In Germany, Jews began to be systematically excluded from the universities. On one occasion, Mahler and her sister were arrested and jailed, simply as a routine act of harassment designed to force Jews out of Munich. Hitler's Kapp Putsch occurred during the time that she was studying in Munich (Stepansky, 1988).

Mahler completed her university education in Vienna, where she obtained her medical qualification in 1923 and began work as a medical researcher and paediatrician. During this period, she was introduced to August Aichhorn, a senior member of Freud's circle, who was the leader of Austria's child guidance movement and specialized in psychoanalytic work with delinquent adolescents. Mahler recalled that

> Aichhorn was a mysterious man who led a strange and charmed life. A character once striking and elusive, he prided himself on his contacts with the criminal underworld of Vienna and, often enough, seemed able to turn these contacts to good use. I recall discussions with him in which, in a quasi-serious vein, he spoke of attending "gang" meetings in which youths plotted their illegal activities. He spoke the delinquent's language, so to speak, and could make these children feel so comfortable that they would share with him their secrets without any fear of betrayal. [Stepansky, 1988, p. 51]

Mahler, by now a practising paediatrician, resolved to become a psychoanalyst. Ferenczi fixed it for her to obtain a training analysis with Helene Deutsch, one of the most powerful members of the Vienna Society. The analysis was abruptly terminated by Deutsch, who pronounced Mahler "unanalysable" (i.e. too extremely disturbed to benefit from psychoanalytic treatment). Deutsch's verdict would normally have been the death-knell for any aspiration to become a psychoanalyst, but the delinquent Aichhorn concocted a plan to take her secretly into analysis with him:

> His envisioned scenario, enacted in due course, was that he would confront the institute's committee on education with the fact of our analytic work as a fait accompli and, with grand dramatic flourish, pronounce it a success: "Her analysis goes excellently; she will be a prominent analyst". [Mahler, in Stepansky, 1988, pp. 67–68]

The plan worked. In 1933, the year of Ferenczi's tragic death from pernicious anaemia, Margaret Mahler obtained her qualification to practise psychoanalysis.

Mahler practised as a child analyst in Vienna and opened her own psychoanalytic well-baby clinic, the Ambulatorium Rauscherstrasse. After the *Anschluss* of 1938, the Viennese analysts organized to help Jewish members escape. Mahler fled first to England and, with the help of a loan from Ernest Jones, arrived in New York in the autumn. She continued both her analytic practice and her research activities in the United States. Her first child analytic patients in the new country were referred by Benjamin Spock ("Doctor Spock"), with whom she established a warm friendship.

Mahler's work came to concentrate on child psychosis. At this time, there had been very little work on the subject, and virtually none by psychoanalysts. Leo Kanner had recently coined the term "early infantile autism", and Lauretta Bender had pioneered research into childhood schizophrenia. Mahler rechristened Kanner's category "infant autistic psychosis" and differentiated it from another psychotic disorder, "infant symbiotic psychosis". Mahler and her co-workers developed a triadic treatment plan that involved the participation of the mother, in the hope that she would learn from the analyst how to engage therapeutically with her child. Mahler founded a therapeutic nursery in collaboration with Manuel Furer in 1950 at the Albert Einstein Medical School, which was moved to buildings in New York's Greenwich Village in 1956 and rechristened the Masters Children's Centre.

In 1962, the Masters Centre launched an ambitious project for the study of normal psychological development. The research made use of participant and non-participant observers of mother–infant interactions, filming, and regular interviewing of both parents. Mahler's reputation as a psychoanalytic theorist rests largely on the results of this study, which she and her colleagues chronicled in *The Psychological Birth of the Human Infant* (Mahler, Pine, & Bergman, 1975), as well as in various papers. Mahler sought to combine rigorous observational studies of mothers and infants with the "representational" perspective of Edith Jacobson, with whom she had entered analysis, apparently during the early 1960s, and who discussed the ideas that were to appear in *The Self and the Object World* (Jacobson, 1964) with Mahler (Stepansky, 1988).

The Masters project focused on two related maturational processes: separation and individuation. Separation is the process of establishing *physical* autonomy (acquiring mobility, co-ordination, etc.). Individuation is the *psychological* process of coming to recognize that one is a separate, individual human being distinct from one's mother. Because these normally proceed hand-in-hand, Mahler (1975) referred to them together as "separation–individuation".

The first stage is that of *normal autism*, which lasts from the age of 2 to 3 months. Mahler believed that the normal autistic baby has no sense of self or other, and no psychological relationship with its mother. This is quite similar to Freud's (1914c) thesis of an initial stage of "auto-erotism" during which there are neither self nor object representations.

The next stage is that of *normal symbiosis*, which persists until about the sixth month of life. Normal symbiosis is the stage of "oneness" in which the baby exists in a "dual unity" with its mother. The first "good" mental representations are formed in which mother and baby are undifferentiated. On the level of behaviour, the baby develops the social smile in response to the human face, moulds its body to the contours of its mother when held, and shows other signs of attunement. It is from this matrix that the process of separation–individuation proceeds.

Mahler believed that children who suffer from autistic infantile psychosis, which can be detected very early in the first year, are developmentally arrested in the stage of normal autism. They are unable to move on to "bond" with the mother in symbiotic fusion. Symbiotic psychotic children are stuck in the stage of normal symbiosis. They are afraid of differentiation. Unlike Winnicott, Mahler did not regard child psychosis as having a simple environmental cause. She believed that psychosis normally involves an innate, presumably genetic, factor.

The next stage of Mahler's scheme is called the stage of *separation–individuation*. This is the period during which the child is psychologically born out of the condition of undifferentiated symbiosis. The phase of separation–individuation is divided into four sub-phases: differentiation (or "hatching"), practising, rapprochement, and constancy.

The sub-stage of *differentiation* is the stage of the "lap baby" who has acquired some mobility and coordination, and it extends from about 5 to about 10 months of age. It is at this time that the infant "hatches" out of the symbiotic egg. The baby begins to make comparative scans of persons in its environment and may show displeasure or even anxiety in response to the presence of strangers. Stranger reactions (Spitz, 1957) and comparative scanning of others suggest that during the differentiation sub-stage the baby is forming a mental representation of his mother as an individual. The baby also begins to explore its environment.

During the sub-phase of *practising* (approximately 10 to 16 months) the senior baby/junior toddler gains greater mobility and begins to move away from its mother, euphoric with new-found athletic prowess. Mahler believed that the characteristic elation and self-assurance of the normal practising toddler is due to its implicit belief in an "invisible bond" uniting infant and mother. The toddler's sense of invulnerability in a wide world is generated by his or her tacit faith in the illusion of oneness (Mahler et al., 1967).

The twin forces of a physical engagement with the world beyond mother and the infant's own accelerating cognitive development conspire to puncture this bubble, ushering in what Mahler calls the sub-phase of *rapprochement*, which lasts approximately until the age of 3 years. "The grandiose conqueror", writes Mahler, "who felt one with the world is more or less suddenly overwhelmed by his sense of aloneness, smallness and separateness" (cited in Kaplan, 1978, p. 13).

> As a child first becomes aware of his status as a separate, helpless, and very small individual...there comes, whether gradually or suddenly, a concomitant realisation that he is very much dependent on his mother, that this mother is separate from him, and that she and the father have their own interests and lives. The toddler realises, in short, that he is by no means the centre of the universe. [Mahler, cited in Stepansky, 1988, p. 149]

The temper-tantrums of the "terrible 2s" are outward signs of this inner crisis. The narcissistic collapse experienced by toddlers during the rapprochement sub-phase is a precondition for the development of a sound sense of reality: "The crushing disillusionments of the crisis period will not be replaced by new illusions of omnipotence but by increasingly realistic ways of valuing the self and estimating the power and worth of others" (Kaplan, 1978, p. 227). The toddler gradually learns to countenance its own separateness, individuality and vulnerability as well as the separateness and individuality, of others.

According to Mahler, the rapprochement sub-phase is massively significant, and its negotiation decisive for future mental health.

Mahler (McDevitt & Mahler, 1980) specifies several factors that may interfere with the successful resolution of the rapprochement crisis, such as a high level of impingement, unreliability, or unavailability on the part of the mother; a traumatically sudden collapse of the child's illusions of omnipotence; and excessive trauma and overly intense, early castration anxiety.

The final stage of separation–individuation is called "on the way to emotional object constancy" and is the life-long process of creating and re-creating a sense of one's own selfhood in relation to the selfhood of others, as well as coping with the inevitable threats to one's autonomy and individuality.

Otto Kernberg

Otto Kernberg has made major contributions to topics as diverse as differential diagnosis, the development of self and object representations, the psychology and psychopathology of organizations, and psychoanalytic technique. In this chapter we will concentrate on the work for which Kernberg is best known: his ideas on the dynamics and treatment of what has come to be called the "borderline personality organization".

Kernberg was born in Central Europe but was trained in Latin America before building an impressive career in the United States. It is hardly surprising that he would strive to find some way of integrating Kleinian thinking—which was the dominant force in Latin American psychoanalysis—with mainstream American psychoanalysis. Kernberg's particular clinical focus made this even more important.

The notion of a form of severe psychopathology sharing characteristics with both the psychoneuroses and the psychoses has a long psychoanalytic history. Perhaps the most impressive of the early attempts to clarify these matters was Reich's monograph *The Impulsive Character* (1925) described in chapter nine. Credit is usually given to Deutsch (1942) for the earliest description of the dynamics of the borderline condition, although Reich preceded her by almost twenty years. Stern (1938) is often credited with introducing the term "borderline" (e.g. Goldstein, 1985).

Kernberg (1975) uses the term "borderline personality *organization*" because he believes that the borderline disorder is a form of character pathology. Even though borderline people may display very different symptoms, their personality is structured in fundamentally the same way.

Kernberg's account of the dynamics of the borderline personality relies heavily on a model of the development of self and object representations derived from the work of Mahler, Jacobson, and Klein. According to this view, the newborn (normal autistic) baby has no concept of self and other. As representations are formed, they are classified as either "good" or "bad", as Klein suggested. As the baby matures and enters Mahler's normal symbiotic stage, it becomes capable of representing itself as blissfully fused with its mother. During the differentiation sub-stage of separation–individuation, images of self and other become tentatively and precariously distinguished. During the practising and rapprochement sub-stages, the toddler clearly distinguishes the "good" image of itself from the image of the "good" object and the "bad" image of itself from the "bad object". In other words, the state of "splitting" that Klein attributed to the paranoid–schizoid position during the first quarter of the first year *actually* takes place almost a year later. Later still, during the rapprochement sub-stage the toddler draws the "good" and "bad" images together, as Klein described as occurring during the depressive position. What Mahler called the rapprochement crisis is underpinned by the emotional trauma of integrating "good" and "bad" in the toddler's mind. It is only after this integration has been achieved that the child's ego gains sufficient stress to *repress* instinctual impulses. Freudian neurotic disorders have their fixation point at some time later than the rapprochement sub-stage.

According to Kernberg's model, the autistic child has failed to establish an image of itself and its mother fused in satisfaction—

the intrapsychic correlate of symbiotic bonding. The symbiotic psychotic child, on the other hand, cannot tolerate realizing that he or she is distinct from the "good" mother and thus drowns in fusion. What about the practising and rapprochement sub-stages? According to Kernberg, this is the fixation point for the borderline.

The internally divided state of the borderline individual is confirmed by his or her behaviour in analysis. He or she quickly forms a very primitive transference onto the analyst that has a very peculiar character: it oscillates between highly positive and extremely negative modes. At one moment the transference picture is of a "bad" analyst interacting with a "bad" patient, while on another occasion (sometimes in the very same session) a "good" analyst interacting with a "good" patient is enacted. Because the patient makes extensive use of early "psychotic" defences, there is considerable confusion between the personality of the analyst with that of the patient. Transference fantasies are often bizarre, highly aggressive, and experienced with total conviction. It is extremely difficult to distinguish fantasy from memory in borderline productions. The breakdown of interpersonal boundaries and the sense of reality is very frightening for the patient (Kernberg, 1975).

It seems clear that a central goal of treatment must be to integrate dissociated units of the personality; in Kleinian lingo, to help the patient reach the depressive position. Kernberg developed a modified form of psychoanalytic therapy called "expressive psychotherapy" specifically for the treatment of borderline conditions. This involves concentrated work on the primitive defences (projection, projective identification, introjection, denial, and splitting) that maintain dissociation, which are interpreted as soon as they enter the transference. Because the borderline patients' splitting operations are aimed at protecting "good" self and object images from contamination by intense aggression, there is a special emphasis placed on the interpretation of negative transference. Interpretations initially focus on the here-and-now significance of the transference rather than invoking the patient's infantile past. Because the patient makes extensive use of projective identification, the analyst will normally have difficulty sustaining an attitude of neutrality and needs to use his or her countertransferences as a basis for making inferences about the patient. It is striking, given

Reich's priority in describing the borderline personality organization, that Kernberg's technical strictures are uncannily similar to the principles of Reichian character analysis (Reich, 1933a) described in chapter nine.

Heinz Kohut

Heinz Kohut was the leader of what became the most powerful dissident movement in American psychoanalysis: Psychoanalytic Self Psychology. I will approach Kohut through the work of his psychoanalytic "grandfather" Paul Federn, to show that self psychology did not spring *de novo* from Kohut's brain but, rather, represented fruition of an older psychoanalytic tradition.

I briefly touched on the psychoanalytic concept of narcissism in chapter eleven. After Sadger introduced the term into psychoanalysis from sexology, Freud avidly took it up and described a narcissistic stage of development during which one is in love with one's own image. Later, when we learn to love others, our narcissism becomes deferred. Instead of regarding ourselves as perfectly loveable in reality, we hold up to ourselves an *ideal* of perfection, which Freud (1914c) called the "ego ideal". We strive to live up to this ideal and experience self-esteem to the extent that we are able to approximate it.

Freud very occasionally discussed narcissism in relation to what he called *Ichgefühl* ["I-feeling" or "ego-feeling"]—the felt quality of one's own existing. Paul Federn, a senior member of the Vienna Psycho-Analytical Society, made the study of ego-feeling the mainstay of his work. Federn joined Freud's circle in 1902 and remained devoted to Freud and psychoanalysis until 1950, when he sat down behind his couch and put a bullet through his head.

Federn felt that his own pioneering work on ego psychology was unjustly neglected by the ego psychology movement spearheaded by Hartmann (Roazen, 1975). Federn emphasized the *experiential* aspect of the ego, describing the ego as first and foremost an *Erlebnis*, a subjective experience. Federn described himself as a psychoanalytic phenomenologist, who studied variations of ego feeling in both healthy and pathological states.

Federn believed that during the earliest stages of development the entire experiential world is encompassed by the child's ego feeling. Even when objects are cognitively distinguished from the infant's own body, they are *felt* to be part of its own ego. Object love is that which is left after the original medial narcissism recedes in consequence of experiences of disappointment in objects (Federn, 1929).

In healthy people this occurs gradually. Federn (1929) believed that *traumatic* disappointment generates narcissistic pathology. He distinguished between healthy and pathological forms of narcissism and argued that psychoanalysts regard narcissism in too negative a light (Federn, 1936). Federn was one of the first psychoanalysts to treat psychotics and narcissistically disturbed individuals, and he argued that such people have a *deficit* in their narcissism, rather than the surfeit that had previously been assumed. Federn (1949) referred to such disorders as "ego diseases" and claimed that in such cases "the patient feels his self changed, even to a vanishing point" (p. 243).

Federn had analysed some of the most active and brilliant members of the second generation of psychoanalysts, including August Aichhorn. Federn also analysed Eduardo Weiss, the leader of the psychoanalytic movement in Italy, who championed his analyst's neglected ideas. Weiss eventually emigrated to the United States, where he became associated with the Chicago Psychoanalytic Institute, the institute where Heinz Kohut received his training.

Heinz Kohut was born in Vienna in 1913, the only child of assimilated Jewish parents, and was in analysis with Aichhorn in the late 1930s. Kohut studied medicine at the University of Vienna. He was one of the crowd that assembled at the railway station to wave goodbye to Freud in 1938. In 1939, Kohut too fled the Nazi terror, emigrating first to England and then on to the United States. He began a residency in neurology but truncated his medical career in order to become a psychoanalyst. Kohut became a member of the Chicago Psychoanalytic Institute's faculty and was elected president of the Chicago Psychoanalytic Association in 1964. In 1965, he was made vice-president of the International Psycho-Analytical Association.

Kohut's first paradigmatically "Kohutian" paper was his "Introspection, Empathy and Psychoanalysis" (1959), in which he attempted to define the methodological domain of psychoanalytic research. In Kohut's view, the psychoanalytic domain is constrained to those features of mental life that can be apprehended by means of introspection and empathy. Kohut's emphasis on introspection sits more comfortably with the Cartesian tradition culminating in Wundt's introspectionism than with Freud's fierce anti-introspectionism. Kohut was arguably calling for a philosophical shift in psychoanalysis towards a more phenomenological perspective, but instead represented this as a *distillation* of the essence of the psychoanalytic method. There is certainly some resonance with Federn's psychoanalytic phenomenology here.

Kohut's distinctive work began in the context of the treatment of narcissistic disorders. Narcissistic disorders are personality organizations typified by a weak or unstable sense of self and difficulty regulating self-esteem. Freud believed that narcissistic disturbances were inaccessible to psychoanalytic treatment because the narcissist is too self-absorbed to engage in the positive transference considered by Freud to be the motor of psychotherapeutic treatment. Kohut believed that these people *do* engage in positive transferences and that these transferences possess distinctive properties.

Although Kohut began the movement that came to be known as "psychoanalytic self psychology" as a theory of and treatment modality for narcissistically disordered people, his theory and technique were soon extended to encompass all forms of psychopathology. Kohut simultaneously, altered his terminology. Whereas his first book (1971) was couched in the classical Freudian idiom of "narcissism", the second (1977) deployed a fresh theoretical language. It was shortly after the publication of the first book that Kohut discovered that he was suffering from leukaemia, the disease that was to kill him in 1981, and this may well have accelerated his dissident trajectory (Wolf, 1996). In order to minimize confusion, I present Kohut's conclusive version of his approach.

Kohut believed that infants need to experience their care-takers as parts of themselves. This is much the same as what Winnicott meant by the notion of the "subjective object" and Federn by the concept of the "narcissistic object". Kohut described them as *self-objects*. According to Kohut, appropriate selfobject transactions must occur if the infant is to develop a secure sense of self. There are three modes of selfobject experience: mirroring, idealizing, and twinship.

"Mirroring" is the experience of an appreciative audience praising and validating one's accomplishments. When being mirrored, one is indisputably the centre of attention. During moments of mirroring, the infant experiences itself as potent, valuable, and vigorous.

If mirroring involves the experience of a grandiose infant being praised by the less important individuals around him, "idealizing" involves the infant's merging into the security of a strong adult figure. Idealizing is a transcendental experience, providing a feeling of unity with a "higher power".

In contrast with mirroring and idealizing, twinship is a relationship between equals. In twinship we find ourself in another. It is the experience of "being quietly sustained by another in whose presence one feels accepted" (Basch, 1989, p. 15).

Each of these modes of selfobject experience evokes transient experiences of selfhood. Kohut (1971) believed that the mirroring and idealising experiences constellate two "poles" of the self, which he termed the "grandiose self" and the "idealizing parental imago". The twinship experience was not assigned a corresponding self structure, because it was only shortly before his death that he came to regard it as a distinct selfobject mode (Kohut, 1984).

The infant's sense of self is dependent upon the behaviour of its parents. How do these tenuous self experiences become established as a more or less permanent, continuous sense of self? According to Kohut, this comes about by means of "optimal frustration": the non-traumatic disruption of selfobject bonds. When the child is disappointed in its selfobject, this sets in motion a process called "transmuting internalization" which results in the selfobject function being taken over by the child. The child learns to praise himself, to merge with an ideal of perfection, and to acknowledge his kinship with others. The grandiose self matures into a set of ambitions, while the idealized parental imago becomes a system of ideals.

The parallel between Kohut's ideas and those of Winnicott are striking (Bacal, 1989), as are their similarity to Federn's work. Rather like the deeply self-absorbed narcissistic individuals whom he specialized in treating, Kohut was inclined to ignore the contributions of other psychoanalytic writers (Akhtar, 1989).

According to Kohut (1984), we tend to use our analyst as a selfobject to the extent that our self experience has been undermined or damaged by inadequate interpersonal provisions during infancy. We unconsciously use our analyst to obtain the very things that we lacked as children—those selfobject experiences that enable us to feel intact and secure. There are therefore three basic forms of transference: mirror transference, idealizing transference, and twinship transference. Once the analyst has been able to establish empathic contact with the patient, one or more of these transference modalities will emerge.

In the mirror transference, the analyst is treated as an object the only proper function of which is to confirm the patient. In the idealizing transference, the analyst is seen as a superior figure with whom the patient feels merged. In the twinship transference, the analyst is seen as being similar to the patient's idealized image of himself.

Kohut's therapeutic procedure involved allowing selfobject transferences to become securely established, as these provide the patient with a sense of personal wholeness during the analytic hour. Kohut felt that it is therapeutically essential to gratify rather than frustrate the patient's selfobject needs, and like Winnicott he advocated a more relaxed approach to psychoanalytic conduct than his Freudian and Kleinian colleagues would condone.

Once the selfobject relationship has been established, it will sooner or later be disrupted—the analyst will go on holiday, miss a session, say something wrong, or show his inadequacy or unavailability in some other way. This, in turn, will disturb the sense of wholeness established by means of the selfobject transference, leading to reactive phenomena such as "narcissistic rage". Disruptions will also be experienced as repetitions of the disappointments of infancy. The analyst interprets these reactions while maintaining his empathic bond, which results in a restoration of attunement. By staying "with" the patient during these difficult moments, the analyst provides an experience of optimal frustration, which promotes the internalization of selfobject functions. The patient emerges from each such episode a little more whole and a little less dependent upon the analyst for a sense of well-being. Each analysis contains many episodes of this kind. They cumulatively result in psychoanalytic "cure". Although Kohut regards interpretation as an essential ingredient of this process, what makes analysis work is fundamentally the impact of the analytic *relationship* rather than the provision of information.

A number of criticisms have been levelled against psychoanalytic self psychology (Akhtar, 1989; Gedo, 1986, 1989). Like Winnicott, Kohut was an extreme environmentalist. He believed that childhood conflicts come about *only* because of parental failure (Tolpin, 1980). He also believed that the unsavoury aspects of human nature—such as perverse sexuality and destructive aggression—are in fact just reactions to the frustration of selfobject needs, rather than intrinsic features.

Kohut's legacy

Kohut's work gave rise to a dissident psychoanalytic movement that, in spite of being mainly confined to North America, has generated a considerable literature. Contemporary Kohutians do not share the intellectual insularity of their founder, and they have taken pains to explore the relationship between self psychology and other approaches (Detrick & Detrick, 1989). Self psychology has also given rise to an intersubjectivist approach that draws on the traditions of European existentialism and phenomenology (Atwood & Stolorow, 1984).

In common with all of the major writers surveyed in this book, Kohut regarded psychoanalysis as a science (a "new sun among the sciences of man": 1973, p. 684), although unlike Freud—who placed his faith in the principle of the unity of science—he believed that the "human sciences" must be sharply distinguished from the "natural sciences" and that psychoanalysis belongs to the latter and not the former category. But is psychoanalysis a science? And what does it mean when we say something is or is not a science? What is at stake? Philosophers have considered these very questions. The most significant of these appraisals is undoubtedly that proposed by Adolf Grünbaum, to whose work we now turn.

CHAPTER THIRTEEN

Grünbaum shakes the foundations: criticism from the philosophy of science

> The question is not what belief is more pleasing or more comfortable or more advantageous to life, but of what may approximate more closely to the puzzling reality that lies outside us.
>
> Sigmund Freud

The psychoanalytic refugees aided by the American Psychoanalytic Association were merely a small proportion from the wave of asylum-seekers escaping the brutality of National Socialism. Amongst these were a 14-year-old boy named Adolf Grünbaum and his family, who fled from the German city of Köln and arrived in Brooklyn, New York, in 1938.

During his military service in World War II, Grünbaum first worked in a research group and later served in U.S. Army intelligence. Just after the Soviets conquered Berlin, Grünbaum was installed at Heinrich Himmler's former Gestapo Headquarters, where he interrogated German academic prisoners and high-ranking SS and Wehrmacht officers. After the war, he went on to study physics at Yale, and he did his doctoral research on Zeno's paradoxes under Carl Hempel, the great empiricist philosopher of science. Grünbaum went on to establish himself as a world authority on the philosophy of physics (1967, 1968a, 1968b).

Grünbaum was appointed to his first chaired professorship 1956. In 1960, at the age of 37, he was appointed Andrew W. Mellon Professor of Philosophy at the University of Pittsburgh, where he was assigned the task of serving as a magnet to attract major scholars to the Philosophy Department and of establishing a new Centre for the Philosophy of Science, which became a unique and vigorous research centre. In subsequent years, he was awarded many academic honours. There have been two *festschrifts* published in his honour (Cohen & Laudan, 1983; Earman et al., 1993), and in 1986 an issue of the journal *Behavioral and Brain Sciences* devoted almost sixty pages to a debate about Grünbaum's ideas on psychoanalysis.

Before exploring Grünbaum's contributions to the philosophy of psychoanalysis, which even critics admit provide "By far the most important philosophical rejection of the scientific credibility of Freud's work ever to appear" (Levy, 1996, p. 129), we need to examine something of their philosophical background.

Logical empiricism

Vienna of the 1930s was not only the capital of the psychoanalytic empire, it was home to a radical philosophical group known as the Vienna Circle. The Vienna Circle philosophers believed that much existing philosophy was intellectually corrupt, and they wanted to set philosophy on a new and more scientific footing. In order to accomplish this, they drew primarily on two sources of inspiration: the empiricism of the eighteenth-century Scottish philosopher David Hume, and the powerful new approaches to formal logic developed by Gottlob Frege and Bertrand Russell. The Vienna Circle philosophers were also called "logical positivists" or "logical empiricists". The latter *revised* the ideas of the former.

The logical positivists adhered to a "principle of verification", which held that in order for a statement to be meaningful, there must be some way of *verifying* it. They held that statements that are in principle unverifiable are literally *meaningless.* Meaningful statements must therefore be well anchored in observation. Although scientific theories often refer to unobservable entities (e.g. photons), scientists must make certain that their theories have some principled connection to things that we can actually see, hear, and touch. If not, the theory is cognitively empty.

There were points of contact between psychoanalysis and the Vienna Circle. The philosophical temperament of the Circle, its impatience with metaphysical speculation and with woolly thinking, as well as its emphasis on science, corresponded well with Freud's scientifically inspired "anti-philosophical" stance (Smith, in press). Some members of the Circle had come to Vienna specifically in order to undergo psychoanalysis (Neider, 1977), and several of the group attempted to reformulate psychoanalytic theory along logical empiricist lines (Schlipp, 1963). Heinz Hartmann and other members of the Vienna Psycho-Analytical Association maintained contact with the Circle.

The classical logical empiricist critique of psychoanalysis was put succinctly by Ernest Nagel at a conference on philosophy and psychoanalysis convened by the New York University Institute of Philosophy in 1958 (Nagel, 1959). Hartmann had opened the conference with a defence of the scientific status of psychoanalysis. Nagel responded, making the point that

> The reason for my doubts is that the theory is stated in a language that is so vague and metaphorical that almost anything appears to be compatible with it. . . . In short, Freudian formulations seem to me to have so much "open texture," to be so loose in statement, that while they are unquestionably suggestive, it is well nigh impossible to decide whether what is just suggested is genuinely implied by the theory or whether it is related to the latter only by the circumstance that someone *happens* to associate one with the other. [p. 42]

Popper's falsificationism

Strict logical positivism died out both because of incoherent features within the system and because of incisive philosophical criticism from without. One of the most damaging of these critics was a young Austrian schoolteacher who had been a childhood friend Freud's sister Rosa (Popper, 1976). His name was Karl Popper.

Popper disagreed with Vienna Circle philosophers' emphasis on verification. The Circle philosophers believed that theories could be verified by accumulating confirmations, "positive instances" of the theory. The more confirmations, the more probably true the theory was to be regarded. This approach is transparently flawed. Consider Hitler's belief that all Jews are corrupt. Of course it is possible to accumulate instances of Jewish corruption (it is possible to do this with members of *any* ethnic group), but do such observations increase the probability that the statement "all Jews are corrupt" is true? Of course not.

According to Popper (1962), some theories seem attractive precisely because they appear to explain a very great deal. On closer inspection, such theories may be vacuous. In the field of psychology, Popper regarded psychoanalysis as one such all-embracing and yet scientifically empty theory. "I cannot", he wrote, "think of any conceivable instance of human behaviour which might not be interpreted in terms of either theory, and which might not be claimed, by either theory, as a 'verification'" (1983, p. 169). Psychoanalytic theory is *"compatible with everything that would happen"* (1974, p. 985).

Popper felt that this demonstrates that there is something very wrong with the verificationist approach. What if, instead of trying to verify theories, we try to prove them wrong? After all, although any number of confirmations cannot prove a theory right, just one disconfirmation can prove it *wrong*. Returning to our racist example, the sighting of just one honest Jew demonstrates the falsity of the theory that all Jews are corrupt. Scientific theories are in principle *falsifiable*: there can be some way of determining whether they are wrong. Non-scientific theories are *non-falsifiable*: there is no possible way of checking to see whether they are wrong. Popper thus concluded that psychoanalysis is non-scientific, because it is non-falsifiable.

Popper believed that scientists have an intellectual responsibility to try to falsify their theories. Only those that stand up to the test can be provisionally accepted as "true". Although not proven, they are "corroborated".

> When has a Freudian analyst tested the hypothesis that for his particular neurotic patient Oedipal conflicts are unimportant? When has a Kohutian analyst tested the hypothesis that a narcissistic patient has no significant self-defects or had adequate empathic mirroring as an infant? When has a Jungian analyst tested the hypothesis that his patient has no collective unconscious? ... The Oedipus conflicts, self-defects, and collective unconscious are all *assumed* to be true by their respective adherents and are employed to interpret ambiguous and opaque data. [Eagle, 1983, p. 40]

Sidney Hook, a philosopher, raised this issue at a 1958 conference on psychoanalysis and philosophy, asking those psychoanalysts present what kind of evidence would lead them to declare in any individual case that a child did *not* have an Oedipus complex. Hook did not receive a satisfactory reply at the conference. Lawrence Kubie, a highly regarded psychoanalytic theorist, replied that because the Oedipus complex is unconscious, no form of observable behaviour could possibly demonstrate its absence!

Grünbaum's critique

Grünbaum did not initially become embroiled in the philosophical debates around psychoanalysis because of a special interest in the subject (although he had already made significant contributions to the philosophy of psychology). Grünbaum entered the fray because of key disagreements with Popper's philosophy. Psychoanalysis was in the first instance an arena in which Popper's views could be challenged. In the process, he became the world's foremost philosophical critic of psychoanalysis and published numerous works devoted specifically to this subject (e.g. Grünbaum, 1977, 1979, 1984, 1986, 1993, 1997) which have given rise to considerable debate.

Grünbaum agrees with Popper that psychoanalysis is gravely defective as a science, although he disagrees with Popper that this is because psychoanalytic ideas are non-falsifiable. Grünbaum notes that Freud changed his mind on many occasions in the face of what he took to be disconfirming evidence. In any case, irrespective of Freud's own position, there are a number of psychoanalytic hypotheses that are clearly falsifiable. For example, Freud's (1911c) claim that paranoia is caused by repressed homosexuality might be taken to imply that it is not possible for a consciously homosexual person to simultaneously be paranoid. Instances of truly paranoid homosexuals would therefore falsify Freud's thesis (Grünbaum, 1984). In response to Hook's question, just because the oedipal hypothesis may not be falsifiable this does not entail that all or even most psychoanalytic claims are unfalsifiable.

If the problem is not one of falsifiability, what exactly is wrong with psychoanalysis? In order to grapple with this question, we need to consider the way that Freud tried to underwrite his theories. One of Freud's early strategies can be called the "jigsaw puzzle argument", an argument that Freud used in 1896 to defend his seduction theory:

> It is exactly like putting together a child's picture puzzle: after many attempts we become absolutely certain in the end which piece belongs in the empty gap; for only that one piece fills out the picture and at the same time allows its irregular edges to be fitted into the edges of the other pieces in such a manner as to have no free space and to entail no overlapping. In the same way, the contents of the infantile scenes turn out to be indispensable supplements to the associative and logical framework of the neurosis, whose insertion makes its course of development for the first time evident, or even, as we might often say, self-evident. [1896c, p. 205]

He also used the same argument to justify the psychoanalytic method of dream interpretation (1923c [1922], p. 116).

Less than two years after writing his "jigsaw puzzle" justification of the seduction theory, he *rejected* that very theory as mistaken. It is clear therefore that this strategy is not good enough, for reasons that are not hard to discover. Although a correct explanation must establish coherence (like the puzzle piece), not all explanations that establish coherence are sound. The establishment of a coherent picture is a necessary but not a sufficient condition for regarding a hypothesis as true. If the jigsaw puzzle argument was not adequate to support the seduction theory, then it is obviously not able to support the practice of dream interpretation either.

Grünbaum (1984) demonstrates that Freud brought another strategy to bear upon the problem. Its *locus classicus* is the *Introductory Lectures on Psychoanalysis* (Freud, 1916–17).

> After all his [the patient's] conflicts will only be successfully solved and his resistances overcome if the anticipatory ideas he is given tally with what is real in him. Whatever in the doctor's conjectures is inaccurate drops out in the course of the analysis; it has to be withdrawn and replaced with something more correct. [p. 52]

In other words, Freud believed that it is only when an interpretation ("anticipatory idea") *tallies* with a real unconscious idea that the interpretation has a healing effect. If it works, it must be true. Grünbaum calls this the *tally argument*. The tally argument has three premises:

1. only psychoanalysis can provide correct knowledge of the mental causes of neurotic symptoms;
2. correct insight is necessary for psychotherapeutic cure;
3. at least some people are cured of their neurosis by psychoanalytic treatment.

If true, these secure the conclusion that at least some psychoanalytic interpretations are true.

Freud had good reason to doubt the soundness of the second of these premisses, since he had begun his career as a Bernheimian hypnotherapist who removed his patients' symptoms by means of suggestion and was also aware of the phenomenon of spontaneous remission (Nunberg & Federn, 1962–1975, Vol. 1).

As we have seen in chapter seven, Freud openly acknowledged that there is inevitably a strong element of suggestion in psychoanalytic treatment, which is brought about by the positive transference. As Freud remarked, the patient gives up resistances *"to please us.* Our cures are cures through love" (Freud, cited in Nunberg & Federn, 1962–1975, Vol. 1, pp. 98–99).

The role of suggestion in psychoanalysis raises an awkward question. Might the curative effect of psychoanalytic interpretations flow from their suggestive power rather than from their truth? Unlike many later psychoanalysts, Freud (1916–17) took this objection seriously and was thus faced with two rival hypotheses purporting to explain the curative effect of psychoanalytic interventions. It was vitally important for him to rule out the suggestion hypothesis, for otherwise psychoanalytic theory would be bereft of empirical support. He attempted to neutralize the suggestion hypothesis by claiming that the patient's positive transference, which is the cause of his or her suggestibility, is eventually eliminated by means of the analyst's interpretation of its infantile origins. As Grünbaum was quick to point out, this strategy is viciously circular. How are we to know that the purported resolution of the positive transference is not just another effect of suggestion?

The fact that there are so many diverse and often mutually contradictory psychoanalytic approaches (some of which have been discussed in the present text), all claiming to be giving a true account of the aetiology and dynamics of psychological disorders, adds plausibility to the suggestion hypothesis. Freudians, Kleinians, Kohutians, and the rest all assert that the truth of their theories is attested to by their therapeutic successes. Given the fact that they contradict one another, it is logically impossible for *all* of these theories to be true; however, if an erroneous theory leads in curative interventions, it follows that the therapeutic effect of psychoanalytic interventions cannot depend on whether or not they tally with what is real in the patient.

Grünbaum (1984, 1993) argues that it is apparently *impossible* to test psychoanalytic theories validly on the couch, although he does not rule out the future development of a scientifically sound research design (Grünbaum, 1986). In essence, the psychoanalyst believes that if the patient accepts and avows as true the interpretations of his or her symptoms and resistances (and what the analyst regards as "true" will at least be compatible with and at most deduced from his or her preferred theoretical beliefs), he or she will be "cured". This implies that, with the best will in the world on the part of the analyst, there remains insidious pressure on the patient to fall in with the analyst's way of thinking. Data taken from the therapeutic situation are useless for objectively validating psychoanalytic theories because they are "epistemically contaminated" by that very situation. If this is the case, then how can we possibly test psychoanalytic propositions? Grünbaum argues that such testing must be extra-clinical, making use of controlled experimentation and epidemiological research. He then goes on to show that even if it were not the case that clinical data are epistemically contaminated, both Freud's theory of repression and the conclusions that he draws from the free-association method are scientifically ill-founded (Grünbaum, 1984, Part II).

All of this leads to the devastating conclusion that psychoanalytic practitioners do not as yet have substantial grounds for giving credence to their theories. Psychoanalytic claims are more like articles of faith than scientific hypotheses.

One response to the scientific criticisms offered by Grünbaum and others is to argue that psychoanalysis is not a natural science and should therefore be exempt from these justificatory norms. Psychoanalysis, it is claimed, is an "interpretative art" rather than a scientific enterprise. Grünbaum (1984, 1993) has demonstrated that this approach does violence to the content of the subject. Freud was a philosophical naturalist and materialist who believed in the empiricist doctrine of the unity of science. He regarded his brainchild as a natural science, as did most if not all of the major contributors whom I have discussed in preceding chapters. Other critics, such as the philosopher Jürgen Habermas (1971), assert that although Freud and others have regarded psychoanalysis as a natural science they are mistaken. Again, Grünbaum (1984, 1993) has taken great pains to highlight the numerous logical and exegetical fallacies of this position.

A second rejoinder is to aver that Grünbaum inappropriately or tendentiously confines his analysis to Freud's work, which has been superseded by more sophisticated and coherent forms of psychoanalysis (Flax, 1981). Grünbaum (1984) has met this criticism, pointing out that post-Freudian psychoanalytic developments do not provide any solutions to the *methodological* difficulties that beset Freud and which Freud (unlike many later theorists) struggled in vain to resolve. Eagle (1983, 1993) develops this point in considerable detail and goes on to suggest that the situation has in fact *degenerated* since Freud's time: "It seems to me", he writes, "that, on the contrary, Freud's writings and formulations for the most part, are paragons of precision and clarity compared to much current writing in so-called object relations theory and psychoanalytic self psychology" (p. 48). Erwin (1997) states with respect to Klein's theory that "the problem is not merely that many years after Klein formulated her hypotheses, they still lack supporting evidence. The more serious problem is this: How could we get such evidence *ever*, even if the conjectures were true" (p. 692).

By the same token, why should we be confident in the claims that psychoanalytic self psychologists make about the mental life of infants? The same holds true of Winnicott.

> Winnicott, unlike the typical self psychologist, did observe many infants in his role as a paediatrician, but how did he discover what was going on in their minds? His answer is that he did not make his "discoveries" by observing children. Instead he claims (1960, 594) that it is ". . . from the study of the transference in the analytic setting that it is possible to gain a clear view of what takes place in infancy itself." [Erwin, 1997, p. 692]

But if psychoanalytic views on the psychology of childhood are ultimately reconstructions based on data from the adult treatment setting, and it is this very material that Grünbaum has argued is too contaminated to underwrite psychoanalytic theories, then doubt must be cast on these as well!

Grünbaum (1993) acknowledges that his arguments may be deeply threatening to psychoanalytic clinicians, who

> react with dismay when confronted by a fundamental challenge to their cherished assumption. . . . Very understandably, those who see their doctrine in jeopardy may find it more difficult to be receptive to my demurrer than it is for me to issue it. . . . After all, whatever the fortunes of my polemic against Freud's clinical arguments and against post-Freudian variants on them . . . in the marketplace of ideas, my own professional craft as a philosopher is not put at risk by the outcome. [p. xi]

Notwithstanding its immense critical impact, Grünbaum does not regard his work as destructive. Psychoanalytic theorists and practitioners

> owe it to themselves to consider my doubts. . . . In the first place, I do *not* rule out the possibility that, granting the weakness of Freud's major clinical arguments, his brilliant theoretical imagination may nonetheless have led to correct insights in some important respects. Hence, I allow that a substantial vindication of some of his key ideas may perhaps yet come from well-designed extraclinical investigations, be they epidemiologic or experimental. Conceivably, it might even come from *as yet unimagined* new clinical research designs. . . . In the second place, if such a reliable new footing is ever to be achieved for Freud's theory, it is essential to have a clear appreciation of the range and depth of the difficulties besetting its extant defences. Analysts ignore these defects at their peril. [p. xi]

Grünbaum's influence

Grünbaum continues to contribute to the debate on the scientific status of psychoanalysis. His work has had a profound impact on other philosophers (e.g. Erwin, 1996; Levy, 1996), on critics of psychoanalysis (e.g. Crews, 1995; Webster, 1995), and on philosophically aware psychoanalysts and psychologists (e.g. Eagle, 1983; Edelson, 1984, 1988).

While Grünbaum was developing his philosophical critique of psychoanalysis from without, Robert Langs, an American psychoanalyst, was developing principles of clinical reasoning, theory, and technique which would provide a powerful and deeply unsettling critique of conventional forms of psychoanalysis from within. Although Langs was at the time unfamiliar with Grünbaum's work, his concern with the problem of the clinical validation of psychoanalytic hypotheses would lead to the development of a model for psychoanalytic clinical research that does not fall foul of Grünbaum's cogent objections.

CHAPTER FOURTEEN

Langs's raw message: communicative psychoanalysis

All sorrows can be borne if you put them into a story.

Isak Dinesen

Robert Langs was born in Brooklyn, New York, in 1928. He studied medicine at the Chicago Medical School, from which he graduated in 1953, and went on to train as a classical Freudian psychoanalyst at the Downstate Psychoanalytic Institute in New York, obtaining his psychoanalytic qualification in 1968. During the period between graduating from medical school and qualifying, Langs pursued research into the effects of LSD, dreams, and early memories (e.g. Langs, 1959, 1966; Langs & Linton Barr, 1962).

The making of a maverick

Langs's early psychoanalytic publications evince an interest in the interplay between the mind and the external world. In Langs's first psychoanalytic book, the two-volume *The Technique of Psychoanalytic Psychotherapy* (Langs, 1973–1974), he stressed that events occurring in the mind of the patient—associations, phantasies, resistances, and recollections—may be best understood as *responses* to stimuli. It was around this time that he began investigating the role of the most proximal of these stimuli: the behaviour of the analyst.

There are three other themes in *The Technique of Psychoanalytic Psychotherapy* that should be singled out for mention. The first of these is the problem of validation. Langs discussed the importance of evaluating interpretations on the basis of patients' responses to them, although at this point he limited himself to presenting conventional analytic views, such as those canvassed by Freud (1937d). Langs was also beginning to ponder the hypothesis that human beings can be unconsciously perceptive and sagacious.

Langs also argued that psychoanalysis can be injurious and that analysts can bring about "iatrogenic" (physician-caused) syndromes. For example, he wrote of "iatrogenic paranoia" that:

> This syndrome, which represents a failure in the therapeutic alliance with emphasis on the loss of basic trust in the therapist, is usually a response to direct (usually verbal), inappropriate, repetitive aggressions or seductions against the patient. The paranoid-like reaction may include some partial distortions on the patient's part or, more often, be an essentially correct appraisal of the therapist, which the latter erroneously assesses as distorted. [Langs, 1973–1974, Vol. 2, p. 342]

Over the next few years, Langs both refined his approach and systematically investigated the relevant psychoanalytic literature on technique. This exploration took him to British theorists such as Klein, Bion, and Winnicott, as well as to idiosyncratic American writers like Harold Searles (see Smith, 1991). "At the moment", wrote Searles (1975),

> ... it is fair to say that psychoanalytic literature is written ... with the assumption that the analyst is healthy and therefore

does not need psychological help from the patient, who is ill and therefore needs psychological help from, and is unable to give such help to, the analyst. . . . In my own practice of psychoanalytic therapy and in my supervision of such work on the part of my colleagues, I have found over and over that stalemates in the treatment, when explored sufficiently, involve the analyst's receiving currently a kind of therapeutic support from the patient of which both patient and analyst have been unconscious. Thus ironically, and in the instances when this status quo does not become resolved, one can indeed tragically, in those very instances wherein the analyst is endeavouring most anguishedly and unsuccessfully to help the patient . . . at an unconscious level the analyst is most tenaciously clinging to this very mode of relatedness as being one in which he, the analyst, is receiving therapy from the patient, without the conscious knowledge of either of them. [p. 382]

Langs's early investigations culminated in the publication of *The Bipersonal Field* (1976a), the first book on what he would later call the "communicative approach" to psychoanalytic psychotherapy. Like the four texts that were to follow in rapid succession (Langs, 1978, 1979, 1980, 1981), *The Bipersonal Field* consists of verbatim transcripts of supervisory seminars in which basic clinical concepts were hammered out and tested. Langs was developing a new methodology. In these seminars he used his theory to make predictions about what patients would do and say, and he then tested these against clinical data.

Langs's emphasis was now firmly on the disruptive potential of the analyst and the patient's unconscious sensitivity to this. The analyst's interventions are seen as shaping both the form and the content of the patient's communications. Even resistance was no longer seen as caused by forces operating purely within the patient:

If you think of this solely in intrapsychic terms, you will hold the patient responsible for the blockage, intervene accordingly, and the patient will become angry, because at some level she will know that you have contributed to the problem. She . . . will feel that you are blaming her and not accepting your own responsibilities in this situation. She will sense that you are placing some of your problems into her—projectively identifying them into her. [1976a, p. 57]

As he honed his methodology and acquired more extensive supervisory experience, Langs reached the conclusion that disruptive, insensitive, and self-serving interventions are the rule rather than the exception in psychoanalytic practice. The reception that he received was not a friendly one. "In this case", comments Lothane (1985), "the establishment chose silence. Obliteration is a fate worse than excommunication" (p. 195).

A theory of unconscious communication

The technique of listening to and forming hypotheses about the meaning of what has been said has been largely neglected by psychoanalytic writers.

According to Langs, there are two fundamental forms of verbal communication: the narrative mode and the non-narrative mode. In the narrative mode, we tell stories (concrete descriptions of real or imaginary events). The non-narrative mode is more abstract. The psychologist Jerome Bruner (1986) calls these the "narrative" and "paradigmatic" modes. According to Bruner, these two modes of speech correspond to two distinct modes of thinking, a view with which Langs concurs.

As an illustration, consider the following examples of narrative and relatively non-narrative, taken from psychotherapy sessions (Bucci, 1997).

I can't stand fruit with bad spots on it. It gives me the creeps. So I picked up that pineapple and it looked so nice, and then my finger went right through inside it, into this brown, slimy, mushy stuff, and my stomach just turned over. [p. 188]

This passage is highly narrative. It describes a scene, a situated episode: the reader can *picture* what is going on. Contrast it with the following:

I love people and I like to be with people. And right now I feel very bad because I can't be with them and do the things I would like to do. But I'm looking forward to a happier and healthier future and—I don't know what else to say. What else can I talk about? Well, I've had a very eventful life, I think. I've worked practically all my life and I love people. [p. 188]

This material possesses little narrative content. One cannot mentally *picture* an event or series of events corresponding to it: it is barren of verbal *imagery*.

According to Langs's theory, it is only narrative communication that encodes unconscious meaning. When a patient tells a story, no matter how apparently trivial or irrelevant, this may convey an unconscious message. On the other hand, when the patient engages in ruminative, reflective, or abstract discourse, no matter how profound, this will be devoid of encoded unconscious meaning.

The mind and the world

According to Freud's usual view, unconscious mental processes are largely segregated from external reality. They consist of drive-cathected memories and phantasies and defences against these. Dominated by the pleasure principle, these processes are essentially irrational. This view is also implicitly or explicitly espoused by most post-Freudian psychoanalytic theorists. Alongside his "official" view, Freud entertained other, opposing possibilities. His first theory of screen memories was one such example, as was his thesis about unconscious perception in the psychoanalytic situation (chapter seven).

Langs's work follows in the tradition of Freud's first screen memory theory and his later ideas on unconscious perception. When analyst and patient meet in the consulting-room, both of them unconsciously begin to *investigate* one another. According to communicative psychoanalysis, we are unconsciously deeply attuned to the subtle nuances of interpersonal exchanges. Indeed, we have a far better grasp of these matters unconsciously than we do consciously. Langs calls the hypothesized mental system responsible for this the "deep unconscious system".

Triggers and themes

Langs conjectured that the stories told during analytic sessions are responses to events occurring within the immediate therapeutic environment. The patient's discourse is not simply a manifestation of the contents of his or her mind: it is co-determined by the behaviour of the analyst and the state of the psychoanalytic setting.

The therapeutic environment is described as a *"trigger"* for unconscious processes in the patient. A trigger is an event or situation that brings about an unconscious response. According to the communicative approach, the deep unconscious system "locks in" on a trigger and rapidly identifies its implications and properties. The *meanings* of the trigger are unconsciously expressed in a disguised, encoded fashion through the narratives that spontaneously spring into the patient's mind. An early example of this sort of analysis is Freud's treatment of his own dream of 3 October 1897. Freud's associations led him to memories of the nanny who maltreated him and stole money from the family. Freud believed that this memory was unconsciously selected to represent unsavoury features of his *contemporary* relationship with his psychoanalytic patients: he abused them and stole their money.

Because each intervention is a new trigger, the first story following an intervention can be treated as an unconscious commentary on that intervention. Here is an example. A psychoanalyst says to her patient that she thinks that the patient should come to analysis more often, increasing the number of sessions from two to three times a week. The patient replies that this might be a good idea and, before long, finds himself recounting the plot of the film *Jaws*. The patient is particularly interested in describing how the film portrays the voracious shark lurking in coastal waters and dragging swimmers to their doom. In this sequence, the patient at first responds manifestly to the analyst's intervention, informing us of his conscious evaluation of the intervention. The subsequent narrative gives us access to his unconscious evaluation. In order to interpret a narrative, we must extract its theme. In this instance, there is a theme of "voracious attacks". We then recontextualize the theme by linking it to the analyst's intervention. It is as though the patient were unconsciously saying, "You, analyst, are voraciously attacking me". This can be fleshed out by linking it to the trigger: "In asking me to increase my sessions you, analyst, are voraciously attacking me." This is a strong but not unreasonable image of the analyst, given that an increase in the number of sessions will increase her income. The analyst is greedy: she is a "shark". This is what Langs calls the *raw message* of the story.

A similar approach to understanding narrative communication was independently discovered by Robert Haskell, an American psychologist who observed what he calls "subliteral" communication in small groups, and he developed a detailed methodology for analysing it (Haskell, 1987a, 1987b, 1987c, 1988, 1989a, 1989b, 1990, 1991). According to Haskell (1982), the deep structures underpinning subliteral narratives "are determined to a great extent by affective concerns, expectations, and the physical structure and environment of the group" (p. 183). It is these deep psychological structures that "generate the syntactic *selection* and *assignment* of a linguistic string of words (surface structure)" (p. 183).

According to Langs, these causal sequences are deeply lawful. Communicative theory claims that whenever an analyst unilaterally suggests an increase in the number of sessions per week, the patient will tend to respond with negatively toned narratives, typically involving themes of greed or exploitation, and that this will occur even if the patient consciously considers the suggestion to be unobjectionable. The law-like relationship between triggers and narratives allows one to make predictions about the course of psychoanalytic sessions.

How is this to be explained? Langs infers on the basis of these observed regularities that we all share criteria against which we unconsciously evaluate the behaviour of others. Any "deviation" from these standards raises unconscious objections, which are expressed as negatively toned narratives. The deep unconscious system tracks interpersonal engagements and registers departures from these norms. It is as if we unconsciously ask ourselves, "Is this person seeking to harm or exploit me, or are they acting in my best interests?"

Langs's method of listening to and interpreting unconscious communication suggests that patients unconsciously regard a great deal of what their analysts do as exploitative, self-serving, and harmful. The communicative approach provides us with a novel and disturbing perspective on conventional psychoanalytic methods.

The frame

The psychoanalytic situation is held together by a set of rules (Mooij, 1982). These "ground rules" make psychoanalysis what it is. They identify the roles of the two participants, their privileges and responsibilities, the constraints upon their activities, and the way that they can use the "equipment" of the analytic setting (the room, the couch, and so on). The ground rules of psychoanalysis distinguish it from all other activities. The ground rules and setting of analysis are referred to as the "frame" (Milner, 1952).

According to Langs, the deep unconscious system is almost entirely concerned with the frame. In other words, patients unconsciously "zero in" on the most fundamental features of the analytic setting and relationship. On the conscious level, people's expectations of therapy are extremely diverse: some want their analyst to offer frequent interpretations, others crave silence, some long for flexibility, others seek rigour. On the unconscious level, this does not appear to be the case. In fact, each of us seems to adhere unconsciously to the same key criteria for the frame (Langs, 1998). When the frame is structured in accord with these standards, it is said to be "secured".

The ground rules of the secured frame involve space and time, issues of proximity, issues of exchange, and psychoanalytic role responsibilities. The basic components are as follows:

1. Sessions should always take place in the same room.
2. Sessions should always take place at the same time.
3. Session should last for the same number of minutes.
4. The patient should decide when to terminate therapy.
5. The analysis should be completely private.
6. The analysis should be completely confidential.

7. Contact between analyst and patient should be confined to the consulting-room.

8. There should be no physical contact between analyst and patient.

9. There is a set fee.

10. The patient should pay for all scheduled sessions.

11. The analyst should be present for all scheduled sessions.

12. The analyst should be neutral, striving not to give the patient explicit or implicit directives, blame, or praise.

13. The analyst should be anonymous, striving to convey no personal information, opinions, and so on.

14. The analyst should manage the work at the patient's unconscious behest.

15. The analyst should take responsibility for his or her deviations and errors and express this in an appropriate interpretative fashion.

According to communicative theory, psychotherapy patients unconsciously inform us, by means of their narratives, that this is how they desire the psychoanalytic situation to be structured. Departures from the secured frame cause the patient unconsciously to select narratives representing the deviation and its implications.

Haskell (1982) describes the impact on a small group of the presence of a researcher taking notes (note-taking is an implicit violation of complete confidentiality).

> For instance, it appears that the affective concern of a trainer taking notes is permuted into (a) talk of journalists, if the aspect of concern is an authority collecting information for publication, (b) talk of F.B.I. or C.I.A. files if the aspect of concern is the authority "spying" for future evaluative purposes, (c) talk of novelists, where the aspect of concern is that what is being written may not be true (a novel = fiction), or (d) talk of archivists, where the aspect of concern is that what is being written will be stored away for future group researchers. [p. 185]

In another research project, the transcript of a tape-recorded psychotherapy session was sent to a number psychotherapists who were to write a commentary on the session from their various theoretical viewpoints for inclusion in a book. Despite the patient's manifest agreement to participate in the project, she produced narratives about lying naked on an operating table and of suffering a gang rape (Jacobs, 1996).

Even though the secured frame seems to be unconsciously desired by most of us, it also generates special anxieties. This feature of the analytic situation seems to have been noted first by the Kleinian analyst José Bleger (1967), who argued that the frame has the power to evoke profound psychotic anxieties. According to Langs (1997), the secured frame evokes existential death anxiety, the dread of certain annihilation. Because the secured frame has the power to activate these anxieties, it is an inherently unstable structure. Both analysts and analysands experience the need to modify the frame so as to pre-empt or eliminate the dread that it may evoke. Framework deviations may evoke a different form of death anxiety: predatory death anxiety. Predatory death anxiety entails the possibility of escape from danger and therefore involves mechanisms of fight, flight, seduction, and submission.

Clinical validation

Communicative psychoanalysts believe that the analyst should be guided by the patient's deep unconscious communications. This is made possible by the disciplined procedure of interpreting narratives in relation to their triggers. "Clinical validation" is the process that allows psychoanalysts to determine the correctness (or otherwise) of their interventions.

I have already described how communicative psychoanalysts use the first displaced narratives following an intervention as a commentary describing the basic properties of that intervention. Here is a brief clinical example illustrating this point. A patient in psychoanalytic therapy described a complex, tangled relationship between herself, her husband, and her husband's lover. The therapist interpreted this in terms of the Oedipus complex. The patient said that the interpretation sounded credible and then went on to discuss her GP. "He doesn't know how to give a diagnosis", she says "He's confused. I had flu and went to him, but the medicine he gave me was useless." This is an example of *non-validation*. The first narrative after the interpretation involved the theme of some-one who is unable to identify the nature of a problem, who is confused, and who provides a useless treatment. According to communicative theory, this patient was unconsciously saying "You, therapist, have offered me an incorrect interpretation. You are confused, and what you say to me is useless."

An intervention is clinically *validated* when the patient re-sponds with a positively toned narrative involving themes such as insight, helpfulness, kindness, and so on. It is quite rare for inter-ventions to be validated. Here is an example of a clinical validation given in response to a sound communicative interpretation.

"I stopped at my mother's place yesterday. I really had to confront her. You know, she usually dismisses me and says that I should pull myself together, but this time she sat there and listened to everything I said. It was great. She thought about everything I said and didn't get defensive."

Communicative therapists consider an interpretation to be cor-rect only when it has been validated by the patient. Conscious agreement is irrelevant to this. In fact, analysands often express conscious assent to an interpretation whilst unconsciously rejecting it, or vice versa. Encoded validations normally occur only in very special circumstances. According to Langs, non-communicative psychoanalysts rarely receive encoded validation for their efforts.

Doing communicative psychoanalysis

Langs's theory of psychoanalytic technique is too intricate for a detailed account within the confines of this chapter. I limit myself here to describing enough of the method to convey something of its flavour.

Because of their concern with establishing a secured frame, communicative psychoanalysts apply special selection criteria when considering a prospective patient. Communicative analysts do not accept referrals from their own patients, or accept patients with whom they have had extra-therapeutic contact (or with whom they are likely to have such contact) as all such arrangements are antagonistic to an atmosphere of security and trust within the therapeutic relationship.

It is for similar reasons that communicative analysts do not approve of assessment by a third party. This very common practice not only poses a severe threat to confidentiality, but also saddles the patient with an experience of rejection (being "passed on"). Communicative analysts also refrain from discussing a referral with the person who has made the referral, and they avoid reading referral notes. Communicative psychoanalysts normally carry out their own assessments. It is during this "consultation" session that the analyst sets out the ground rules and role expectations of both analyst and analysand, so that that an informed choice can be made.

Having taken on a patient, the communicative psychoanalyst tries to create conditions favourable to free and open unconscious communication. This is done by maintaining a secured frame and remaining mainly silent. In fact, the establishment of an appropriate setting and keeping silent are the two most fundamental forms of intervention. This may seem strange, as these are both non-verbal activities, but according to Langsian thinking an "intervention" is *any* act of commission or omission that is causally relevant to the patient's behaviour (Langs, 1981).

Most of the verbal interventions used in other forms of psychoanalysis are regarded as unacceptable by communicative practitioners. Communicative psychoanalysts do not ask questions, engage in confrontations, or solicit clarifications, as these forms of intervention do not consistently elicit derivative validation. Verbal intervention is mainly confined to interpretation. But even here, the options are limited. The communicative psychoanalyst offers neither transference interpretations, classical reconstructions, and resistance interpretations, nor interpretations of symbolism (although the patient's past is addressed insofar as it is reproduced in resonance with contemporary triggers). Communicative interpretations try to explain narratives in light of their triggers: they attempt to specify how the patient has unconsciously made sense of some feature of the analytic situation. The analyst does *not* interpret the patient's stories as expressions of transference. He or she is required to "take it on the chin" and take on board the patient's perspective. Interpretations are offered only in the presence of some indication that the patient requires one (e.g. the patient is in a state of resistance or distress).

The technique of decoding narratives is quite different from making inferences about patients on the basis of the manifest content of their discourse. It is possible, for example, to infer that a patient has difficulty with "authority figures" on the basis of his report of coming into conflict with his line manager. Taking a larger Freudian leap, an analyst might infer from such an account that the patient has difficulties in his relationship with his father. The communicative psychoanalyst uses narrative reports differently. He or she maps the narrative onto some specific feature of or event within the psychoanalytic setting. Perhaps an example (taken from Smith, 1991) will clarify this.

> The patient is an adolescent girl. The main trigger was the fact that the therapist had spoken on the telephone to the patient's mother, and had not discussed this with her. The patient offered narratives concerning her relationship with a girl named Jessica involving themes of deception and the presence of third parties. The therapist responded with erroneous, counter-transference-laden interpretations which were not validated by the patient, who became increasingly distressed and withdrawn as the session went on. The patient moved on to a poignant account of shutting herself in her room and talking to her teddy bears. Eventually, the therapist said:
>
> > You started off your session today expressing your disappointment and anger with Jessica. You describe her as being weak. Instead of telling you up front what was wrong she got her mother to call the school. By doing this she brought other people into something which concerned just you and her. Also, last week when you met at the cinema she pretended that your meeting was a chance meeting even though you knew that she had overheard your arrangements with Julia. You felt that she was unwilling to admit to this and it seems important to you that people are honest.

You also described how you could only talk to your teddy bears as they were the only ones with whom you could have a unique, safe relationship without bringing anyone else in. I think you might feel betrayed by me because not only have I had some contact with your mother when she called me but I have not mentioned this to you. You seem to be stressing that your mother, or anyone else, should not be involved in this relationship. It should be like the relationship you had with your teddy bears or else you feel betrayed. [p. 226]

This is a well-crafted communicative interpretation. The therapist interpreted the patient's stories as commentaries on her violation of confidentiality. After the interpretation, the patient mentioned how her parents asked her questions about the therapy, and then she said:

I can talk to Julia. She really understands. We really get on. She really is my best friend. It's not that we don't argue but she seems to know when I'm upset. When I go all quiet she will eventually come up to me and asks what is wrong so we can talk about it. [p. 227]

Although the interpretation of narratives is certainly important in the communicative approach, the management and rectification of the frame is even more significant. Words are cheap, and we unconsciously judge one another on the basis of our *actions*. It is therefore important to rectify framework deviations whenever possible as well as interpreting them. The analyst who interprets a frame deviation without setting it right is justly seen by his or her patient as inconsistent and dishonest.

Madness and cure

One criticism of communicative psychoanalysis is that it ignores the causal role of childhood events. This criticism is ill informed. The rejection of the concept of transference is not tantamount to a rejection of the importance of early experiences. It is simply a rejection of Freudian claims about how this influence is transmitted. Communicative psychoanalysis rejects the thesis that we indiscriminately and inappropriately *impose* our memories on the present.

As an alternative to the theory of transference, it may be more correct to say that during the course of our development we learn to adapt to certain interpersonal situations. These adaptations lead to certain unconscious sensitivities. For example, a child growing up in a home suffused with violence may develop an acute unconscious sensitivity to the violent properties of interpersonal transactions. Because the child must learn to anticipate violence, he or she has developed an exquisitely attuned unconscious "violence detector". Were this child to enter psychoanalytic treatment, one would expect him or her to be selectively sensitive to the specifically violent implications of the analyst's behaviour. The child's deep unconscious system is like a radio receiver tuned by experience to pick up certain emotional wavelengths more readily than others. But is this not just the same as the concept of transference? No, it is not. Selective sensitivity is not the same as the imposition of phantasy. According to this approach, the unconscious developed in much the same way as the immune system. Unconscious sensitivities are reinforced by experiences in much the same way that the production of antibodies is reinforced by the presence of pathogens.

It is also sometimes suggested that communicative psychoanalysis cannot be curative because it does not provide the patient with information about his or her repressed past. This criticism is driven by an uncritical acceptance of the Freudian model of cure. Even if it is the case that early experiences are responsible for the emergence of psychopathology, it does not follow from this that explicit discussion or interpretation of these factors is a necessary condition for cure.

It seems clear that communicative psychoanalysts implicitly regard the process of cure as brought about by relational factors. They do not, on the whole, believe that conscious acceptance of an interpretation is necessary in order for it to have a therapeutic effect. It may simply be that communicative psychoanalysis works by creating conditions favourable to a natural healing process. Although the literature had discussed the process of "cure" in terms of insight, the inherent healing properties of the secured frame, and the introjection of a frame-securing analyst, it is fair to say that the approach does not yet have a detailed, testable theory of psychological cure. This is not necessarily to its discredit. It is more scientifically sober to say that one does not clearly understand a phenomenon than to invent fanciful theories to fill in the cognitive gap. The history of medicine is largely the history of incorrect ideas about how treatments work.

Langs (1982) believes that psychotherapists and psychoanalysts produce changes by a variety of means, some of which are rather unflattering. For instance, in the process of cure through nefarious comparison, patients experience a sense of personal relief in the realization that their analyst is as least as psychologically disturbed as they are. This thesis is not entirely without psychoanalytic precedent. Blanton (1971) recalls the following remarks by Freud:

> "Do you know why psychiatrists go into their speciality?" he continued. "It is because they do not feel that they are normal, and they go into this work because it is a means of sublimation for this feeling—a means of assuring themselves that they are really normal. Society put them in charge of the mentally abnormal, and so they feel reassured." [pp. 46–47]

Langs also believes that all forms of psychotherapy extract their price, and that in assessing the value of psychotherapy we must balance the benefits accrued against the harm inflicted, just as we would in any medical treatment. There is a strong tendency within the psychoanalytic profession to ignore the harm that treatment may bring about.

An answer to Grünbaum

Communicative psychoanalysis provides a strategy for testing psychoanalytic theories "on the couch" that does not fall foul of Grünbaum's (1984) objections.* According to Grünbaum's tally ar-

---

*Langs's work additionally makes it possible to use communicative variables for quantitative research into verbal behaviour both inside and outside the psychoanalytic situation (e.g. Langs, Badalamenti, & Thompson, 1996; Langs, Udoff, Bucci, Cramer, & Thompson, 1993).

gument (chapter thirteen), Freud tried to use therapeutic success as a means of underwriting psychoanalytic theory—psychoanalysis must be true, because it works. Leaving aside the basic question of whether psychoanalysis really does work better than rival modalities, there was a basic problem confronting this strategy. When psychoanalysis does work, how do we know that it works because it is true? It might work only because of its suggestive power! Freud admitted that there was a powerful component of suggestion in the psychoanalytic situation, and he could not in good faith dismiss the criticism, but, as Grünbaum (1984) shows, he was never able successfully to come to grips with it.

Grünbaum cogently argues that unless the role of suggestive influence can be ruled out, most clinical "confirmations" of psychoanalytic hypotheses must be regarded as having little evidential value. This problem arises from the causal circularity of the testing situation: we are testing psychoanalytic theory by means of events in psychoanalytic therapy. The therapy muddies the epistemological waters. Evidence on behalf of the theory garnered from the therapy is potentially or actually contaminated by the causal impact of the analyst's expectations.

But what if we were to test a psychoanalytic theory using clinical data from a *rival* therapeutic approach. Could we not test, say, Freudian theory using Jungian clinical data? This approach would successfully evade Grünbaum's objections, as any suggestive influence would *reduce* the likelihood of confirmation. But even though the prospect of testing psychoanalytic theories "on the couch" once again seems possible, the procedure itself seems *prima facie* unworkable. Just what aspects of Freudian theory could one possibly test using Jungian data? I am not at all certain that conventional psychoanalytic theories are sufficiently robust and generalizable to be tested in this fashion. The situation is different with respect to communicative psychoanalysis. Communicative psychoanalysis makes predictions about how frame events give rise to narratives. These hypotheses can certainly be tested against non-communicative data. For example, given non-communicative session S, a knowledge of the initial conditions, and an account of the trajectory of the session up to time T, it is possible to use communicative psychoanalytic theory to deduce predictions about the first narrative themes after T. Another possibility is to examine the incidence of particular narrative themes in non-communicative therapies sharing an identical framework deviation and comparing this with the incidence of the same theme within a control group. For instance, communicative theory predicts that there should be a high incidence of narratives of death, loss, and separation voiced by patients in time-limited therapy as compared with a control group. Such a research project would be quite easy to implement and analyse.

Langs's influence

Langs's work has heightened psychoanalysts' awareness of the role of the frame. His work on unconscious communication has had some impact on contemporary practice (e.g. Casement, 1985; Dorpat, 1985; Dorpat & Miller, 1992). The growing awareness of the abusive potential of psychoanalysis and psychotherapy owes a great deal to Langs's pioneering work. In recent years, Langs has devoted himself to the scientific investigation of psychoanalytic interactions and has collaborated with mathematicians to this end (this research is summarized in Langs et al., 1996). Many features of communicative psychoanalysis are readily testable. It also has clear points of contact with the work of cognitive scientists such as Haskell (as discussed earlier) and provides an interesting response to Grünbaum's powerful indictment of psychoanalytic research on the couch. Unfortunately, it has, by and large, been ignored by researchers and philosophers alike.

Coda

Unfortunately, however, people are seldom impartial where
ultimate things, the great problems of science and life, are
concerned. Each of us is governed in such cases by deep-
rooted internal prejudices, into whose hands our speculation
unwittingly plays. Since we have such good grounds for being
distrustful, our attitude towards the results of our own
deliberations cannot well be other than one of cool
benevolence.

Sigmund Freud

Psychoanalysis has had an extraordinary history. It was a
child of a great intellectual and spiritual revolution—the
naturalization of the human mind—which has still not yet
reached its culmination. It is a history of compelling visions of the
human condition devised by colourful, creative, and sometimes
anguished individuals. It is a history of controversy and strife.

Nevertheless, during the century of its existence, psychoanalysis has not so much developed as expanded. It has not clearly

attained a better and better grasp of the nature of psychic reality. Instead, it has given rise to the co-existence of rival schools of thought that engage in dialogue neither with one another nor with Nature herself. However emotionally appealing, such ecumenicism breeds intellectual stagnation.

As there is at present no evidence-based way of choosing one psychoanalytic approach over another, practitioners are forced to make their choices on subjective grounds. But if affiliation to one psychoanalytic approach or another normally owes more to taste than to research, the spread of psychoanalytic ideas may owe more to epidemiology than to evidence. Dawkins (1993) speaks of such self-replicating belief systems as "viruses of the mind". The victim of such a virus

> ... typically finds himself impelled by some deep, inner conviction that something is true, or right, or virtuous; a conviction that doesn't seem to owe anything to evidence or reason, but which, nevertheless, he feels as totally compelling and convincing. [p. 20]

Science progresses by ruthlessly pitting rival theories against decisive evidence, and the collapse of an established idea is an occasion for general excitement rather than consternation. But psychoanalysis clings to its beliefs instead of attempting collectively to test them objectively. With minimal resources for rational debate and research, the gap between opinion and evidence results in a craving for authority. "The issues that divide analysts", writes Cioffi (1979), "are couched in a rhetoric that doesn't allow of rational, impersonal discussion" (p. 504).

Psychoanalysis is strong on bold and imaginative theorizing, but weak on making disciplined links between these theories and observations of the phenomena that it purports to explain. But although it suffers from multiple intellectual handicaps, it is still "the only game in town" when it comes to understanding our emotional life.

Psychoanalysis is not *condemned* to its insularity. The need for collective intellectual effort with colleagues from related disciplines (of which Freud was acutely aware) is further underscored by what we know about the size of the problem of understanding the human mind.

Churchland (1984) instructively compares the history of psychology with the history of astronomy. The astronomers of ancient Greece knew that the universe was big. They worked out that the astronomical bodies were perhaps a few thousand miles distant from the earth. Then, in the third century BC, Aristarchos of Samos disturbed things. He calculated that the moon must be *hundreds of thousands* of miles away, that the sun must be *millions* of miles away and that the stars must be *many thousands of millions* of miles away. As Churchland dryly puts it "An expansion of this magnitude changes one's perspective on things" (p. 249).

Today, we are in a position analogous to that of Aristarchos of Samos with respect to the mind. In fact, as Churchland points out, cognitive scientists are now able to make a rough calculation of the size of mental space.

Before I continue, pause for a moment and take a silent guess at the estimated size of mental space. The figure is astonishing. At a *conservative* estimate, our brains are capable of something like $10^{100,000,000,000,000}$ configurations of neural activation. If you wanted simply to type this number out in full, with all of its zeros, you would need a rather large piece of paper. Stake a stab at how large the sheet of paper would have to be to accommodate this figure. Would it stretch to the end of your street? To Bangalore? To the North Pole? Would it stretch all the way around the world or to the moon and back? Assuming that each numeral was only three millimetres wide, the entire number would be millions upon millions of kilometres long! In fact, the piece of paper would have to be so long that *it would extend all the way to the limits of the known astronomical universe and back many millions of times!* The magnitude represented by this numeral is greater than the number of all the grains of sand on all the beaches in the world. It is greater than the number of all the stars in all the galaxies of space. Think of it: ten to the hundred-million-millionth power! You will get some small intimation of the immensity of mental space if I tell you that physicists have calculated that the total number of elementary particles in the entire astronomical universe is a paltry 10^{87}.

Psychoanalysis is a research programme that was noble in its inspiration but faulty in its execution. It has become derailed, but not fatally so. In trying to understand the human mind, psychoanalysts are trying to understand something awesomely vast.

Crude speculation and dogmatic assertion are not equal to the task.

> There was once a chap who wanted to know the meaning of life, so he walked a thousand miles and climbed to the high mountaintop where the wise guru lived. "Will you tell me the meaning of life?" he asked.
>
> "Certainly," replied the guru, "but if you want to understand my answer, you must first master recursive function theory and mathematical logic."
>
> "You're kidding."
>
> "Not really."
>
> "Well then . . . skip it."
>
> "Suit yourself."
>
> [Dennett, 1982, p. 9]

If psychoanalysis is to have the future that it deserves, this option of lazy ignorance must not be chosen. We must get down to the task of exploring in earnest the vastness of mental space.

REFERENCES

Abraham, K. (1921). Contributions to the theory of the anal character. In: *Selected Papers on Psychoanalysis*. London: Hogarth Press, 1973. [Reprinted London: Karnac Books, 1989.]

_____ (1924a). The influence of oral erotism on character-formation. In: *Selected Papers on Psychoanalysis*. London: Hogarth Press, 1973. [Reprinted London: Karnac Books, 1989.]

_____ (1924b). A short study of the development of the libido viewed in the light of mental disorders. In: *Selected Papers on Psychoanalysis*. London: Hogarth Press, 1973. [Reprinted London: Karnac Books, 1989.]

_____ (1925). Character formation on the genital level of the libido. In: *Selected Papers on Psychoanalysis*. London: Hogarth Press, 1973. [Reprinted London: Karnac Books, 1989.]

Akhtar, S. (1989). Kernberg and Kohut: a critical comparison. In: D. W. Detrick & S. P. Detrick (Eds.), *Self Psychology: Comparisons and Contrasts* (pp. 329–363). Hillsdale, NJ: Analytic Press.

Altschuler, M. D. (1965). *Roots of Modern Psychiatry: Essays in the History of Psychiatry*. London: Grune & Stratton.

Appignanesi, L., & Forrester, J. (1992). *Freud's Women*. London: Wiedenfeld & Nicolson.

Arrizabalaga, J., Henderson, J., & French, R. (1997). *The Great Pox: The French Disease in Renaissance Europe.* Cambridge, MA: Yale University Press.

Atwood, G. E., & Stolorow, R. D. (1984). *Structures of Subjectivity.* Hillsdale, NJ: Analytic Press.

Bacal, H. A. (1989). Winnicott and self psychology: remarkable reflections. In: D. W. Detrick & S. P. Detrick (Eds.), *Self Psychology: Comparisons and Contrasts* (pp. 259–275). Hillsdale, NJ: Analytic Press.

Balint, M. (1932). Character analysis and new beginning. In: *Primary Love and Psycho-Analytic Technique.* New York: Liveright. [Reprinted London: Karnac Books, 1986.]

_____ (1968). *The Basic Fault: Therapeutic Aspects of Regression.* London: Tavistock.

Basch, M. F. (1989). A comparison of Freud and Kohut: apostasy or synergy? In: D. W. Detrick & S. P. Detrick (Eds.), *Self Psychology: Comparisons and Contrasts.* London: Analytic Press.

Beard, G. M. (1869). Neurasthenia, or nervous exhaustion. *Boston Medical and Surgical Journal, 3:* 217–221.

Bettelheim, B. (1983). *Freud and Man's Soul.* New York: Alfred A. Knopf.

Bibring, E. (1934). The development and problems of the theory of the instincts. *International Journal of Psycho-Analysis* [1941], 22: 102–131.

Blanck, G., & Blanck, R. (1994). *Ego Psychology Theory and Practice.* New York: Columbia University Press.

Blanton, S. (1971). *Diary of My Analysis with Sigmund Freud.* New York: Hawthorn.

Bleger, J. (1967). Psycho-analysis of the psychoanalytic frame. *International Journal of Psycho-Analysis, 48:* 511–519.

Bloch, E. (1908). *The Sexual Life of Our Time in Its Relation to Modern Civilisation,* translated by M. Eden Paul. London: Rebman.

Boadella, D. (1973). *Wilhelm Reich: The Evolution of his Work.* London: Vision.

Bonomi, C. (1997). Freud and the discovery of infantile sexuality: a reassessment. In: T. Dufresne (Ed.), *Freud under Analysis: Essays in Honor of Paul Roazen.* New York: Jason Aronson.

Borch-Jacobsen, M. (1996). *Remembering Anna O.: 100 Years of Psychoanalytic Mystification.* London/New York: Routledge.

Bromberg, N., & Small, V. V. (1984). *Hitler's Psychopathology.* New York: International Universities Press.

Bruner, J. (1986). *Actual Minds, Possible Worlds.* Cambridge, MA: Harvard University Press.

Bucci, W. (1997). *Psychoanalysis & Cognitive Science: A Multiple Code Theory*. London: Guilford Press.

Butler, S. (1880). *Unconscious Memory: A Comparison between the Theory of Dr Ewald Hering . . . and "The Philosophy of the Unconscious" by Dr Edward von Hartmann, with Translations from these Authors*. London: David Bogue.

Casement, P. (1985). *On Learning from the Patient*. London: Tavistock.

Casper, J. L. (1852). Über Nothsucht und Päderastie und deren Ermittelung seitens des Gerichstarztes. *Vierteljahrschrift für gerichtliche und öffentliche Medicin*, 1: 21–78.

Chodorow, N. (1989). *Feminism and Psycho-Analytic Theory*. Cambridge, MA: Polity Press; New Haven, CT: Yale University Press.

Churchland, P. (1984). *A Neurocomputational Perspective*. Cambridge, MA: Bradford/MIT.

Cioffi, F. (1974). Was Freud a liar? *The Listener*, 7 February, pp. 172–74. [Reprinted in: *Journal of Orthomolecular Psychiatry*, 5: 275–280.]

_____ (1979). Freud: new myths to replace the old. *New Society*, 20 November, pp. 503–504.

Cocks, G. (1985). *Psychotherapy in the Third Reich: The Göring Institute*. Oxford: Oxford University Press.

Cohen, R. S., & Laudan, L. (Eds.) (1983). *Physics, Philosophy and Psychoanalysis*. Dirdrecht: Reidel.

Crews, F. (1995). *The Memory Wars: Freudian Science in Dispute*. New York: New York Review Imprints.

Davidson, A. I. (1990). Closing up the corpses: diseases of sexuality and the emergence of the psychiatric style of reasoning. In: G. Bools (Ed.), *Meaning and Method: Essays in Honor of Hilary Putnam* (pp. 295–325). Cambridge: Cambridge University Press.

Davis, M., & Wallbridge, D. (1981). *Boundary & Space: An Introduction to the Work of D. W. Winnicott*. London: Karnac Books.

Davis, W. (1995). *Drawing the Dream of the Wolves: Homosexuality, Interpretation and Freud's "Wolf Man"*. Bloomington, IL: Indiana University Press.

Dawkins, R. (1976). *The Selfish Gene*. Oxford: Oxford University Press.

_____ (1993). Viruses of the mind. In: B. Dahlbom (Ed.), *Dennett and His Critics*. Oxford: Basil Blackwell.

Decker, H. (1991). *Freud, Dora, and Vienna 1900*. New York: Macmillan.

Dennett, D. (1982). Philosophy according to Nozick. *New Boston Review*, 7: 9–11.

Deutsch, H. (1942). Some forms of emotional disturbance and their relationship to schizophrenia. *Psychoanalytic Quarterly, 11*: 301–321.

Detrick, D. W., & Detrick, S. P. (Eds.) (1989). *Self Psychology: Comparisons and Contrasts*. Hillsdale, NJ: Analytic Press.

Dorpat, T. (1985). *Denial and Defence in the Therapeutic Situation*. New York: Jason Aronson.

Dorpat, T., & Miller, M. (1992). *Clinical Interaction and the Analysis of Meaning*. Hillsdale, NJ: Analytic Press.

Eagle, M. (1983). The epistemological status of recent developments in psychoanalytic theory. In: R. S. Cohen & L. Laudan (Eds.), *Physics, Philosophy and Psychoanalysis: Essays in Honor of Adolf Grünbaum* (pp. 31–57). Dordrecht/Boston: D. Reidel.

Eagle, M. (1993). The dynamics of theory change in psychoanalysis. In: J. Earman et al. (Eds.). *Philosophical Problems of the Internal and External Worlds: Essays on the Philosophy of Adolf Grünbaum*. Pittsburgh, PA: University of Pittsburgh Press.

Earman, J., et al. (Eds.) (1993). *Philosophical Problems of the Internal and External Worlds: Essays on the Philosophy of Adolf Grünbaum*. Pittsburgh, PA: University of Pittsburgh Press.

Edelson, M. (1984). *Hypothesis and Evidence in Psychoanalysis*. Chicago, IL: University of Chicago Press.

Edelson, M. (1988). *Psychoanalysis: A Theory in Crisis*. Chicago, IL: Chicago University Press.

Eissler, K. R. (1978). Creativity and adolescence: the effect of trauma on Freud's adolescence. *Psychoanalytic Study of the Child, 33*: 461–517.

Ellis, H. (1897). *Studies in the Psychology of Sex, Vol. 1: Sexual Inversion*. London: University Press.

———— (1901). *Studies in the Psychology of Sex, Vol. 2: Sexual Inversion*. London: University Press.

Erwin, E. (1993). Philosophers on Freudianism: an examination of replies to Grünbaum's *Foundations*. . In: J. Earman et al. (Eds.). *Philosophical Problems of the Internal and External Worlds: Essays on the Philosophy of Adolf Grünbaum*. Pittsburgh, PA: University of Pittsburgh Press.

———— (1996). *A Final Accounting: Philosophical and Empirical Issues in Freudian Psychology*. Cambridge, MA: Bradford/MIT.

———— (1997). Psychoanalysis: past, present and future. *Philosophy and Phenomenological Research, 57* (3): 671–696.

Federn, P. (1929). The ego as subject and object in narcissism. In: *Ego*

Psychology and the Psychoses (pp. 283–322). London: Karnac Books, 1977.

_____ (1936). On the distinction between healthy and pathological narcissism. In: *Ego Psychology and the Psychoses* (pp. 323–364). London: Karnac Books, 1977.

_____ (1949). Depersonalisation. In: *Ego Psychology and the Psychoses* (pp. 323–364). London: Karnac Books, 1977.

Ferenczi, S. (1909). Introjection and transference. In: *Sex in Psycho-Analysis*. New York: Basic Books, 1950.

_____ (1913). Stages in the development of the sense of reality. In: *Selected Papers of Sandor Ferenczi, Vol. 1.* New York: Basic Books.

_____ (1933). The confusion of tongues between adults and the child. In: *Final Contributions to the Problems and Methods of Psycho-Analysis.* London: Hogarth Press. [Reprinted London: Karnac Books, 1980.]

Fermi, L. (1968). *Illustrious Immigrants: The Intellectual Migration from Europe 1930–41.* Chicago, IL: University of Chicago Press.

Flaubert, G. (1874). *The Temptation of Saint Anthony*, translated by K. Mrosovsky. London: Penguin, 1983.

Flax, J. (1981). Psychoanalysis and the philosophy of science: critique or resistance? *Journal of Philosophy, 78*: 561–569.

Freud, A. (1936). *The Ego and the Mechanisms of Defence.* London: Hogarth Press. [Reprinted London: Karnac Books, 1992.]

Freud, S. (1887–1904). *The Complete Letters of Sigmund Freud to Wilhelm Fliess,* translated and edited by J. M. Masson. Cambridge, MA: Belknap Press.

_____ (1891b). *On Aphasia: A Critical Study*, translated by E. Stengel. New York: International Universities Press, 1953.

_____ (1891d). Hypnosis. *S.E.*, 1. [*The Standard Edition of the Complete Psychological Works of Sigmund Freud* (24 volumes), ed. James Strachey. London: Hogarth Press and the Institute of Psycho-Analysis, 1953–1964.]

_____ (1892–94). Preface and footnotes to the translation of Charcot's *Tuesday Lectures. S.E.*, 1.

_____ (1895d) (with Breuer, J.). *Studies in Hysteria. S.E.*, 2.

_____ (1896a). Heredity and the aetiology of the neuroses. *S.E.*, 3.

_____ (1896b). Further remarks on the neuro-psychoses of defence. *S.E.*, 3.

_____ (1896c). The aetiology of hysteria. *S.E.*, 3.

_____ (1899a). Screen memories. *S.E.*, 3.

_____ (1900a). *The Interpretation of Dreams. S.E.*, 4 & 5.

_____ (1901a). *On Dreams. S.E.,* 5.

_____ (1901b). *The Psychopathology of Everyday Life. S.E.,* 6.

_____ (1904a). Freud's psycho-analytic procedure. *S.E.,* 7.

_____ (1905d). *Three Essays on the Theory of Sexuality. S.E.,* 7.

_____ (1905e). Fragment of an analysis of a case of hysteria. *S.E.,* 7.

_____ (1906a). My views on the part played by sexuality in the aetiology of the neuroses. *S.E.,* 7.

_____ (1908b). Character and anal erotism. *S.E.,* 9.

_____ (1909d). Notes upon a case of obsessional neurosis. *S.E.,* 10.

_____ (1910a [1909]). Five lectures on psycho-analysis. *S.E.,* 11.

_____ (1910c). *Leonardo da Vinci and a Memory of His Childhood. S.E.,* 11.

_____ (1910d). The future prospects of psycho-analytic therapy. *S.E.,* 11.

_____ (1910h). A special type of choice of object made by men. *S.E.,* 11.

_____ (1911c). Psycho-analytic notes on an autobiographical account of a case of paranoia (dementia paranoides). *S.E.,* 12.

_____ (1912b). The dynamics of transference. *S.E.,* 12.

_____ (1912e). Recommendations to physicians practising psycho-analysis. *S.E.,* 12.

_____ (1912–13). *Totem & Taboo. S.E.,* 13.

_____ (1913i). The disposition to obsessional neurosis. *S.E.,* 12.

_____ (1914c). On narcissism: an introduction. *S.E.,* 14.

_____ (1914d). On the history of the psycho-analytic movement. *S.E.,* 14.

_____ (1914g). Remembering, repeating and working-through (further recommendations on the technique of psycho-analysis, II). *S.E.,* 14.

_____ (1915a). Observations on transference-love (further recommendations on the technique of psycho-analysis, III). *S.E.,* 14.

_____ (1915c). Instincts and their vicissitudes. *S.E.,* 14.

_____ (1915d). Repression. *S.E.,* 14.

_____ (1915e). The unconscious. *S.E.,* 14.

_____ (1916–17). *Introductory Lectures on Psycho-Analysis. S.E.,* 15–16.

_____ (1917e). Mourning and melancholia. *S.E.,* 14.

_____ (1920g). *Beyond the Pleasure Principle. S.E.,* 18.

_____ (1923b). *The Ego and the Id. S.E.,* 19.

_____ (1923c [1922]). Remarks on the theory and practice of dream-interpretation. *S.E.,* 19.

_____ (1923e). The infantile genital organisation. *S.E.,* 19.

_____ (1924d). The dissolution of the Oedipus complex. *S.E.,* 19.

_____ (1925). Letter to Stefan Zweig. In: *Letters of Sigmund Freud, 1873–1939*, edited by E. L. Freud, translated by J. Stern. London: Hogarth Press, 1970.

_____ (1925d). *An Autobiographical Study. S.E.*, 20.

_____ (1925h). Negation. *S.E.*, 19.

_____ (1926d). *Inhibitions, Symptoms and Anxiety. S.E.*, 20.

_____ (1926e). *The Question of Lay Analysis. S.E.*, 20.

_____ (1927c). *The Future of an Illusion. S.E.*, 21.

_____ (1927e). Fetishism. *S.E.*, 21.

_____ (1930a). *Civilization and Its Discontents. S.E.*, 21.

_____ (1931b). Female sexuality. *S.E.*, 21.

_____ (1933a). *New Introductory Lectures on Psycho-Analysis. S.E.*, 21.

_____ (1937c). Analysis terminable and interminable. *S.E.*, 23.

_____ (1937d). Constructions in analysis. *S.E.*, 23.

_____ (1940a). *An Outline of Psycho-Analysis. S.E.*, 23.

_____ (1940b). Some elementary lessons in psycho-analysis. *S.E.*, 23.

_____ (1950a [1887–1902]). Project for a scientific psychology. *S.E.*, 1.

Friedlander, B. (1904). *Die Renaissance des Eros Uranios*. Berlin: Verlad "Renaissance".

Gedo, J. E. (1986). *Conceptual Issues in Psychoanalysis*. Hillsdale, NJ: Analytic Press.

_____ (1989). Self psychology: A post-Kohutian view. In: D. W. Detrick & S. P. Detrick (Eds.), *Self Psychology: Comparisons and Contrasts* (pp. 415–429). Hillsdale, NJ: Analytic Press.

Glatzer, H. T., & Evans, W. N. (1977). On Guntrip's analysis with Fairbairn and Winnicott. *International Journal of Psychoanalytic Psychotherapy*, 6: 80–98.

Goldstein, W. N. (1985). *An Introduction to the Borderline Conditions*. New York: Jason Aronson.

Groddeck, G. (1923). *The Book of the It*, translated by V. M. E. Collins. London: Vision Press, 1949.

Grosskurth, P. (1986). *Melanie Klein: Her World and Her Work*. London: Karnac Books.

Grünbaum, A. (1967). *Philosophical Problems of Space and Time* (2nd edition). Boston: Reidel.

_____ (1968a). *Geometry and Chronometry in Philosophical Perspective*. Minneapolis, MN: University of Minnesota Press.

_____ (1968b). *Modern Science and Zeno's Paradoxes* (2nd edition). London: Allen & Unwin..

_____ (1977). How scientific is psychoanalysis? In R. Stern, L.

Horowitz, & J. Lynes, (Eds.), *Science and Psychotherapy* (pp. 219–254). New York: Haven Press.

_____ (1979). Is psychoanalytic theory pseudoscientific by Karl Popper's criterion of demarcation? *American Philosophical Quarterly, 16*: 131–141.

_____ (1984). *The Foundations of Psychoanalysis: A Philosophical Critique.* Berkeley, CA: University of California Press.

_____ (1986). Is Freud's theory well-founded? *Behavioral and Brain Sciences, 9* (2): 266–281.

_____ (1993). *Validation in the Clinical Theory of Psychoanalysis: A Study in the Philosophy of Psychoanalysis.* Madison, CT: International Universities Press.

_____ (1997). One hundred years of psychoanalytic theory and therapy: retrospect and prospect. In: *Mindscapes: Philosophy, Science and the Mind.* Pittsburgh, PA: University of Pittsburgh Press.

Habermas, J. (1971). *Knowledge and Human Interests.* Boston, MA: Beacon Press.

Hale, N. G. Jr. (1995). *The Rise and Crisis of Psychoanalysis in the United States: Freud and the Americans, 1917–1985.* Oxford: Oxford University Press.

Hare, E. H. (1962). Masturbatory insanity: the history of an idea. *Journal of Medical Science, 108*: 1–25.

Hartmann, H. (1939). *Ego Psychology and the Problem of Adaptation.* New York: International Universities Press.

_____ (1950). Comments on the psychoanalytic theory of the ego. In: *Essays on Ego Psychology.* New York: International Universities Press, 1964.

Haskell, R. E. (1982). The matrix of group talk: an empirical method of analysis and validation. *Small Group Behaviour, 13*: 165–191.

_____ (1987a). Giambattista Vico and the discovery of metaphor. In: R. E. Haskell. (Ed.), *Cognition and Symbolic Structures* (pp. 67–82). Norwood, NJ: Ablex Publishing.

_____ (1987b). A phenomenology of metaphor: a praxis study into metaphor and its cognitive movement through semantic space. In: R. E. Haskell (Ed.), *Cognition and Symbolic Structures* (pp. 257–292). Norwood, NJ: Ablex Publishing.

_____ (1987c). Social cognition and the non-conscious expression of racial ideology. *Imagination, Cognition and Personality, 6* (1): 75–97.

_____ (1988). Small group "fantasy theme" analysis: anthropology and psychology. A comparative study of a psychosocial structure of a ritual ceremony. *Journal of Psychohistory, 16*: 61–78.

_____ (1989a). Analogical transforms: a cognitive theory of the origin and development of equivalence transformation, Part I. *Metaphor and Symbolic Activity, 4*: 247–259.

_____ (1989b). Analogical transforms: a cognitive theory of origin and development of equivalence transformation, Part II. *Metaphor and Symbolic Activity, 4*: 257–277.

_____ (1990). Cognitive operations and non-conscious processing in dream and waking reports. *Imagination, Cognition and Personality, 10*: 65–84.

_____ (1991). An analogical methodology for the analysis and validation of anomalous cognitive and linguistic operations in small group (fantasy theme). Reports. *Small Group Research, 22*: 443–474.

Heimann, P. (1950). On counter-transference. In: *About Children and Children No Longer*. London: Routledge.

Higgins, M. B., & Raphael, C. (1967). *Reich Speaks of Freud*, translated by T. Pol. London: Souvenir Press.

Hinshelwood, R. D. (1994). *Clinical Klein*. London: Free Association Books.

Hirschmüller, A. (1978). *The Life and Work of Josef Breuer*. New York: New York University Press.

Hook, S. (Ed.) (1958). *Psychoanalysis, Scientific Method and Philosophy*. London: Transaction.

Jacobs, M. (Ed.) (1996). *In Search of Supervision*. London: Sage.

Jacobson, E. (1964). *The Self and the Object World*. New York: International Universities Press.

Jacoby, R. (1983). *The Repression of Psychoanalysis: Otto Fenichel and the Political Freudians*. Chicago, IL: University of Chicago Press.

Jones, E. (1918). Anal-erotic character traits. *Journal of Abnormal Psychology, 13*.

_____ (1953). *The Life and Work of Sigmund Freud, Vol. 1*. London: Hogarth Press.

Joseph, B. (1985). Transference: The total situation. In: E. B. Spillius (Ed.), *Melanie Klein Today: Developments in Theory and Practice. Vol. 2: Mainly Practice*. London: Routledge, 1988.

Jung, C. G. (1933). Editorial. In: *Collected Works, Vol. 10: Civilisation in Transition*, translated by R. F. C. Hull, edited by H. Read, M. Fordham, & G. Adler. Bollingen Series XX. New York: Pantheon, 1964.

Kahr, B. (1996). *D. W. Winnicott: A Biographical Portrait*. London: Karnac Books.

Kaplan, L. J. (1978). *Oneness & Separateness: From Infant to Individual*. New York: Simon & Schuster.

Kernberg, O. (1975). *Borderline Conditions and Pathological Narcissism*. New York: Jason Aronson.

Kerr, J. (1994). *A Most Dangerous Method: The Story of Jung, Freud and Sabina Spielrein*. London: Sinclair Sevenson.

King, P., & Steiner, R. (Ed.) (1990). *The Freud–Klein Controversies: 1941–45*. London: Routledge.

Klein, M. (1920). Der Familienroman in statu nascendi. *Internationale Zeitschrift für Psychoanalyse*, 1920.

_____ (1921). The development of a child. In: *Love, Guilt and Reparation and Other Works 1921–1945*. London: Hogarth Press and the Institute of Psycho-Analysis. [Also in: *Writings, Vol. 1*, 1975.]

_____ (1926). The psychological principles of early analysis. In: *Love, Guilt and Reparation and other Works 1921–1945*. London: Hogarth Press and the Institute of Psycho-Analysis. [Also in: *Writings, Vol. 1*, 1975.]

_____ (1932). *The Psycho-Analysis of Children*, translated by A. Strachey. London: Hogarth Press and the Institute of Psycho-Analysis, 1975. [Also in: *Writings, Vol. 4*, 1961.]

_____ (1933). The early development of conscience in the child. In: *Love, Guilt and Reparation and Other Works 1921–1945*. London: Hogarth Press and the Institute of Psycho-Analysis. [Also in: *Writings, Vol. 1*, 1975.]

_____ (1935). A contribution to the psychogenesis of manic-depressive states. In: *Love, Guilt and Reparation and Other Works 1921–1945*. London: Hogarth Press and the Institute of Psycho-Analysis. [Also in: *Writings, Vol. 1*, 1975.]

_____ (1946). Notes on some schizoid mechanisms. In: *Envy and Gratitude and Other Works 1946–1963*. London: Hogarth Press and the Institute of Psycho-Analysis. [Also in: *Writings, Vol. 3*, 1975.]

_____ (1952a). The origins of transference. In: *Envy and Gratitude and Other Works 1946–1963*. London: Hogarth Press and the Institute of Psycho-Analysis. [Also in: *Writings, Vol. 3*, 1975.]

_____ (1952b). Some theoretical conclusions regarding the emotional life of the infant. In: *Love, Guilt and Reparation and Other Works 1946–1963*. London: Hogarth Press and the Institute of Psycho-Analysis. [Also in: *Writings, Vol. 1*, 1975.]

_____ (1957). Envy and gratitude. In: *Envy and Gratitude and Other Works 1946–1963*. London: Hogarth Press and the Institute of Psycho-Analysis. [Also in: *Writings, Vol. 3*, 1975.]

_____ (1963). Some reflections on "The Orestia". In: *Love, Guilt and Reparation and Other Works 1946–1963*. London: Hogarth Press and the Institute of Psycho-Analysis. [Also in: *Writings, Vol. 1*, 1975.]

_____ (1961). *Narrative of a Child Analysis. The Writings of Melanie Klein, Vol. 4*. London: Hogarth Press, 1975 [reprinted London: Karnac Books, 1996].

_____ (1975). *Love, Guilt and Reparation and Other Works 1921-1945. The Writings of Melanie Klein, Vol. 1* (ed. R. Money-Kyrle with B. Joseph, E. O'Shaughnessy & H. Segal). London: Hogarth Press [reprinted London: Karnac Books, 1992].

_____ (1975). *Envy and Gratitude and Other Works. The Writings of Melanie Klein, Vol. 3* (ed. R. Money-Kyrle with B. Joseph, E. O'Shaughnessy & H. Segal). London: Hogarth Press [reprinted London: Karnac Books, 1993].

Kohut, H. (1959). Introspection, empathy and psychoanalysis. *Journal of the American Psychoanalytical Association, 7*: 459–483.

_____ (1971). *The Analysis of the Self*. New York: International Universities Press.

_____ (1973). The future of psychoanalysis. In: P. Ornstein (Ed.), *The Search for the Self*. New York: International Universities Press.

_____ (1977). *The Restoration of the Self*. New York: International Universities Press.

_____ (1984). *How Does Analysis Cure?* Chicago, IL: University of Chicago Press.

Krafft-Ebing, R. von (1894). *Psychopathia Sexualis*. Stuttgard: F. Enke.

Kuppfer, E. von (1899). *Lieblingsminne und Freundesliebe in der Weltlitteratur*. Leipzig: M. Spohr.

Laing, R. D. (1959). *The Divided Self*. Harmondsworth: Penguin, 1965.

Langs, R. J. (1959). A pilot study of aspects of the earliest memory. *Archives for Neurology and Psychiatry, 81*: 709.

_____ (1966). Manifest dreams from three clinical groups. *Archives of General Psychiatry, 14*: 634–643.

_____ (1973–74). *The Technique of Psychoanalytic Psychotherapy*. New York: Jason Aronson.

_____ (1976). *The Bipersonal Field*. New York: Jason Aronson.

_____ (1978). *The Listening Process*. New York: Jason Aronson.

_____ (1979). *The Therapeutic Environment*. New York: Jason Aronson.

_____ (1980). *Interactions: The Realm of Transference and Counter-transference*. New York: Jason Aronson.

_____ (1981). *Resistances and Interventions: The Nature of Therapeutic Work*. New York: Jason Aronson.

_____ (1982). *The Psychotherapeutic Conspiracy*. New York: Jason Aronson.

_____ (1997). *Death Anxiety and Clinical Practice*. London: Karnac Books.

_____ (1998). *Ground Rules of Psychotherapy and Counselling*. London: Karnac Books.

Langs, R. J., Badalamenti, A., & Thompson, L. (1996). *The Cosmic Circle: The Unification of Mind, Matter and Energy*. New York: Alliance Publishing.

Langs, R. J., & Linton Barr, R. (1962). Placebo reactions in a study of lysergic acid diethylamide (LSD–25). *Archives of General Psychiatry*, 6: 369–383.

Langs, R. J., Udoff, A., Bucci, W., Cramer, G., & Thompson L. (1993). Two methods of assessing unconscious communication in psychotherapy. *Psychoanalytic Psychology, 10*: 1–13.

Levine, I. (1923). *The Unconscious: An Introduction to Freudian Psychology*. London: L. Parsons.

_____ (1926). *Das Unbewusste*, translated by A. Freud & S. Freud. Leipzig: Internationaler Psychoanalytischer Verlag.

Levy, D. (1996). *Freud among the Philosophers*. London: Yale University Press.

Little, M. (1951). Countertransference and the patient's reaction to it. *International Journal of Psycho-Analysis, 32*: 32–34.

_____ (1985). Winnicott working in areas where psychotic anxieties predominate: a personal record. *Free Associations, 3*: 9–43.

Lothane, Z. (1985). Robert Langs: the communicative approach. In: J. Reppen (Ed.), *Beyond Freud: A Study of Modern Psychoanalytic Theorists* (pp. 175–203). Hillsdale, NJ: Analytic Press.

Maclean, G., & Rappen, U. (1991). *Hermine Hug-Hellmuth: Her Life and Work*. London: Routledge.

Macmillan, M. (1991). *Freud Re-Evaluated: The Completed Arc*. Amsterdam: North Holland.

Mahler, M. S., Pine, F., & Bergman, A. (1975). *The Psychological Birth of the Human Infant*. New York: Basic Books. [Reprinted London: Karnac Books, 1989.]

McDevitt, J. B., & Mahler, M. S. (1980). Object constancy, individuality and internalization. In: S. I. Greenspan & G. H. Pollock (Eds.), *The Course of Life, Vol. 1: Infancy and Early Childhood* (pp. 135–139). Washington, DC: U.S. Government Printing Office.

Meisel, P., & Kendrick, W. (Eds.) (1986). *Bloomsbury/Freud: The Letters of James and Alix Strachey, 1924–1925*. London: Chatto & Windus.

Millikan, R. G. (1984). *Language, Thought and other Biological Categories*. London: Bradford/MIT.

_____ (1993). *White Queen Psychology and Other Essays for Alice*. London: Bradford/MIT.

Milner, M. (1952). Aspects of symbolism and comprehension of the not-self. *International Journal of Psycho-Analysis, 33*: 181–185.

Mooij, A. (1982). *Psychoanalysis and the Concept of a Rule: An Essay in the Philosophy of Psychoanalysis*. London: Springer-Verlag.

Nagel, E. (1959). Methodological issues in psychoanalytic theory. In: S. Hook (Ed.), *Psychoanalysis, Scientific Method and Philosophy*. London: Transaction.

Neider, H. (1977). Gespräch mit Heinrich Neider: Persönliche Errinerungen an den Wiener Kreis. *Conceptus*, 1.

Nietzsche, F. (1878–80). *Human, All Too Human*, translated by R. J. Hollingdale. London: Cambridge University Press, 1986.

Nunberg, H., & Federn, E. (Eds.) (1962–1975). *Minutes of the Vienna Psycho-Analytic Society, Vols. 1–4*. New York: International Universities Press.

Pfister, O. (1913). *The Psychoanalytic Method*, translated by C. Rockwell Payne. London: Kegan Paul, 1915.

Popper, K. (1962). *Conjectures and Refutations*. New York: Basic Books.

_____ (1974). Replies to my critics. In: *The Philosophy of Karl Popper, Vol. 2*, edited by P. A. Schlipp. La Salle, IL: Open Court.

_____ (1976). *Unended Quest: An Intellectual Autobiography*. Glasgow: Fontana.

_____ (1983). *Realism and the Aim of Science*, edited by W.W. Bartley, III. Totowa, NJ: Rowman & Littlefield.

Ramas, M. (1980). Freud's Dora, Dora's hysteria: the negation of a woman's rebellion. *Feminist Studies, 6* (3): 488–489.

Rank, O. (1911). Ein Beitrag zum Narzissismus. *Jahrbuch Psychoanal. Psychopathol. Forschungen, 3*: 401–426.

_____ (1932). *Art and Artist: Creative Urge and Personality Development*, translated by C. F. Atkinson. New York: Alfred A. Knopf.

Rayner, E. (1990). *The Independent Mind in British Psychoanalysis*. London: Free Association Books.

Reich, W. (1920). A case of pubertal breaching of the incest taboo. In: *Early Writings, Vol. I*, translated by P. Schmitz. New York: Farrar, Strauss & Giroux, 1975.

_____ (1925). The impulsive character: a psychoanalytic study of ego pathology. In: *The Impulsive Character and Other Writings*, translated by B. Koopman. New York: New American Library.

_____ (1927). *Die Funktion des Orgasmus*. Vienna: Internationaler Psychoanalytischer Verlag.

_____ (1929). *Dialectical Materialism and Psychoanalysis*, translated by A. Bostock. *Studies on the Left, 6* (4).

_____ (1933a). *Character Analysis*, translated by V. Carfagno. New York: Touchstone, 1972.

_____ (1933b). *The Mass Psychology of Fascism*, translated by V. Carfagno. London: Souvenir Press, 1972.

_____ (1936). On Freud's eightieth birthday: our congratulations to Freud on his birthday. In: *Reich Speaks of Freud*. London: Souvenir Press.

_____ (1942a). *The Discovery of the Orgone, Vol. I: The Function of the Orgasm*, translated by T. P. Wolfe. New York: Orgone Institute Press.

_____ (1942b). *The Function of the Orgasm*, translated by V. R. Carfagno. New York: 1975.

_____ (1967). *Reich Speaks of Freud*. London: Souvenir Press.

Roazen, P. (1975). *Freud and His Followers*. New York: Alfred A. Knopf.

_____ (1985). *Helene Deutsch: A Psychoanalyst's Life*. New York: Doubleday.

_____, & Swerdloff, B. (1995). *Heresy: Sándor Rado and the Psychoanalytic Movement*. London: Jason Aronson.

Rodman, F. R. (Ed.) (1987). *The Spontaneous Gesture: Selected Letters of D. W. Winnicott*. London: Harvard University Press.

Sadger, I. (1910). Analerotik und Analcharakter. *Die Heilkunde*.

Sartre, J.-P. (1943). *L'etre et le néant*. Paris: Gallimard.

Schatzman, M. (1976). *Soul Murder: Persecution in the Family*. Harmondsworth: Penguin.

_____ (1992). Freud: who seduced whom? *New Scientist*, 21 March, pp. 34–37.

Schiller, F. (1795). *On the Aesthetic Education of Man in a Series of Letters*, edited and translated by E. M. Wilkinson & L. A. Willoughby. Oxford: Clarendon, 1967.

Schimek, J. G. (1987). Fact and fantasy in the seduction theory: a historical review. *Journal of the American Psycho-Analytic Association, 35*: 937–965.

Schleiner, W. (1997). *Medical Ethics in the Renaissance*. Washington, DC: Georgetown University Press.

Schlipp, P. A. (Ed.) (1963). *The Philosophy of Rudolf Carnap*. London: Cambridge University Press.

Schrenck-Notzing, A. von (1895). *Therapeutic Suggestion in Psychopathia Sexualis (Pathological Manifestations of the Sexual Sense), with Especial Reference to Contrary Sexual Instinct*, translated by C. G. Chaddock. Philadelphia: F. A. Davis, 1895.

Searles, H. F. (1975). The patient as therapist to his analyst. In: *Countertransference and Related Subjects*. Madison, CT: International Universities Press.

Segal, H. (1967). Melanie Klein's technique. In: B. B. Wolman (Ed.), *Psychoanalytic Technique: A Handbook for the Practising Psychoanalyst*. New York: Basic Books.

Sharaf, M. (1983). *Fury on Earth: A Biography of Wilhelm Reich*. London: Hutchinson.

Shaw, J. C., & Ferris, G. N. (1883). Perverted sexual instinct. *Journal of Nervous and Mental Diseases, 10*: 185–204.

Smith, D. L. (1985). Freud's developmental approach to narcissism: A concise review. *International Journal of Psycho-Analysis, 66*: 489–497.

_____ (1991). *Hidden Conversations: An Introduction to Communicative Psycho-Analysis*. London: Routledge.

_____ (in press). *Freud's Philosophy of the Unconscious*. Dordrecht: Kluwer Academic Publishers.

Spitz, R. A. (1953). Authority and masturbation. *Yearbook of Psycho-Analysis, Vol. 9*. New York: International Universities Press.

_____ (1957). *No and Yes: On the Genesis of Human Communication*. New York: International Universities Press.

Stepansky, P. E. (1988). *The Memoirs of Margaret S. Mahler*. London: Collier Macmillan.

Sterba, R. (1978). Unpublizierte Diskussionsbemerkungen. *Jahrbuch der Psychoanalyze, 10*: 214.

Stern, A. (1938). Psychoanalytic investigation and therapy in the borderline group of neurosis. *Psychoanalytic Quarterly, 7*: 467–475.

Strachey, A. (1925). Report of Melanie Klein's Berlin lecture. In: P. Meisel & W. Kendrick, *Bloomsbury/Freud: The Letters of James and Alix Strachey, 1924–1925*. London: Chatto & Windus, 1986.

Sulloway, F. (1979). *Freud: Biologist of the Mind*. New York: Basic Books.

Szasz, T. (1963). The concept of transference. *International Journal of Psycho-Analysis, 44:* 432–433.

Tolpin, M. (1980). Discussion of "Psychoanalytic Developmental Theories of the Self: An Integration" by M. Shane & E. Shane. In: A. Goldberg (Ed.), *Advances in Self Psychology* (pp. 47–68). New York: International Universities Press.

Tower, L. (1956). Countertransference. *Journal of the American Psycho-Analytic Association, 4:* 224–255.

Ulrichs, K. H. (1898). *Forschungen über das Rätsel der mannmännlichen Liebe* [12 vols. of 1864–1879], edited by M. Hirschfeld. Leipzig: Max Spohr.

van Deusen, E. H. (1868–1869). Observations on a form of nervous prostration, (neurasthenia), culminating in insanity. *American Journal of Insanity, 25:* 445–461.

Veith, I. (1977). Four thousand years of hysteria. In: M. Horowitz, (Ed.), *Hysterical Personality.* New York: Jason Aronson.

Ward, J. (1896–1898). Excerpt from *Naturalism and Agnosticism.* In: G. N. A. Vesey (Ed.), *Body and Mind.* London: George, Allen & Unwin.

Webster, R. (1995). *Why Freud Was Wrong: Sin, Science and Psychoanalysis.* London: HarperCollins.

Winnicott, D. W. (1949). Mind and its relation to psyche-soma. *Collected Papers: Through Paediatrics to Psycho-Analysis.* London: Tavistock, 1958. [Reprinted: London: Karnac Books, 1996.]

———— (1951). Transitional objects and transitional phenomena. In: *Collected Papers: Through Paediatrics to Psycho-Analysis.* London: Tavistock, 1958. [Reprinted: London: Karnac Books, 1996.]

———— (1954). Metapsychological and clinical aspects of regression within the psycho-analytical set-up. In: *Collected Papers: Through Paediatrics to Psycho-Analysis.* London: Tavistock, 1958. [Reprinted: London: Karnac Books, 1996.]

———— (1956a). On transference. *International Journal of Psycho-Analysis, 37:* 386–388.

———— (1956b). Paediatrics and childhood neurosis. In: *Collected Papers: Through Paediatrics to Psycho-Analysis.* London: Tavistock, 1958. [Reprinted: London: Karnac Books, 1996.]

———— (1960). Ego distortion in terms of true and false self. In: *The Maturational Processes and the Facilitating Environment: Studies in the Theory of Emotional Development.* London: Hogarth Press and the Institute of Psycho-Analysis, 1976. [Reprinted: London: Karnac Books, 1995.]

_____ (1962a). A personal view of the Kleinian contribution. In: *The Maturational Processes and the Facilitating Environment: Studies in the Theory of Emotional Development*. London: Hogarth Press and the Institute of Psycho-Analysis, 1965. [Reprinted: London: Karnac Books, 1995.]

_____ (1962b). Ego integration in child development. In: *The Maturational Processes and the Facilitating Environment: Studies in the Theory of Emotional Development* (pp. 56–63). London: Hogarth Press and the Institute of Psycho-Analysis, 1965. [Reprinted: London: Karnac Books, 1995.]

_____ (1963). Communicating and not communicating leading to a study of certain opposites. In: *The Maturational Processes and the Facilitating Environment: Studies in the Theory of Emotional Development*. London: Hogarth Press and the Institute of Psycho-Analysis, 1965. [Reprinted: London: Karnac Books, 1995.]

_____ (1968). Communication between infant and mother, mother and infant, compared and contrasted. In: *What Is Psycho-Analysis?* London: Balliére, Tindall & Cassell. [Also in *Babies and Their Mothers*. London: Free Association Books, 1987.]

_____ (1971). Playing: a theoretical statement. In: *Playing and Reality*. Harmondsworth: Penguin, 1980.

Wolf, E. (1996). The Viennese Chicagoan. In: A. M. Siegel (Ed.), *Heinz Kohut and the Psychology of the Self* (pp. 7–18). London: Routledge.

INDEX